Out in the Country

INTERSECTIONS
Transdisciplinary Perspectives on Genders and Sexualities

GENERAL EDITORS
Michael Kimmel and Suzanna Walters

Sperm Counts:
Overcome by Man's Most Precious Fluid
Lisa Jean Moore

The Sexuality of Migration:
Border Crossings and Mexican Immigrant Men
Lionel Cantú, Jr.
Edited by Nancy A. Naples and Salvador Vidal-Ortiz

Moral Panics, Sex Panics:
Fear and the Fight over Sexual Rights
Edited by Gilbert Herdt

Out in the Country:
Youth, Media, and Queer Visibility in Rural America
Mary L. Gray

Out in the Country

Youth, Media, and Queer Visibility in Rural America

Mary L. Gray

NEW YORK UNIVERSITY PRESS

New York and London

NEW YORK UNIVERSITY PRESS
New York and London
www.nyupress.org

Library of Congress Cataloging-in-Publication Data
Gray, Mary L.
Out in the country : youth, media, and queer
visibility in rural America / Mary L. Gray.
p. cm. — (Intersections: transdisciplinary perspectives
on genders and sexualities)
Includes bibliographical references and index.
ISBN-13: 978-0-8147-3192-5 (cl : alk. paper)
ISBN-10: 0-8147-3192-9 (cl : alk. paper)
ISBN-13: 978-0-8147-3193-2 (pb : alk. paper)
ISBN-10: 0-8147-3193-7 (pb : alk. paper)
1. Gay youth—Kentucky. 2. Rural population—Kentucky. I. Title.
HQ76.27.Y68G73   2009
306.76'608350973091734—dc22   2009006120

New York University Press books are printed on acid-free paper,
and their binding materials are chosen for strength and durability.
We strive to use environmentally responsible suppliers and materials
to the greatest extent possible in publishing our books.

Manufactured in the United States of America
c   10 9 8 7 6 5 4 3 2 1
p   10 9 8 7 6 5 4 3 2

For Catherine, our nieces and nephews,
and in memory of Grandma Doree,
the mother of all PFLAG moms.

Contents

Acknowledgments

I am deeply indebted first and foremost to the individuals who shared their stories for this project. Without their participation and encouragement, this book would not have been possible. I would like to particularly thank Natalie Reteneller, for her tireless spirit and many hours of thoughtful reflection. She has been an inspiration, as have the Louisville Youth Group youth leaders and mentors. The insights of AJ, Mary Bird, Gina Cooper, Jakob McDougale, Michelle B., Ed and Jane McCurley, and Shaun A., Joe B., and Dale Green were invaluable.

This research was funded, in part, by a fellowship from the Sexuality Research Fellowship Program of the Social Science Research Council supported by the Ford Foundation. An earlier research award from the Gay and Lesbian Alliance Against Defamation's Center for the Study of Media and Society also contributed to the completion of this project.

While living in Kentucky, I could not have asked for a group of more supportive colleagues than those I found at the University of Louisville and the University of Kentucky. The faculty and staff of the Women's and Gender Studies Program and Professors Susan Kelly, Carol Mattingly, and Rick Zimmerman were generous sources of strength and wonderful role models.

I am grateful to the many teachers and colleagues who have sustained me. Geof Bowker, Steve Epstein, Larry Gross, Leah Lievrouw, Vince Rafael, Michael Schudson, Ellen Seiter, Susan Leigh Star, Olga Vasquez and the University of California at San Diego Communication Department's staff, graduate students, and faculty were especially patient and nurturing with my growth as a scholar. I have garnered wonderful mentoring from my Social Science Research Council fellowship adviser, Joshua Gamson, and engagement with friends and scholars Ron Day, John De Cecco, Mark Deuze, Betsi Grabe, Rae Greiner, Judith Halberstam, Karen Hossfeld, Toi James, Esther Newton, David Delgado Shorter, Carrie Sloan, Heide Solbrig, Matthew Stahl, Fred Turner, Zak Szymanski, and Nina Wakeford.

Colleagues associated with the Society of Lesbian and Gay Anthropologists are priceless. If it hadn't been for SOLGA, I doubt I'd still be in academics. Indiana University's Department of Communication and Culture has been a dream academic home. All the faculty and staff contributed to the growth and polish of this manuscript in immeasurable ways. I want to particularly thank Dick Bauman and Barb Klinger for comments on pieces of this puzzle and Yeidy Rivero and Phaedra Pezzullo for cocktails when I didn't know what to do with those pieces of the puzzle. The Gender Studies Department at IU has been a second academic home. Marlon Bailey, Sara Friedman, Colin Johnson, and Brenda Weber are nothing short of inspiring as colleagues. Ilene Kalish, and her staff at NYU Press, helped me step into the shoes of the writer. Thank you for your keen editorial eye and your seemingly indefatigable patience. A special thanks to Suzanna Walters, whose tireless cajoling and sharp intellect kept me giving more than I thought I could give. Thank you for your thoughtful comments and patience. Without Verda Hamparson's emotional support and the editorial prowess of Doris Brosnan and Andrew Brosnan, I would likely still be working out the rough outlines of this manuscript and am therefore forever in their debt. I want to extend a special note of thanks to Leigh Star. She believed in me, gently coaxed me in productive directions, and helped me understand the contributions I could make as a scholar. Leigh gave me a strong sense of lineage and intellectual heritage that I will always treasure and look forward to passing on to my own students.

To the Tuckers and the Guthries—I wouldn't be here without you. Thank you. Catherine Guthrie has been my rock and soft place to land for the length of my scholarly career. Every day, she has made me feel more loved, wise, and at peace with the world and my place in it. I would not be the person, scholar, or writer I am today without her. May I have a lifetime to show my appreciation and love.

Preface

Never Met a Stranger

When I talk about researching what gay visibility in the media means to rural youth claiming a queer sense of identity, most people want to know how I ever found enough kids to ask. They also ask if, as a queer-identifying woman, I was scared traveling around "the middle of nowhere" asking about such things. First, you have to understand that I'm the kind of person who has, as the saying goes, "never met a stranger." While children raised in cities might learn to manage the press of strangers through distance and aloofness, my small-town upbringing taught me to assume the (ladylike) posture of pre-emptive friendliness. Far from feeling estranged out in the country (and sometimes embarrassed to admit this to my urbane friends), I felt at home.

Growing up in California's Central Valley, I was surrounded by twangy, dustbowl-singed drawls as thick as any I would encounter while doing my research in rural Kentucky and the small towns scattered along its Illinois, Indiana, West Virginia, and Tennessee borders. My inclination to use "y'all" allowed me to fit in fairly seamlessly with my new surroundings. My white skin, gender neutrality (or, at least, not notably butch by country standards), and familiarity with small towns helped me feel at ease with the people I met and the circuitous rhythms of country life. I sensed that the experiences of youth living in presumably simple and isolated places would shed light on how profoundly complicated, mobile, and mediated rural youth identities are because of my intimate familiarity with these places. Such communities produce far more complex, dynamic experiences and expressions of sexuality and gender than characterizations about rural America lobbed from the Left or the Right. I meandered through regions of the mid-Southern swath of the United States as a stranger but with a deep sense of acquaintance.

As a kid, I saw the same familiar faces day after day. California's multi-culturalism complicated the racism that structured my small social world. My Central California town was not that small (a population of 15,000 in the early 1970s that exploded to more than 60,000 by the time I left it), but it was small enough that its white, Latino, Laotian, and Hmong residents could not easily avoid one another. We shared the same neighborhoods, schools, and style of weathering ranch tract houses. We were no more than a half-hour away from the outskirts of a city of more than 200,000 people, but it was the only sizable city for hours in either direction and agricultural land buffered our town's connections to it. There were too few locals for anyone to remain anonymous for very long or get lost in the crowd. At least, that was how I was raised to feel about where I lived.

I moved away from my hometown at the age of 18 not because I felt exhausted by its smallness (although several of my childhood friends left for that reason), but because I received a state scholarship to attend a respected university only three hours away. While the few lesbian couples with kids at my school showed me I could pursue a domestic life with another woman if I did so quietly, I wasn't really sure what else there was to do locally beyond struggle to raise children and make ends meet. Even so, I don't know that I felt going to college meant I was leaving home in any permanent sense. I remember thinking I would come and go to visit family and friends and make my way back with a college degree that might make the struggle to get by easier.

By my junior year, I could see that my college education would make it difficult for me to move back home after all. I had acquired a new language to critique the social and political inequalities that I once ignored or grudgingly accepted. It was much harder to confront the tacit sexism and sexual conservatism, racism, and classism that typically left me speechless on visits home. My inability to translate my frustrations to family only deepened my feelings of disorientation and alienation. I was also too naïve and inexperienced with grassroots organizing to recognize or seek out local challenges to these inequalities with which to align and connect. I wrote off my small town as insufferably stifling, much as rhetoric about "the rural" and "Red states" does today.

It was around this time that I learned about the political action group Queer Nation through friends and articles in gay and lesbian magazines. A few gay-identifying friends, inspired by Queer Nation, had recently come out as queer. Because I hadn't found my way into a lesbian-identified community (beyond fledgling attempts to date women in various sports leagues around town), I had no "lesbian" identity to shed. I laid claim to a "queer" identity just as Queer Nation's nearby San Francisco chapter dissolved in 1991. Perhaps, like those before me who chose to identify as "gay" rather than "homosexual" or "lesbian" rather than "gay woman," coming out as queer seemed to verbalize the politics of my desire. It also gave voice to my desire for political change. No word other than "queer" described my sense of self and no other has felt quite right since.

Unsure of where to live or how to do political work after college, I moved with friends to San Francisco and entered a graduate program in anthropology just as the Internet bubble was beginning to swell. I joined other queer-identifying activists in their late teens and early twenties committed to and hoping to mobilize San Francisco's burgeoning queer-youth movement. We saw ourselves as a political force to be reckoned with in our own right rather than a vulnerable, suicide-prone population in need of protection. The World Wide Web, launched in 1992 and made more widely accessible in 1993 through graphical web-browsing software like Mosaic and, later, Netscape, seemed like an obvious strategy to reach our demographic, at least the ones in college with free e-mail accounts and access to networked computers.

My work co-founding and co-moderating a Usenet newsgroup for lesbian, gay, bisexual, and transgender (LGBT) identifying youth led to collaborations with other youth on website projects by and for youth and, later, to a job building communities for an Internet startup called PlanetOut, a commercial website created to attract lesbian, gay, bi, and trans people. While working on the design of PlanetOut's community spaces and finishing a master's thesis on narratives of queer-youth activism, I began to wonder what the everyday skirmishes in places that did not have a strong network of youth services looked like and tried to make sense of why we knew so little about them. Certainly communities and youth activists in these places were doing important work. What happens to kids who read these online resources in places that don't have the capacity to organize and coordinate with youth services and the broader infrastructure of support one takes for granted living three blocks from the Castro? Were these youth able to do much more than read what we post? They have access to representations that are affirming, but, at the same time, none of these images reflect their local surroundings. The 1998 murder of Matthew Shepard in the college town of Laramie, Wyoming (population 27,000), brought to the fore that city-based queer-youth social movements seemed able to do little more than pity and demonize those living outside of urban centers.

Recognizing the serendipity of my own queer identity—how much my own identifications had to do with the language available to me at the time and the timing and context of claiming queerness—I decided that the only way to figure out how identities might be organized for political work outside of cities was to go there myself and ask which city-based strategies worked and which seemed out of place.

At the heart of my intellectual curiosity was a political aim. Youth-driven models of organizing online ignored how reliant queer-youth organizing was on the infrastructure of urban-based nonprofit organizations, whether for mere meeting space or for access to computers and donated software programs to surf and post to the web. They also presumed media make a difference in kids' lives no matter where one lived. If media were to be of any use as an organizing tool, we needed to start with the question—rather than the presumption—of their utility and consider when, how, where, and why media technologies stood in for other political work that seemed too hard to do otherwise.

As a media scholar, I set out to gather the details of rural young people's everyday negotiations of lesbian, gay, bisexual, and transgender identities and engagements with mass and new media, through informal conversations, extensive interviews, and tagging along to see what I might see out in the country. I did so with an eye toward using this project to question my own assumptions about the power of media to effect change. I hope this book will expressly de-center media as the object of analysis in new media research and add to an argument for greater ethnographic attention to the uptake and meaning of media in our everyday lives. But having traveled to this project from my experiences growing up in a town seen as too small or too inconsequential (if it were visible at all) to matter, I also hope to challenge LGBT scholars' and activists' presumptions that cities are the predestined or exclusive catalysts of change. Keeping cities as the unquestioned center of our inquiries belies the reality that we have barely scratched the surface of the social terrains that warrant our intellectual and political attention.

1

Introduction

There Are No Queers Here

I snaked my way through I-64 traffic, past two car wrecks and several police speed traps to reach Frankfort, Kentucky, by 8:20 that icy February morning in 2002. A regional field organizer from the Kentucky Fairness Alliance (KFA), a statewide lesbian, gay, bisexual, and transgender (LGBT) advocacy organization, had arranged for me to lobby with a dozen young people and four adults from Berea, a Central Kentucky town of 9,800 people, and I was running almost a half-hour late. I quickly found my fellow advocates crowded around a table in the Kentucky State Capitol's smoky basement cafeteria. They stood out among the gray-haired white men in dark-blue suits who filled the low-ceilinged, fluorescent-lit room silently chain-smoking as they read their morning papers.

The all-white group from Berea sat tightly packed together with their backpacks and winter coats piled on the floor around their feet. An even mixture of young men and women wore Berea College or Berea High sweatshirts. The four adult allies affiliated with the Berea chapter of Parents and Friends of Lesbians and Gays (PFLAG) had the tired-but-supportive faces of elders trying to keep up with their younger counterparts' exuberance. As I walked toward them, a tall man in his early fifties with a neatly trimmed salt-and-pepper beard stood up, smiled, and said in a resonating baritone, "You must be Mary." He held out both his hands to shake mine as the youth seated around him also smiled, waved up at me from their seats, and made room for me to squeeze in among them. The excited pitch of the discussion about lobbying strategy and talking points suggested that they were well into a second round of coffee.

After apologizing for being late, I introduced myself, sat down, and asked them if this was the first time they had lobbied together. Two of the younger members of the group smiled widely and said "no," then launched into the following story. The year before, in 2001, a small group

1

of the same young people from Berea College, a private Christian school, met with their state house representative, Lonnie Napier, during Religious Leaders Lobby Day. The KFA and progressive clergy involved in KFA's Religious Organizing Project co-sponsored the event to educate lawmakers about LGBT issues in the state. "None of us had ever met a government representative before," said Jeremy, a Berea College senior. "I know Napier's family owns a lot of property around town, but I'd never met him in person." The Berea students certainly did not expect their meeting with a local government representative to become a media spectacle.

Jeremy and his friend Seth broke out in laughter as they recounted their barbed exchanges with Representative Napier. "He let me and a couple other guys into his office and then started throwing Bible quotes at us, saying we'd been badly influenced by TV and the Internet. It was weird. He just went off. Then, he tells us he doesn't have to be educated about LGBT issues because there aren't any gays living in Berea!" Napier's claim—professed to two of his gay-identifying constituents—floored Jeremy and Seth. More than 15 people regularly attended the Berea LGBT student group's monthly meetings and many more belonged to its online discussion list. "Berea's got to be the gayest place in Kentucky, outside of Louisville and Lexington!" Seth asserted before returning to the topic of last year's lobbying efforts. Apparently Napier carried the conversation with the Berea students out onto the State Capitol building's steps in range of a local camera crew and reporter covering the 2001 Lobby Day event. The students said that the next day's evening news featured images of Napier shaking his finger in the face of a white young man clutching his backpack straps and looking bewildered as Napier unleashed his fire-and-brimstone condemnations of the gay lifestyle.

LGBT Lobby Day events are quintessential examples of how a politics of visibility can work as a political force in public life. Private citizens coalesce as a community of LGBT people at these events to demonstrate their strength in numbers. Together, they seek to effect change through a public call for social recognition and equal representation. I was intimately familiar with the Berea students' strategies because I was once a queer-youth activist. I moved to San Francisco after college and joined a cadre of dynamic youth leaders, all in our late teens and early twenties, drawn as much to the city's politics as its social scene in the mid-1990s. A range of not-for-profit youth advocacy organizations, like San Francisco's Stop AIDS Project and the Lavender Youth Recreation and Information

Center, provided meeting space and other raw materials for our organizing, but a tight circle of queer-youth activists led the effort to craft and run rallies like California's first LGBT Youth Lobby Day, held January 3, 1996, on Sacramento's State Capitol building steps and in its rotunda.

Hundreds of youth activists from around California bused in or drove to the Capitol for that first Lobby Day to advocate for the passage of what would become, four years later, Assembly Bill 537, a law to protect K-12 students from harassment based on sexual orientation and gender identity.[1] A few of the event's organizers, myself included, hailed from small towns, transplants from California's mountain ranges and farming communities. Others grew up in the rural corners of Midwestern and Southern "flyover" states that many city dwellers cannot find on a map. The expectations of conformity and the lack of civic engagement (unless one counts church picnics) that we associated with our upbringings made the idea of publicly reveling in a queer sense of difference ("Let your freak flag fly!") almost unimaginable. Caught up in the excitement of that first Youth Lobby Day, and as only young activists can sometimes believe, we felt we could accomplish anything through these public demonstrations of defiant visibility and collective action.

But the Berea students' Lobby Day experience, which I will return to in the next chapter, demonstrates the dilemmas rural young people face when they rely on similar strategies of visibility and assertions of difference deployed by their urban peers. Unlike urban gay and lesbian communities able to mobilize significant numbers of people and dollars to generate visibility, rural youth and their allies live and work in communities and legislative districts that prioritize solidarity, rely on familiarity, and lack the public or private resources to underwrite sustained, visible dissent to assert queer difference. These are also places where media representations of LGBT people outpace the tangible presence of locally organized constituencies able to or invested in prioritizing queer recognition.

This book addresses how young people in the rural United States who lay claim to LGBT identities confront the politics of gay visibility, expectations, and constraints that define and shape the recognition of LGBT-identifying people in popular culture and public life. I take an interdisciplinary approach to examine how rural queer and LGBT-identifying youth, contrary to popular narratives of escape to urban oases, stand their ground to name their desires and flesh out their local meaning. I take stock of the strategies they use to create belonging and visibility in communities where they are not only a distinct minority but also popularly represented as out of place. To do so, they must lean on the structures of rural life, particularly the dynamics of class, gender, race, and location. In equal measure, they also use mainstream and new media representations to piece together what counts as an "authentic" LGBT identity and integrate these depictions of "realness" into rural settings. I argue that LGBT-identifying youth and their allies use their status as "familiar locals" as well as tenuous access to each other, public spaces, and media-circulated representations of LGBT identities to rework the boundaries of public recognition and local belonging. They rally these resources not to combat isolation from their senses of self, but to weather the demands a politics of gay visibility poses outside of cities. Along the way, their experiences attenuate claims that political strategies of gay visibility and recognition have brought us universally to the brink of a "post-gay" moment.

I push against assuming that a politics of visibility can lead to what sociologist Steven Seidman characterizes as life "beyond the closet" because, as scholar Eve Sedgwick among others notes, visibility operates as a binary: in order for someone to be visible, to "come out," there must always be a closet *someplace* where others clamor or struggle to get out.[2] The rural United States, as I will argue below, operates as America's perennial, tacitly taken-for-granted closet. Examining the assumptions that tether LGBT identities to cities and closets to rural communities opens the door to critique the privileging of some queer identities over others that the politics of gay visibility can produce.

I bring together gay and lesbian studies of community and identity, social theories of public spaces, and studies of media reception, particularly the role of new media in everyday life, to frame how sociality, location, and media shape the visibility of LGBT-identifying young people living in rural areas of Kentucky and along its borders. With the help of these academic conversations, refracted through the lens of ethnography—the qualitative study of research participants' interactions and perspectives—I set the stage for readers to consider how strategies of visibility that currently drive mainstream gay and lesbian social movements in the United States work out in the country. More broadly, I lay the groundwork to make the case that this ethnographic study of rural LGBT-identifying and questioning youth contributes to larger debates regarding young people's contemporary experiences of sexual and gender identity and the mediation of public engagement in a digital era.

Never Met a Stranger

Small-town life, so the story goes, engenders a kind of "never met a stranger" friendliness—a popular Southern euphemism I heard often during my time out in the country. It is a pervasive ethos, what cultural theorist Raymond Williams might have called a "structure of feeling," that makes it easy to presume you have known the person ahead of you in the grocery store checkout lane all your life.[3] This imagined, affable familiarity animates both the repulsion and fascination many urbanites—particularly queer-identifying ones—feel toward the rural. They might ask, why would any self-respecting lesbian, gay, bisexual, or transgender person forego the expansive safe havens of urban enclaves like the Castro in San Francisco, Boystown in Chicago, the Village in Manhattan, Brooklyn's Park Slope, Florida's Key West and Miami, and West Hollywood in Los Angeles for the suffocating myopia of the sticks?

At the heart of the antipathy between familiarity and queerness is the belief that discovering a sense of one's queer self requires three things: the privacy to explore one's queer differences beyond the watchful eyes of those who presume to know everything about one; a visible community able to recognize and return one's queer gaze; and the safe space to express queer difference without fear of retribution. These conditions considered pivotal to reaching that last stage of identity development called "coming out" are presumed to be part of a city's fabric (even if, at times, thread-bare) while veritably absent out in the country. Even if one questions the availability or existence of these conditions to most urban dwellers, without question rural youth negotiate queer desires and embodiments under different logistical realities.

Unlike their urban and suburban peers, young people living between the metropoles of San Francisco, Chicago, and Manhattan face vastly different access to agencies serving lesbian, gay, bisexual, and transgender-identifying youth. Many also live beyond the reach of publicly funded LGBT health programs, community-based support agencies, and visible constituencies able to finance, nurture, and augment such services.[4] The dearth of capital and community-based resources also means that gatekeepers, like Berea's Representative Lonnie Napier, can make all the difference. Powerful individuals wield a disproportionate amount of power in setting local agendas and therefore the conditions for LGBT visibility. This leaves little recourse or incentive to risk one's local acceptance by registering dissent. Age, obligations to family, and limited economic opportunities left the rural youth I met with little choice in the matter but to stay put and make do.

But the ubiquitous presumption that only urban centers can properly foster the kinds of visibility considered essential to LGBT identities and community organizing drove me to ask: What are the queer sexual and gender possibilities in places where the operative assumption is that one has never met a stranger? If access to a visible community of sexual and gender difference is central to the story of urban queer cultural formation, how do the expectations and experiences of prosaic familiarity, central to the organization of rural communities, produce and articulate queerness differently? Where, when, and how do rural youth who seek support for their sense of gender or sexual difference acquire a vocabulary for specifically LGBT identities? And, with the rapid but unequal incorporation of new information technologies into the lives of rural youth and their support agencies, what difference does the Internet's increasing presence—and presumed ubiquity—make to youth negotiating the politics of LGBT visibility in small towns across Kentucky and its rural Appalachian borders?

Epistemologies of LGBT Visibility: Gay and Lesbian Studies of Community and Identity

The contemporary story of gay identity formation in the United States is that it started in (and could not have happened without) a city. Historian John D'Emilio's now classic argument posited that capitalism's mobilizing forces reorganized same-sex desire into a visible and viable social identity. Masses of young, single individuals discovered new erotic as well as economic opportunities as they migrated from farms to cities at the turn of the 19th century, crescendoing in the post–World War II era.[5] D'Emilio argued that the anonymity of U.S. cities provided same-sex desiring people with networks of connection. These new "homophile movements," as they were called, defied medical discourses that defined same-sex desires as an individual pathological defect and transformed homosexuality into a collective identity.[6] Historians like George Chauncey in his book *Gay New York*, for example, added greater nuance to this argument, noting that the racially and class-stratified sexual circuits of gay life in New York City organized more through habits or patterns of congregation than through anonymity.[7] Nonetheless, the cityscape took center stage as the key site for the rise of gay and lesbian identity and community formation.

Out of this amassing of desire came a visible political movement inspired by the strategies of the new social movements for civil and wom-
en's rights that took root in the 1950s, 1960s, and 1970s.[8] Through a range
of political and social strategies, not the least of which was savvy use of
mainstream and alternative media, gay- and lesbian-identifying activists
of this era demanded legitimacy.[9] Urban chapters of activist organizations
like the Gay Liberation Front and later the Gay Activists Alliance fought
nationally on projects ranging from the repeal of sodomy laws that en-
trapped anyone seen to traffic in the "perversion" of "unnatural" sexual
acts to reforms of the American Psychiatric Association's classification of
homosexuality as a mental illness. While some activists, certainly radical lesbian feminists, sought broader social revolution through liberation
from the confines of heterosexuality, others fought for recognition and
validation of gay and lesbian people to live and love just like everyone
else.[10] These "wars of position" would later be characterized as a struggle
between liberationist and assimilationist politics.[11] Both positions, however, work from an assumption that visibility and political dissent operate
the same way across space and time and are readily available and universally valued no matter where one might live. Cities are imagined to draw
out and bind together the nameless throngs of same-sex desiring and gender-variant people to build visibility and political power. This particular
history of gay and lesbian visibility positions the city's capacities to make
space for queer difference and consolidate capital as necessary precursors
to modern lesbian and gay identity formation.

D'Emilio and other social constructivist scholars, building on earlier
feminist critiques, meant to challenge biological assumptions about sexuality and gender roles, and open them to cultural inquiry.[12] But as sociologist Steven Seidman observed, "As much as these [social construction
studies of gay and lesbian community formation] challenged essentialist
or universalistic understandings of homosexuality, they contributed to a
politics of the making of the homosexual minority" (Seidman 1996, 9).
The political gains of gay and lesbian organizing made in the 1970s and
1980s buoyed U.S. scholars, particularly gay- and lesbian-identifying ones,
to legitimate homosexuality as an object of historical and cross-cultural
social formation rather than an individual pathological defect.

Community studies expanded cultural and historical understandings of
gay and lesbian urban enclaves and established gay and lesbian studies as
legitimate fields of study in the social sciences and the humanities.[13] Kath
Weston, in her exhaustive 1993 review of the anthropological literature

resulting from this boon in gay/lesbian scholarship, characterizes this time period as a shift from incidental "subrosa" references to homosexuality and gender variance as deviations from the norm to a salvage anthropology of "ethnocartography" consumed with locating and redeeming (predominantly male) homosexuality's centrality to social life.[14]

Some of the most important and influential work in and beyond lesbian and gay anthropology, such as anthropologist Esther Newton's groundbreaking studies of male drag performers and, later, lesbian community in New York's Cherry Grove on Fire Island, theorized the particularities of place, gender, class, and race as critical to understanding the shape identities take. Newton's pioneering scholarship and that of others, exemplified by the work of linguistic anthropologist William Leap, laid the foundation for conceptualizing U.S. lesbian and gay urban public life as performative, constructed through the interactions of spaces, politics, and subjects rather than rooted in any intrinsic qualities or characteristics of lesbian- and gay-identifying people.[15] The ethnographies of U.S. lesbian and gay community life that followed could no longer discount or downplay the pivotal role spatial relations played in the particularities and cultural meaning of individuals' claims to the word "gay" or "lesbian." At the same time, none of these studies ventured beyond urban communities.

And certainly the need to respond to the tragedies of the AIDS pandemic through much of the late 1980s and 1990s further drove anthropologists and social workers to the urban epicenters of the AIDS crisis. These activist-scholars used their research to challenge the popular representations of HIV/AIDS as a "gay disease" while unpacking the ways institutionalized forms of discrimination and oppression in our national health care and public health systems intersected to accelerate the disease's spread among gay- and bisexual-identifying men and men who have sex with men but do not identify as gay or bisexual.[16]

More recently anthropologists working outside the United States and with diasporic communities have called into question what gay visibility means and looks like in a global context.[17] Evie Blackwood's work with *tombois* in West Sumatra and Megan Sinnott's research of *toms* and *dees* in Thailand, for example, draw attention to how individuals' expressions of female sexual desire and embodiment interlock and work through cultural understandings of gender roles.[18] Tom Boellstorff's research on *lesbi* and *gay* Indonesians argues that through what he calls a framework of "dubbing," Indonesians take up the fragmented discourses of lesbian and gay identities circulating in mass media and transform them into locally particular experiences of subjectivity.[19] Martin Manalansan's landmark ethnographic study of gay Filipino men living in the diasporic spaces of New York City calls into question any stable, universal gay or lesbian subject, noting how established norms of gay and lesbian cultures are constantly translated and transformed in specific locations.[20] The growth in transgender studies scholarship further complicates how the experiences of transgender people and, as David Valentine argues, the category of transgender itself fit into the coherency of a steady, equally fought march toward non-normative sexual and gender visibility.[21] Yet all of these studies, to varying degrees, inadvertently carry forward assumptions that cities are the "habitus" of queerness wherever one travels.[22] This book is the first contemporary ethnographic study of queer rural life in the United States and the first to consider how the saturation of gay visibility in the media might, particularly through the experiences of young people, challenge presumptions of queerness' proper place.

De-centering Metronormativity

As historical anthropologists James Clifford and George Marcus suggest, a narrative that consistently presumes the absence or impossibility of particular "social forms . . . demands analysis as a narrative structure" (Clifford and Marcus 1986, 112). These narratives do the cultural work of keeping one story visible at the expense of others.[23] Community histories of U.S. gay minorities cohere through and hinge on unrelenting narratives that imagine rural spaces as "gay America's closet," the premodern trappings that must be "left behind to reach gay culture and community formation in the cities" (Howard 1999, 63). The rhetoric of the countryside's "isolation" from gay identity, implicit in this progress narrative (how are you going to keep them down on the farm once they've seen gay Paris?!), helped stabilize gayness as an inherent trait just waiting for the right (urban) conditions to come together so it could come out and proudly shine. Gay visibility is simultaneously given a spatial location and a social value in this formulation. In other words, the narrative of rural to urban migration graphed gay visibility as a political accomplishment onto the space of the city. A politics of visibility needs the rural (or some *otherness*, some *place*) languishing in its shadow to sustain its status as an unquestionable achievement rather than a strategy that privileges the view of some by eliding the vantage point of others.

The language researchers use to describe rural queer experience often presumes pre-existing, yet alienated, sexual and gendered subjects who seek belonging in their own skin and a connection to gay culture that exists in an urban elsewhere.[24] By extension, such representations frame rural queer-youth sexualities and genders as "lacking" or "incomplete." A few researchers have questioned the curious sidestepping of the rural as a site for investigation of queer sexualities and genders. Anthropologist Kath Weston, for example, noted the importance of a rural/urban binary to queer sensibilities of gay urban migration.[25] Deploying Benedict Anderson's concept of an imagined community, Weston argued that the contrasting images of "escape from the isolation of the countryside . . . to the anonymity of the urban landscape . . . [f]rom the start . . . were embedded in the gay subject" (Weston 1995, 274). More recently, queer theorist Judith Halberstam coined the phrase "metronormativity" to characterize this peculiar tendency to conflate the urban with visibility and sexual enlightenment that "reveals the rural to be the devalued term in the urban/rural binary governing the spatialization of modern U.S. sexual identities" (Halberstam 2005, 36–37).[26]

Some academic disciplines have been more attentive to the neglect of the rural in thinking through what difference place might make to expressions of queer sexualities and genders.[27] Jon Binnie and Gil Valentine note in their review of the cultural geography literature addressing lesbian, gay, and bisexual sexualities how the handful of rural sexuality studies "demonstrate how much we take for granted that lesbian and gay lives are lived in the urban environment" (Binnie and Valentine 1999, 178). Indeed, their summary begins with an overview of where geographies of sexuality have gathered the most data—North American cities—such as the commonly cited study of gay and lesbian space in San Francisco by Manuel Castells and Larry Knopp's extensive analyses of political economies of gay men's gentrification of urban spaces.[28] The only collection of cultural geography essays that moves beyond the landscapes of the city is *Decentring Sexualities: Politics and Representations Beyond the Metropolis*, edited by Richard Phillips, Diane Watt, and David Shuttleton.[29] The anthology draws from disciplines such as literary and cultural studies, queer studies, history, and law but does not offer a sociological or ethnographic take on its subject matter.

Despite the recognized neglect of rural spaces noted by a range of scholars, there remain relatively few extended studies of queer sexualities and genders in the rural United States. Two notable exceptions that contribute to the cultural understanding of U.S. rural queer sexualities and genders centrally inform this book. I will elaborate on the theoretical contributions of these texts throughout this book, but let me briefly offer an overview here. *Men Like That: A Southern Queer History*, John Howard's vibrant analysis of Mississippi's queer history between 1945–1985, as told through oral histories, draws a picture of male-male desires in the common spaces of house, church, and school in stark contrast to the images of the South as devoid of sexual and gender difference (Howard 1999). Howard's detailed accounts of the racial and sexual lines that order queer male homoerotic desires in the South and centrality of circulation rather than congregation that characterize the making of queer spaces in rural communities directly challenge presumptions that rural spaces cannot sustain rich queer cultures. *The Stranger Next Door: The Story of a Small Community's Battle over Sex, Faith, and Civil Rights*, sociologist Arlene Stein's ethnographic study of a small Oregon lumber town in the 1990s, found that local "culture wars" over sexuality, particularly gay and lesbian people's rights to protection from discrimination, echoed deeper anxieties about the community's economic and social stability and race and class tensions (Stein 2001). Stein brings a similar theoretical complexity to lives lived queerly in rural spaces and, importantly, speaks to how central race and class are to the expressions of queer sexualities and genders in places organized around getting along and discomfort with strangers.

To date, no studies have focused specifically on youth in the rural United States and their negotiations of a queer sense of self and the expectations of visibility that have become a feature of modern LGBT experience and popular culture.[30] This ethnography is an attempt to intervene and refocus our attention. These case studies of rural sexualities and genders offer fresh vantage points to consider the links among larger structural issues, such as statewide social-service funding and regional race and class relations, media representations, and day-to-day processes of individual presentations and negotiations of identity.

Queering the Effects of Media Visibility

If visibility is imagined to be the road to acceptance for LGBT-identifying people, much of that recognition circulates through representations in the media. Films, television characters, press accounts of social movements, AIDS reporting, plays, books, and the Internet are where most stories of queer desires transpire. These representations translate queer desires into

LGBT-specific identities and give them a proper locale, typically the city. As such, media are the primary site of production for social knowledge of LGBT identities. It is where most people, including those who will come to identify as LGBT, first see or get to know LGBT people. In other words, media circulate the social grammar, appearance, and sites of LGBT-ness.

Arguably, media's social force seems heightened (sometimes hyped?) in rural places not because of a complete absence of LGBT-identifying or queer-desiring individuals with whom rural youth might identify, but because of the way rurality itself is depicted as antithetical to LGBT identities. Mass media consistently narrate rural LGBT identities as out of place, necessarily estranged from authentic (urban) queerness. These images teach rural youth to look anywhere but homeward for LGBT identities. Should we presume rural queer and questioning youth treat new media technologies as the latest vehicles of escape? Is it possible that, for the rural youth who stay put, new media serve not primarily as "opportunities for the formation of new communities . . . spanning vast distances" but as opportunities to create and consolidate networks much closer to home that are otherwise absent from mass-media representations?[31]

One of the difficulties in researching the role media play in the cultivation of a rural queer sensibility is that it is all too easy to fall back on the presumed properties of the technologies themselves to the exclusion of the social contexts that give technologies meaning.[32] Historically, technological innovations in the modern era simultaneously raise society's hopes and stoke its fears.[33] But no technology comes prepackaged with a set of "good" or "bad" traits. Unfortunately, until the novelty of a "new technology" tapers off or is displaced by something newer, media-effects researchers and cultural critics alike cycle through fixations on the good, bad, and ugly that come hidden inside the box—whether it is a radio, a television, or the Internet. This has produced a lineage of media scholarship tightly focused on communication technologies as things that produce effects rather than cultural elements of the complexity of human interactions and our relationships with/to innovation itself.[34] These debates over media's strong or weak effects rage on regardless of the media in question.

However, the tenor of these intellectual deliberations reaches a fervent pitch when questions turn to media's potential influence on children. Young people have always been the screens onto which society projects its greatest fears. Film historian Greg Waller, for example, points out the ways early discussions of the nickelodeon concerned issues of effects on children and their moral character.[35] More recently, with the advent of everything from MySpace to Gameboys, new technologies are presented in popular culture as sources of distraction, violence, or allure that threaten the sanctity and safety of children. Judith Levine argues that rather than accept the statistical reality that children are more vulnerable to sexual harm at the hands of immediate family members, society projects its fears onto strangers, seeing media as one of several tools used to lure unsuspecting children. A case in point is the "pedophile panic" that spurred the drafting of the 1996 Communications Decency Act (Levine 2002, 20–44). This panic led to institutionalizing parental surveillance through codes for films and music, as well as v-chips and Internet-filtering software. These preventive measures presume and perpetuate the notion that media have direct and very negative effects on children. Prevention logic suggests one can curtail certain behaviors by regulating access to these media or the content of media itself. Of course, the reality is far more complicated.

Interventions: Breaking the Media-Effects Habit

Out in the Country bridges ethnographic approaches to media from an anthropological perspective and reception or audience studies in the field of communication.[36] Ethnographers of the media sometimes forget they are, as Janet Staiger argues, "doing textual analysis" through the interpretation of fieldnotes, interviews, and other mainstays of the ethnographic tool kit (Staiger 2005, 13). Losing sight of this can sometimes lead to framing media as taken-for-granted tools rather than texts with histories and politics to be unraveled.[37]

Media studies tends to approach the question of representations of social influence of media as a matter of impact. We think the medium itself carries certain properties and, therefore, inherent powers. New media promise to bring about change—slipping it in around mass culture. We attach cultural weight to it as we look to blogs to address our mistrust of mainstream journalism or turn to distance learning to address the increasing costs of higher education. But new media are part of mass culture—the stories they circulate remediate the stories already out there. Often, new media studies perpetuates a "media effects" approach. For example, we might be tempted to imagine that new media technologies allow rural gay kids to escape their rural communities and find refuge and recognition online. But framing the question like this leads us down a dead-end road of inquiry unable to explore how rural queer and questioning youth engage and transform media as they respond to expectations of visibility and the structures of familiarity that organize their offline experiences. Focusing on new media as spaces that produce online worlds fails to respond to the call of critical cyberculture researchers to examine how "[o]ffline contexts permeate and influence online situations, and online situations and experiences always feed back into offline experience" (Baym 2006, 86). Media scholars like Nancy Baym call on us to "recognize that the internet is woven into the fabric of the rest of life" (Baym 2006, 86).

What we learn from reception and audience studies in media studies, particularly work done with and about youth from theorists like Ellen Seiter and Sonia Livingstone, is that youth engage media in far more complicated ways than we assume.[38] Seiter and Livingstone respond to and challenge work that assumes media are deleterious to kids based on presumptions about the particular effects of the medium. They apply an ethnographic and qualitative approach to complicate what "effects" might look like in the lives of young people by studying their everyday uses of media. They treat young people, much as work in new childhood studies and critical youth studies do, as active agents but also a culturally constructed demographic.

What we learn from reception studies, particularly among young people, tends to be adult-centered and adult-monitored; it is driven by questions parents have about their children's consumption of media and focused on demonstrating how deleterious media are to kids—their negative effects. Some work challenges this. Ellen Seiter, for example, pioneered scholarship in children's use of the media that worked to understand not only how children make meaning in their lives through their use of media, but also how parental anxieties over children's media use spoke more broadly to societal tensions over what constituted "proper parenting," particularly the mother's role as moral guide. But much of the work on reception studies focuses tightly on the conditions for viewing, centered on the moment of reception itself. How can we break out of this narrow focus to see the more complicated relationships between media and their meaning in our everyday lives? One way is through ethnographic approaches that contextualize media engagements as part of a broader social terrain of experience. Performances of identities require tools. What tools are out there for rural youth to pick up if they seek to express a sense of self that doesn't square up with the heteronormative expectations around them? What allows for an iteration of a sexual or gender identity that is constructed in popular culture as antithetical to their rural communities? What kind of visibility can be performed here and through what means? What are the limits of these iterations? What do we need to politically tweak to make queer sexualities and genders more habitable to rural youth? It might be specific enunciations of identity, or it might be creating a politics that does not see visibility as the primary goal, therefore allowing an affinity and political kinship to take center stage.[39]

Remediating Media Reception and Cyberculture Studies

This book underscores the continued, pressing need to understand media reception not as a singular one-way passive act but as constellations of active moments of engagement saturated in histories and contemporary experiences of raced, classed, and placed identities.[40] When rural young people watch a TV show or surf the Internet, their sense of who they are, how others see them, and where they live is always part of the picture. To capture a more contextual notion of media reception, I situate the production, consumption, and circulation of media representations and new media technologies within the broader social conditions of rural life— most notably the dynamics of class, gender, race, and location. These conditions afford different access to technology use and social identifications. Paying attention to how rural young people deal with the material realities of their lives challenges theoretical models of media use that presume anything conclusive or universal can be claimed about media's "effects."

The politics of LGBT visibility's demanding refrain to "come out, come out, wherever you are" echoes the rhetorical invocations of disembodied freedoms and escapist anonymity attributed to the "effects" of the Internet. I use the examples of youth turning to online coming-out stories and personal ads to complicate these libratory discourses popularly associated with discussions of "cyberspace." LGBT-identifying rural young people use new media not to escape their surroundings but to expand their experience of local belonging. They use new media to enhance their sense of inclusion to broader, imagined queer communities beyond their hometowns. They also experience new media as one among several ephemeral moments of public space and belonging. They effectively—though not without cost—suture the queer social worlds they find in their hometowns, on television, and online.

These young people's strategies offer models for rethinking the relationships among visibility, public spaces, and media, particularly in a digital era. The day-to-day uses of new media as source materials for identity work also highlights the frayed and fragile edges of a politics of LGBT visibility in communities that battle for basic resources and struggle for community recognition in the broader U.S. political landscape. Without question, new media were central to understanding the distributed and collective underpinnings of modern queer identities among rural youth in the United States. In making this assertion, I am not claiming, as early Internet enthusiasts did, that new media produce new identities.[41] In fact, I am arguing that the more compelling issue warranting investigation here is the critical link between modern identity categories and the circulation of popular discourses vis-à-vis "new" media. Unfortunately, new media studies often neglects how technologies reflect, reproduce, and are embedded with a given society's gender and sexual mores and ethics.[42] So, instead of asking whether technologies intrinsically offer political promise for queer youth in rural places, I examine how technologies are used (and not used) across multiple sites for queer-identity work. Under what sociopolitical conditions do online youth communities make sense? How are broader possibilities of identity representation both enabled and disabled by engagement with these technologies?

This study addresses how these technologies take part in producing and circulating queer categories as well as how the materiality of rural young queer life increasingly—although differentially—involves entanglements with online spaces. I sidestep actually defining "new media" because it is as elastic a category as "rural," "queer," or "youth." While the newness of the media may be relevant, one can never tell from a distance or from the texts themselves what kind of relevance it will have. For rural queer youth, it arguably matters more that today's media markets are saturated with specific popular discourses defining LGBT identity politics that conspicuously exclude them. Broadcast television programs, like *Queer Eye for the Straight Guy,* as well as niche-market consolidation of queer-owned Internet and print media, such as PlanetOut Partners (owners of Gay.com and PlanetOut.com) and Liberation Publications (publishers of *Out, The Advocate,* and Alyson Books), distribute a more standardized image of LGBT people today than early homophile organization publications.

My two contributions to studies of new media and their relationship to social knowledge production draw on the same logic of de-centering. Just as I seek to bring the rural out of the margins, I aim to de-center media as the object of analysis and to shift to a deep contextualization. I theorize the relationship between media and identities as sociotechnical, never imagining that social identities happen through unmediated processes. I confound distinctions between online and offline to answer the call by critical cyberculture scholars mentioned above. I also draw on media scholars Bolter and Grusin's argument of remediation.[43] New media circulate old stories entwining or commingling aesthetics of media forms to keep some narratives and forms of storytelling prioritized over others. In other words, media are products of and do political work.

Young people confound clear boundaries between online and offline worlds by integrating their uses of media and public spaces in everyday processes of identity negotiation and articulation. There's not one site that matters more—they all matter differently at different moments in the narration of the self. I'm looking to de-center media radically to see what else is in the picture—what contexts and conditions make some media engagements and visibilities seem to matter so much, and other times seem irrelevant, to the youth I met. They confound online/offline divides and utopian notions that new media are qualitatively different experiences of sociality because of some inherent quality or properties of the media themselves. As Sonia Livingstone points out, "The simple distinction between offline and online no longer captures the complex practices associated with online technologies as they become thoroughly embedded in the routines of everyday life" (Livingstone 2008, 393–94).[44] I'm looking at how young people confound distinctions between online and offline and how they draw lines between online and offline to negotiate visibility. Not to hide but to be seen. I am questioning whether this is a qualitative shift in the experience of visibility with access to new media or if it remediates old stories about identity. But experiences—reception or media engagement—cannot really separate out the phenomenological, the rhetorical, and the political. Properties of the media and the rhetoric that surrounds them are shot through with political expectations of what they can and cannot, will and will not do. These discourses hint at but cannot tell us what people try to make them do or how they minimize their impact in their lives. Rural young people's uses of new media disrupt clean divisions between online and offline experiences. Their everyday processes of identity integrate uses of new media, from their selection of words in an e-mail to denote their membership or connection to other Gay-Straight Alliance members to sending out action alerts through a PFLAG listserv to organize rides to a lobbying event. In the first half of the book, I am radically de-centering media to see what else might be in the picture of young rural people's engagements with a politics of visibility.

Affirming claims to LGBT identities may comfort a deep sense of alienation some individuals feel when they push against the grain of heterosexuality and gender conformity, but these claims are not (or need not be) the only route to political and social gains for queer lives and social movement in the United States. This book considers how "metronormative" epistemologies of visibility privilege urban queer scenes. The systematic marginalization of the rural as endemically hostile and lacking the cultural milieu necessary for a celebratory politics of difference naturalizes cities as the necessary centers and standard bearers of queer politics and representations. Along the way all those not able, or inclined, to migrate to the city are put at a notable disadvantage not just by the material realities of rural places but also by the shortcomings of queer theory and LGBT social movement in ways we have only recently begun to explore.

Youth Identities Out in Public

The entanglement through much of the 1970s and 1980s of political and intellectual work with mass-mediated representations discussed above gave rise and recognition to gay and lesbian urban communities.[45] These same politics of visibility inspired the field of psychology to produce new theories of sexual identity development to explain the presence of all these gay and lesbian people, particularly teens and young adults, flocking to the counterculture scenes in San Francisco and New York. Psychology as a discipline needed to update its definitions of homosexuality once the American Psychiatric Association removed it from its list of mental illnesses in 1973.[46] Psychologist Ritch Savin-Williams convincingly argues that psychologist Erik Erikson's theories of adolescent identity formation—the dominant identity development model of the discipline at the time—served as the starting point for a veritable cottage industry in "sexual identity" process modeling to account for the presence of all these homosexuals hanging around the city.[47] The premise of Erikson's work is that adolescence is a socially sanctioned life stage of "normative crisis" in which individuals explore and, eventually, integrate facets of their identities, including sexual desires, into a coherent sense of self.[48] The more than two dozen (and counting) models that Savin-Williams documents are variations on a theme that naturalizes the coming-out process as a series of stages or (more or less) linear trajectories that inevitably culminate in the integration of the healthy, happy homosexual respected and recognized from the inside out.[49]

Both Savin-Williams and sociologist Janice Irvine note that the explosion of this literature on the coming-out process contributed to the construction of a monolithic social category, "gay and lesbian youth," particularly as an "at-risk population" in desperate need of rescue.[50] To be sure, there are queer and questioning young people who experience a great deal of pain, frustration, confusion, and eventual relief through their engagements with LGBT identities. The majority of young people I interviewed expressed everything from ambivalence to self-destructive anger when it came to making sense of their sexual and gender identities under the relentless (monotonous) norms of heterosexuality and gender conformity that structured their lives (and those of anyone living in the United States). But, returning to historical anthropologists James Clifford and George Marcus' warning to be suspicious when cultural narratives of social formations seem to persist and repeat, I want to note that the "sexual identity formation" models Savin-Williams and Irvine critique dovetail too much with theories of gay community formation to be serendipitous. In effect, these models and our popular incorporation of their logic into how we think sexual identity works to pathologize experiences of desires and claims to identities—and by extension places—do not conform to a politics of visibility. As a result, researchers typically assume rural youth lack the resources, capacity, and support to actively foster difference in the seeming homogeneity of their small towns.[51]

Theorizing Youth:
Applying Critical Youth Studies to Queer-Youth Identity Work

Rather than presume an absence of critical materials for identity formation, I draw on a sociological tradition that theorizes identity as a highly social, contextual, and collective achievement rather than a psychological expression of an internal process of integration. Far from being the reflection of an inner drive, I argue that youth identities are cultural assemblages that work with the materials on hand.[52] My approach is deeply informed by the scholarship that falls under the rubric of new childhood studies and critical youth studies.[53]

New childhood studies takes adult researchers (perhaps many of today's parents) to task for uncritically applying a developmental paradigm that frames young people's identity practices as playful experimentation rather than seeing these practices as ways of being in the world.[54] Children's and adolescents' articulations of identity are interpreted strictly as rites of passage, paths youth travel on their way to adulthood. Under this rubric, young people's experiences of identity are simultaneously understood as the blossoming of an individual's unique character and, paradoxically, the timely appearance of universal characteristics particular to a phase of the human life course. New childhood studies challenges researchers to work against ahistorical, apolitical accounts and universalizing developmental models of children and adolescents. In its place, new childhood studies offers a critical analysis of the "socially constructed nature of childhood and adolescence" replete with the cultural baggage of adult-centered views of the world (Best 2007, 11).[55]

More recently, building on the work of new childhood studies, critical youth studies uses the insights and tools of cultural studies and critical studies of race, sexuality, and gender to engage children and adolescents as active agents and independent social actors rather than passive "subjects-in-the making" (Best 2007, 11). This approach attempts to foreground how power dynamics, including the researcher's relationship to youth participants, produce the cultural knowledge that shapes our understandings of young people. Working from this premise, critical youth scholars seek to acknowledge adults, children, and adolescents as cultural participants working in and through a dense network of power relations. This is particularly the case when it comes to the culturally charged discussion of youth sexuality. As Susan Driver argues, in reflecting on her own pioneering research examining queer youth's exploration of sexual desire through digital video, youth research must respond to and work against the heteronormative "conventional codes of academic knowledge" that "render ambiguous, indirect, and unstable ways of signifying [queer sexual] desire invisible" (Driver 2007, 308).

Studying rural queer and questioning youth identity formations builds on new childhood studies and critical youth studies in two important ways. Unlike the independence and self-determination that define the queer-youth political culture of national LGBTQ youth advocacy programs or queer-specific, urban-based resources and social services, rural young people's engagements with LGBTQ politics are marked by their interdependence with familiar queer adult advocates and non-LGBTQ allies. Since the 1990s and the visibility of "gay youth" as a cultural category, city-based queer-youth activists that followed my own envisioned their work as autonomous from that of adult queer activists (even though it was contingent on capital trickling down from adults). Rural queer and questioning youth have neither the peers nor the local tax base to imagine such independent political power. This echoes the broader disenfranchisement that challenges all rural-based political organizing efforts. As a result, studying rural queer-youth identities requires critical scholars of youth culture to complicate youth-centered research models to account for adults' active participation in the construction of rural queer-youth identity and community.

I investigate rural queer-youth identities as performative, socially mediated moments of being and becoming or, as queer theorist Lisa Duggan puts it, identity construction as a "process in which contrasting 'stories' of the self and others—stories of difference—are told, appropriated, and retold as stories of location in the social world of structured inequalities" (Duggan 1993, 793). I work against privileging youth experience in ways that could inadvertently essentialize queerness as a stable state of being that some youth possess.[56] Instead, I legitimize rural young people's claims to queer identities as, by definition, always more than "just a phase" or "experimentation" while questioning the presumption that identities ever start with or settle down to rest in the hands of individuals.

My own use of the metaphor of collective labor in a discussion of youth identity—talking about identity as work shared among many rather than the play of any one individual—is meant to recognize that the assembly and articulation of one's sense of self is, like any other social action, as sociologist Anselm Strauss puts it, "work [that] always occurs in contexts" (Strauss 1993, 95–97). Sociologist Barbara Ponse defined identity work as "the processes and procedures engaged in by groups designed to effect change in the meanings of particular identities" (Ponse 1978, 208). Drawing on Strauss and Ponse as well as the youth studies scholarship discussed above, I define queer-identity work as the collective labor of crafting, articulating, and pushing the boundaries of identities. I frame youth sexualities and genders as labor carried out among and through people, places, media texts, and a host of other circuitous routes. Treating identity as work highlights the strategies youth and their allies employ as they encounter the politics of visibility across these various work sites. I argue that rural youth do the collective labor of identity work differently than their urban counterparts not because rural queer youth have it inherently harder, but because they confront different heteronormative/homophobic burdens. They also bear the weight of a politics of visibility that, I argue, was built for city living.

Methods: Locating the Rural

Over nineteen months, between September 2001 and April 2003, and several short follow-up trips in the summers of 2004 and 2005, I drove around (and around, and around) the regions I describe in this book. I traveled more than 40,000 miles crisscrossing and circling the topography of my research site by the end of my work. I rarely stayed in one locale for more than a few days at a time, often driving from one meeting, event, or informal get-together to the next and then circling back to my Louisville apartment in between when at all possible. Sometimes I spent more time traveling to a remote town (discovering how unreliable online maps are for ferreting out KenTennessee's many unincorporated townships) than at an event or with the youth I drove out to meet.

Some readers might wonder why I chose rural communities in Kentucky and along its state borders for this research. Probably like most West Coast latchkey kids of the 1970s and 1980s, reruns of TV sitcoms and old PBS documentaries about President Johnson's War on Poverty framed the few images I had of this region. Even though California is rarely imagined to contain "rural" within its borders, there are plenty of small towns (including my own) in my home state that I could have studied and with which I would have had greater familiarity. But I wanted to exploit the reputed chasm between "the rural" and "the urban" to examine the layered cultural work such a binary produces. First, I wanted locate my research in an archetypal rural space that loomed large in the cultural imaginary of the United States. Doing so would allow me to investigate which stories of everyday life structure the mythology of a clear and clean divide between "rural" and "urban."[57] Related to this, I also sought to question the presumed ubiquity of new media technologies in the United States and to challenge conversations about the digital divide that tend to be narrowly concerned with questions of technology's availability (particularly "elsewhere") rather than social accessibility. While Internet access, for example, may be available in rural areas of the United States, its technological presence cannot (and should not) be easily equated with technological access and equal distribution. Selecting rural U.S. communities as a fieldsite troubled facile, colonialist-inflected distinctions between "developing" and "developed" worlds and what difference technological presence means absent the political conditions and will to ensure its equitable use. If I wanted to bring into relief the unexamined metrocentricity of scholarship on queer identity and community formation, I needed to radically de-center cities from my investigations and let rural young people's experiences and negotiations of queer subjectivity shape my understanding of where cities fit in their lives.

I spent the first two months of my research familiarizing myself with Louisville, Kentucky, and volunteering as an adult mentor with the Louisville Youth Group (LYG), a small nonprofit support organization for gay, lesbian, bisexual, transgender, and questioning young people under 21 years old. LYG's sole employee, a charismatic leader who had co-founded the group as a teenager, coordinated LYG's activities from her donated (unair-conditioned) office space on the third floor of a local church. LYG's youth leaders and its director planned campouts, drag show fundraisers, and Big Brother/Big Sister–type mentoring projects that matched local youth with adults in the community. Its weekly support group meetings moved between another donated church space located downtown and the offices of a well-known area LGBT advocacy organization. I soon realized that many of the youth who regularly attended LYG's weekly meetings traveled from rural counties as far as two hours away, sometimes carpooling with friends, other times driving alone, to take part in the two-hour meetings and post-meeting gatherings in which the group of twenty to twenty-five boisterous teens typically relocated to a nearby fast-food restaurant. The contingent of rural youth who routinely drove one hundred miles each way—typically in one evening—to attend LYG events quickly confounded the simple distinctions I had drawn between rural and urban lives.[58] I needed to be as mobile as the rural young people I hoped to get to know if I wanted to understand their sense of place in the world and its relationship to their identities.

With the help of youth I met at LYG and through regional and state-wide youth and LGBT advocacy agencies, I anchored my research in several small towns and rural communities, most with populations between 900 and as large as 15,000 found in what is referred to by the U.S. Census and Appalachian Regional Commission as the Central Appalachian Region.[59] I also included young people and adult participants living in communities in Kentuckiana, the areas along the Kentucky and Indiana borders of the Ohio River, and the Tri-State region joining Illinois, Kentucky, and Indiana. Most of my time, however, was spent with youth living in Central and Eastern Kentucky, particularly young people in communities nestled deep in the valleys and winding roads that make up the mountainous border that bridges Kentucky and Tennessee, a stretch of

Appalachia called KenTennessee.[60] All place names are pseudonyms, but the features of the areas—such as the commercial, industrial, and physical landscape—are consistent. In some cases the exact town populations mentioned are obscured to protect participants' privacy. All participants' names are changed to provide anonymity to individuals and those easily associated with local groups or well-known local personalities. Most of the names of public figures associated with state and national organizations are unchanged.

Following what anthropologist George Marcus refers to as a practice of "mobile ethnography," or more commonly called "multi-sited ethnography," I focused on a strategy of following the "connections, associations, and putative relationships" that connected the rural youth I met and that they cited as important to them (Marcus 1995, 96–97).[61] Ethnography traditionally seeks a holistic view of a single site—a coherent deep reading of the local. Marcus' notion of mobile ethnography does not seek a holistic view of a specific location. This stretches the usual limits of ethnography not from a local to the global but toward what Marcus sees as an effort to get at the context or social systems embedded in cultural formations, in my case a politics of LGBT identity formation. This approach turned out to be well-suited for looking at how rural LGBT-identifying young people constantly reworked boundaries, both local and virtual, to address the politics of LGBT visibility in places defined by adherence to solidarity through sameness. By contesting the presumed distance between an urban "us" and a rural "them" and facile distinctions between "offline" and "online" social spaces, this mobile ethnography allowed me to challenge the colonialist residues of modern ethnography that uncritically presume and dismiss the rural United States as backwater, outmoded, and isolated though rarely acknowledged as an "other" America deeply marginalized by the processes of modernity and globalization.[62]

It was not hard to find people interested in discussing the experiences of rural young people and how they negotiate a queer sense of sexuality and gender.[63] The area's vibrant network of young people and their advocates were neither confined to their small towns nor as isolated from resources in the way I originally imagined them to be. I met youth, their parents, adults with now-grown gay and lesbian children, social-service workers, church officials, earnest lobbyists like Berea's citizens, and the legislators they lobbied scattered across the region, blurring not only lines between rural and urban but also lines among counties, states, and national organizing efforts.

Most striking in this study were the small numbers of young women and youth of color of different genders available and/or able to participate in this discussion. White teenage men overwhelmingly dominated the friendship circles I tapped for participation in this project. Of the thirty-four youth I interviewed in-depth, thirty-one are white. This racial homogeneity superficially reflects the ethnic makeup and distribution typical of rural communities in these regions described in the chapters that follow. But much like the census data itself, it does not reflect the growing population of immigrant communities of color, particularly undocumented Latino workers and their families who go undercounted and misrepresented.[64] Less than a third of the participants (eleven total) identified as young women, compared to twenty-three young men. I discuss the reasons for the gendering of this difference in this book's Appendix, but, needless to say, it is a severe limitation to this study. Debra Tolman's discussion of sexual desire experienced by young women notes how bisexual- and lesbian-identifying young women feel particularly isolated and may offer some insight as to why they would be reticent to share their stories. Like the young women in Tolman's research, the rural young women I met were "highly aware that a lot was at stake for them because of their desire" (Tolman 2002, 185). Young rural women who identify as lesbian or bisexual or express a desire for other young women commit what Tolman called "a double violation" because "they feel sexual desire and it is for girls" (Tolman 2002, 185). Tolman, citing Rose Weitz, suggests that bisexual or lesbian girls "exempt from the institution of heterosexuality, in fact stand in a very different and threatening relationship to it, by violating its most core principle: that [they] are, by nature, attracted to the opposite gender only . . . these girls have an 'uncontained' sexuality that heightens social anxiety and thus instigates violent reactions" (Tolman 2002, 185). Indeed, several young women I met were willing to talk about their experiences but were unwilling to document them or consent to have them included in this research for fear of "blowing their cover," as more than a few young people put it.

Of the thirty-four youth I formally interviewed, three identified as transgender and all three were white: one 17-year-old female-to-male transsexual, one 17-year-old male-to-female transsexual, and one genderqueer-identifying 19-year-old. In most cases, youth used words to describe their sexualities that were familiar categories: gay and lesbian were the most common terms; bisexual was used occasionally. The median age of youth participants was 16-and-a-half years old.

I attended weekly youth agency meetings, *Queer as Folk* viewing parties, drag show fundraisers staged in barns, and a litany of prayer services among affirming and condemning representatives of the Christian faith. The thirty-four young people between 14 and 24 years old shared their stories through phone and in-person interviews. Our one-on-one conversations typically lasted anywhere from one to three hours. I also captured a handful of interviews from chat-room marathons or a flurry of e-mail exchanges. Among one-third of the interviewees, I used a combination of offline and online interviewing—in most cases using e-mail to follow up on questions generated from face-to-face discussions.[65]

Working Identities: A Note on the Use of Language

I use the term "queer" to characterize the action of identity work, much as Tanya Erzen does in her study of the ex-gay movement, to account for how these social interactions disrupt the norm, even when it might mean striving toward the normative identity category "gay" (Erzen 2006, 14). Like Michael Warner, I also use "queer" "in a deliberately capacious way . . . in order to suggest how many ways people can find themselves at odds with straight culture" (Warner 1999, 38). I frame sexual and gender identities as queer labor carried out between people and places, to map the modern experiences, conditions, and expressions that produce a sense of "authentic" identity. The authenticity of identity from this perspective reads as an ongoing, at times exhausting, dialogue rather than a reflection of reality. It refuses the inclination to be lodged in a singular person, place, or thing.

Some youth did see themselves as consciously queering their community's norms, but far more used "gay," "lesbian," "bisexual," or "transgender" as a noun to name a self-evident, core sense of their identity.[66] Yet, despite efforts to stabilize and normalize their sense of self through concrete labels, rural LGBT-identifying youth and young people questioning their heterosexuality and gender identity necessarily disrupted (in effect, *queered*) their surroundings. Their mere presence defied local and national expectations no matter how much they might conform to the most normative gay and lesbian standards. In doing so, rural LGBT-identifying and questioning youth complicate critiques of "homonormativity"—gay and lesbian conformity and liberal appeals for acceptance—and perhaps signal the need for rethinking what homonormativity means in locales where even queers assume LGBT-identifying people are out of place.[67]

Drawing on scholar Shane Phelan, I maintain that the usefulness of the term "queer" may be that it names "an unstable identity process" (Phelan 1997, 60) less intentionally claimed by individuals than unpredictably carried out through their interactions.

With almost uncanny consistency, regardless of self-identification, young people and their allies spoke more broadly of belonging to "the LGBT community." My use of the term "community" is meant to acknowledge its importance as an organizing principle to the people with whom I worked more than to signal my belief in its existence beyond an aspiration or ideal.[68] When youth referred to others, unless discussing a specific person, they referenced "LGBT (or GLBT) people" collectively— as a bloc constituency. I found it striking that so many youth consistently referenced the lineup of political identities most often cited by our national advocacy organizations. Then I realized that several of these young people regularly read the lesbian and gay community website PlanetOut. com's news headlines and action alerts posted on the Human Rights Campaign and National Gay and Lesbian Task Force websites. I did the same thing as someone trying to follow national debates about the Bush administration's efforts to push the debate around a constitutional amendment banning same-sex marriage or follow which states would be putting an anti-gay marriage measure on their November ballots. The social-service parlance of "LGBT" has become commonplace in the politics of visibility and indexes how deeply steeped some of these youth are in that political culture. So the pervasive use of "LGBT" as a phrase among youth commuting to social-service agencies like urban-based youth groups is not surprising. Like any jargon, it served to mark youth "in the know" and seemed to have been readily picked up by their peers less politically engaged or connected to urban-based social services. The circulation of "LGBT" also marks a strategy rural youth and their urban political counterparts share—a move toward solidarity and a sense of familiarity that precedes connection to an on-the-ground community.

References to a coherent and tangible "LGBT community" speak to the power of nationally mass-mediated conversations to manifest an "imagined community" of lesbian, gay, bisexual, and transgender people whether L, G, B, and T-identifying people are present or not.[69] From LGBT characters on primetime television or in movies to the online community spaces of popular LGBT websites and news coverage of the gay marriage debates, media play a central role in circulating the meaning of "LGBT" identities. These circulations narrow and elide queer experiences of desire as they produce some identity work over others. As anthropologist David Valentine so convincingly demonstrates in his study of the subtle erasures of subjectivity that happen when categories, like "transgender," coalesce in institutions charged with serving the people they name, "If the categories we use to talk about our worlds contribute, at least in part, to how we shape action in the world, then we must think about how they impact on those whose categories might be different from ours" (Valentine 2007, 31).

Roadmap: Chapter-by-Chapter Overview

Each chapter illustrates how dense networks of familiarity and estrangement intersect with places and strategies for negotiating a politics of visibility. These negotiations work out the boundaries of identity for queer and questioning rural youth. The book opens by picking up where the indefatigable Berea citizens' lobbying efforts to be seen by Representative Napier left off. I detail the meaning and use of "family" in the political and social work of local chapters of the national organization Parents and Friends of Lesbians and Gays. This analysis is juxtaposed with a thick description of how one local organization—the Grayson County Homemakers Club—brought the discussion of gay teens to the center of its small town of Leitchfield, Kentucky. Together these two cases demonstrate how both national and local activist communities deploy and complicate metaphors of "family" and legitimate "localness" to strategically move LGBT youth from the category of "queer strangers" to recognizable locals who deserve community support.

Shifting from a focus on the presumed intimacies of home and family, the book lays out examples of public spaces available for identity work in rural communities. It highlights in chapter 3, for example, the battle over Gay-Straight Alliances in rural schools and the struggles of the only rural chapter of the national nonprofit organization Gay, Lesbian and Straight Education Network. Chapter 4 chronicles the experiences of young people doing drag in the aisles of Wal-Mart, and the productive, fragile nature of such performances of identity work in rural communities. These examples illustrate how, in response to rural America's increasingly privatized and impoverished structural conditions, LGBT youth and their allies make the most of the spaces available to them by creating what I described above as boundary publics.

Having firmly established the presence of LGBT-identifying youth in rural spaces, chapter 5 moves to critically examine how rural young people experience online coming-out stories, personals, and LGBT-specific web portals as sites of information—discursive practices toward a lived "queer truth." In concrete ways, young people talked about these media texts—what I call a "genre of queer realness"—as resonances of their own, lived experience as well as evidence of others like them living beyond their small communities.

Chapter 6 examines how two trans-identifying rural young people experience their very different engagements with the same Discovery Channel documentary. The comparison is used to highlight how the dialectic between digital circulations of realness and material conditions of class and location shape queer-identity work. These two analyses suggest that a media-circulated "genre of queer realness" sets particular expectations of normative transgender embodiment. At the same time, the conditions of rural young people's lives—such as class status and its links to physical location and access to health care—importantly reconstitute and transform these popular discourses of what it means to be LGBT-identified and how to go about becoming a "real" lesbian, gay, bisexual, or trans-identifying person.

The concluding chapter ties the book's arguments together to consider how expectations of gay visibility work through and against structures of familiarity, boundaries of public spaces, and engagements with media to produce rural queer-youth identities. I reflect on how the cultural value and weight assigned to visibility position new and mass media as libratory tools that will lead rural queer and questioning youth out of the wilderness of their presumed isolation. Ultimately, *Out in the Country* questions how the taken-for-granted binaries of rural/urban, closeted/visible, and online/offline work together to privilege ideologies of visibility and produce isolation irrespective of where one lives, universally marginalizing queer lives beyond metropoles in the process.

The book's Epilogue returns readers to several rural communities and offers updates on the whereabouts of key participants introduced in the book. It opens with a discussion of the 2004 passage of Amendment 2, Kentucky's state constitutional referendum banning same-sex marriage. I use the fight over this measure, waged right after I completed the research for this book, to assess what Amendment 2 and the broader national fight over gay marriage mean to young rural activists facing arguably more pressing day-to-day political struggles for safe schools and access to LGBT-positive health information and care. Kentucky's skirmish over gay marriage, as it played out in rural communities, underscores the need to more closely examine national gay and lesbian political strategies rooted in assumptions about the power and place of visibility that may operate differently outside of urban environments.

As media scholar Suzanna Walters persuasively argues, LGBT-identifying people are perhaps better seen in the media today than ever before, but we are not necessarily better known (Walters 2001, 10). Rural young people's limited successes deploying a politics of LGBT visibility—drawing on public claims to LGBT identities to disarm naysayers like Representative Napier—underscore the dilemmas of living in an era of unprecedented media visibility ("gay people are everywhere—on TV!") without a national consensus that prioritizes (let alone politically defines) the welfare of LGBT people. Arguably, similar cultural and political pressures compel urban and rural queer folks alike to name their identities and seek validation and legitimacy through acts of public recognition. The politics of visibility that have come to define authentic LGBT identity, however, are tailor-made for and from the population densities; capital; and systems of gender, sexual, class, and racial privilege that converge in cities. Rural youth confront these politics with a shortfall of LGBT-identifying people and dollars. They also depend almost exclusively on non-LGBT-identifying allies and media representations to answer the call to stand up and be recognized.

I do not assume, however, that rural communities are endemically hostile to or unable to make room for queer difference. Instead, building on work exemplified by John Howard and Arlene Stein, I argue that reliance on family, local power dynamics, class and racial politics, and the cultural marginalization that structures these specific rural communities render them ill-suited to strategies of visibility currently privileged by the priorities of the United States' predominantly middle-class, urban-focused gay and lesbian social movement. In working against the assumption that visibility signifies or produces the same kinds of social identities, this book moves the discussion of LGBT youth identity formation away from the private world of individual negotiations of the closet and places it in the thick of a politics of visibility as played out in the rural public sphere.

I hope to challenge pervasive stereotypes of rural places as static and monolithically repressive and push us to rethink metrocentric assumptions of what it means or looks like to be "isolated," in need of "outreach," or "out" in public spaces beyond the city's limits. If we are to improve the quality of life lived queerly from a range of social locations, including rural places, we must, as African American Studies scholar Marlon Ross suggests, "unpack the closet paradigm" (Ross 2005, 179). I take up Ross' directive to consider the consequences of LGBT visibility in communities where one's reputation as a familiar local is valued above all other identity claims in a popular media and political milieu that excludes rural landscapes except as scenes of queer tragedy and horror.

Analytically, rural youth's negotiations of a politics of visibility demonstrate that late-modern identity work engages media and demands a public no matter where you live. Queer-identity work done in places thin on privacy, reliant on familiarity, and shy on public venues for sustained claims to queer difference produce differently—not less—mediated or declarative queer pronunciations than urban LGBT communities. My argument is that the recognition of those pronouncements depends deeply on one's surroundings.

PART I

Queers Here?

Recognizing the Familiar Stranger

2

Unexpected Activists

Homemakers Club and Gay
Teens at the Local Library

The Berea College students introduced in the previous chapter were exceptional advocates. The ecumenical Christian college's mission to provide a free education to Appalachia's poorest but most promising youth drew dynamic student leaders who were likely to be as socially progressive as they were deeply spiritual.[1] But, despite the students' efforts in 2001, Representative Napier was never publicly compelled to explain his claim that no gay people lived in his district. So, in a well-crafted response to Napier's assertion, students at the college conducted a signature drive the weeks preceding the Kentucky Fairness Alliance (KFA) Lobby Day the following year to prove Napier wrong.

After spreading the word about the drive on the lesbian, gay, bisexual, and transgender (LGBT) student group's website and Yahoo Groups discussion list and working in shifts between classes and through the lunch hour at the campus student union, the Berea students gathered more than 400 signed postcards to hand-deliver at KFA's 2002 Lobby Day that called on Napier to acknowledge that LGBT people live in his district. In a town of 9,800, 400 signatures demonstrated that Napier had a visible constituency with which to contend.

When I found the Berea students in the Kentucky State Capitol's basement cafeteria that February morning in 2002, they were finalizing plans for how best to use their stacks of postcards in their appeals to Napier. The KFA arranged for me to shadow the student lobbyists and offer any insights I might have from my experiences as a queer-youth organizer in California. Some of the students quizzed me about life in San Francisco, but they did not seem to assume any of my political work made me an expert here. They had the confidence of youth activists open to suggestions from adult allies but clearly on their own mission.

We wound our way through the maze of stairwells and drab green tiled corridors leading out of the basement to the representatives' offices on the floors above. A KFA staff member had already slipped upstairs to Napier's office and scheduled our group for a brief face-to-face meeting. I followed the three students and one adult Parents and Friends of Lesbians and Gays (PFLAG) member as they filed into the office and presented the postcards to Napier. The representative, a white man in his late fifties with a receding hairline that met thin wisps of unnaturally brownish-orange hair, shifted awkwardly in his high-back black leather chair as the students enthusiastically described the success of their postcard campaign. Napier thumbed through the neon-yellow cards held together by thick rainbow-colored rubber bands, then quickly passed them to his legislative aide. He thanked the young people for their time as he rose from behind his desk and moved toward the door. Seth, a white 17-year-old Berea freshman, shuffled forward and formally asked Napier to reconsider his opposition to the statewide Fairness Bill that, if passed, would add sexual orientation and gender identity to Kentucky's nondiscrimination statutes. Clearing his throat and putting on the broadest smile he could muster, Napier placed his hand on Seth's shoulder and said, "Son, I'm sorry, because I know you don't agree with me on this. But I don't believe in supporting gay people's rights, because it's bad for families."

Longtime PFLAG-Berea member Ed McCurley wryly responded, "Whose families, Representative Napier?" Ed began recounting the difficulties his own son had as a gay man growing up in their county. Before Ed could continue, Representative Napier's assistant, a blond-haired white woman not much older than the Berea students wearing the stately pearls and pantsuit of someone twice her age, said, "I'm afraid we'll have to end here. Representative Napier has to attend to the state's business." The students poured into the hallway to vent about the conversation. Ed confided to me that he expected nothing more out of Napier than the polite rebuff we received but figured it was a start. With a renewed sense of purpose fueled by their anger at Napier's recalcitrance, the students headed to their next round of KFA Lobby Day visits. KFA staffers had already booked the students' appointments, focusing them on the task of thanking the Fairness Bill's handful of stalwart legislative supporters.[2]

Strangely Familiar

Familiarity is the lingua franca of the rural. Community belonging turns
not on appeals to difference deserving equal respect or claims to fictive
kinship ("We are all the same under the skin") but a plea to be seen first
and foremost as a member of your family no matter how different you
may seem. In other words, the politics of visibility out in the country
turns on the fulcrum of "family."[3]

Family is the primary category through which rural community members assert their right to be respected and prioritized by power brokers
like Lonnie Napier. For Representative Napier, queerness was something
that existed elsewhere, a bad influence that invaded from the outside
through media (or too liberal a college education). Because he did not
imagine gay people—or enough of them—could or should be local to his
community, Napier did not feel obliged to pay much attention to matters of LGBT discrimination. The Berea students and PFLAG members
believed that proving gay people existed in their communities was the
first critical step toward LGBT social justice and political advancement.
But existence alone was not enough. Particular categories of recognition
count more than others in a politics of LGBT visibility carried out in rural
communities.

Strangers, those not clearly marked by a familiar family name or presence in the political economies of small towns, are easily dismissed as in-
terlopers meddling in local affairs. Ed McCurley, a tall, thin white man
with a metered drawl honed by his years as a local First Christian Church
Disciples of Christ pastor, understood this. Most of his lobbying experience came from time spent as a volunteer member on his regional Human Rights Commission through the 1970s and early 1980s. He told me
that much of that work was about making white community members
come to see black residents not as strangers but as "locals struggling to
raise their families as much as the next guy." One's credentials as "just another local" are pivotal to the broader politics of rural recognition and
representation.

Invoking "family," as both Lonnie Napier and Pastor McCurley did,
proves to be, literally and figuratively, a key strategy in the politics of
rural LGBT visibility. LGBT-identifying youth and their advocates
routinely draw on the currency of their family ties to legitimate their
right to representation and counter accounts—whether from locals like
Napier or in popular media—that they do not exist. Arguably, this is

a version of the strategy of sameness with a twist ("We're just like everyone else") common to LGBT political organizing.[4] That approach can buy some advances in mainstream recognition, particularly for middle-class, white, gender-normative gays, lesbians, and transsexual people, but it does so at the cost of marginalizing those who resist or cannot fit the expectations of gendered and sexual normalcy this strategy demands. While a strategy of sameness exacts a price in rural communities too, it arguably carries a different exchange rate. Cities are built on a pride in what sociologist Georg Simmel theorized as "the aggregation of so many people with such differentiated interests" produced by the "conditions of metropolitan life" (Simmel 1950, 410). Rural communities, on the other hand, organize around an appreciation for solidarity expressed through blending in. Sameness is neither hard to come by nor much to ask for in a small town. But a semblance of sameness, particularly rooted in family connections, purchases something valued in rural communities: the sense of familiarity and belonging so central to structures of rural life.

Historically, an unspoken agreement operated in rural communities: queer difference was allowed to quietly exist, if not flourish, as long as it did not interfere with one's commitments to family and community. As historian John Howard argues, the imposition of silence around difference and the valuing of silence concerning sexual matters left room for rural individuals to "choose to utilize silences or silencing" to explore their queer sense of difference (Howard 1999, 31). As Howard notes, "Queer discourse . . . relied on a careful etiquette of revelation and (dis) identification" (Howard 1999, 128–29).[5] Of course power relations could, at any arbitrary moment, pin a case of community disruption on queer difference, particularly if it seemed to upset social orders of gender, class, and race that structured rural life. But silences could certainly be queerly productive (Howard 1999, 257–98).

The logic of visibility—"being out and proud"—that organizes contemporary LGBT identities and social movements and saturates media representations of them (genericizing how LGBT people look or politically act) has made it harder, arguably impossible, for queer differences to go unnamed or unspoken in rural places.[6] LGBT-identifying rural young people and their advocates respond to these expectations of visibility while maintaining their commitments to familiarity by articulating their queerness through the norms of their communities, particularly under the rubric of "family."

The Stakes of Family Belonging

Cultural theorist Raymond Williams was one of the first scholars to note that popular representations juxtaposing an idyllic but stagnant countryside with dynamic city life produced a fictional binary that justified the marginalization and plunder of countrysides in the name of modern progress.[7] Presumptions of familiarity, rooted in these mythic notions of rural life as simple and static, do not square with the dramatic upheaval and turbulent realities of rural communities.[8] They do, however, signal the shared anxieties that structure everyday rural life.

In a small town or rural area, family ties transform the strange or the queer into something (someone) recognizable. Even if an individual is a stranger to some, they could be someone's kin.[9] This is not nostalgic sentimentality. The possibility of a local family connection gives every rural resident a claim to community membership. Community standing, and family connections in particular, has tangible consequences. Although compromised by severe cuts in state and federal spending, the tax base and philanthropic reservoirs of urban areas still provide a publicly funded safety net of social services. The industrial restructuring and subsequent outsourcing of manufacturing jobs that began in the 1980s, while certainly damaging to the U.S. national economy, further exacerbated the deeply entrenched economic marginalization experienced by the rural regions of Central Appalachia in which I worked.[10] These areas are defined by a lack of education and job opportunities and poverty rates that run at 22.1%, nearly twice the national average.[11] The relief and assistance provided by homeless and domestic violence shelters, confidential health care, anonymous psychological counseling, food banks, public programs for job placement, and a range of continuing-education programs linked to local employers, though woefully inadequate in cities, are, for the most part, completely absent from the rural landscape.[12] Families are where job information circulates, housing opportunities are extended, and most of the civic services we associate with "public works" happen in rural communities. As such, rural LGBT identity politics rely almost exclusively on public faces that look "just like everyone else" not just to integrate into local communities, but to maintain their access to the bare necessities needed to get by.

Crusading for Family

In the 1970s sociologist Howard Becker turned the definition of social deviance on its head. He argued that social relations of power rather than individual attributes or behaviors determine what (and whom) we label a breach of societal norms. Becker referred to those who write the rules of social order, the codes of recognition that confer legitimacy or abjection, as moral entrepreneurs. Becker contended that two kinds of moral entrepreneurs crusade for social order: rule creators and rule enforcers (Becker 1973, 147). The Berea students and PFLAG members like Pastor Ed saw their struggle for the recognition of LGBT people as a moral crusade. They battled to change the rules of rural social order that defined gay people as out of place and LGBT-identifying youth as victims of nefarious urban sprawl seeping through the television set. Instead, they argued, LGBT individuals deserved acknowledgment and justice as local family members and, thus, recognition as integral community constituents. These crusaders were creative forces in the fight to redefine LGBT youth as "family," but they had considerably less power to enact their definitions on the rule of law.

The Kentucky state representative, on the other hand, trafficked in both kinds of moral entrepreneurship. Representative Napier took his cues as a rule creator from popular conservative religious rhetoric that labeled homosexuality an excessive, sinful lifestyle and from popular representations of homosexuality as an exclusively urban phenomenon, a moral decay that city dwellers brought on themselves.[13] But thanks to his family's long history in the area (and the wealth and connections that accompany it), Napier corners the official market as a rule enforcer. He, like many of his counterparts in Kentucky's most rural state electoral districts, is a career rule enforcer. He has held his representative's seat since 1985. Voter disaffection and economic realities render rural representatives de facto legislative rule enforcers. Less than half the voter-eligible population of Kentucky votes, and rural districts rarely draw more than 30% of their residents registered to vote. In truth, there is little outright competition for the role of rule enforcer. The more rural a Kentucky state representative's district, the more likely it is that he (and 87 of Kentucky's 100 state representative seats are held by men) is an incumbent facing no electoral opponent.[14] To put this in perspective, note that, as in other low-tax-base states, even though the salaries are not comparable to what lawyers and businesspeople might make in the private sector, it pays to be a Kentucky public official.[15] That said, there are disproportionately fewer citizens in rural communities with the means to run for and hold public office. The limited number of local positions of political power—and circumscribed power at that—actually intensifies the power dynamics, particularly the strategic use of "legitimacy"—claims to one's status as a local, at the rural community level (McAreavey 2006, 96–97). It is precisely the heightened sense of familiarity through proximity, the spatial dynamics of rural so- cial relations of power, or what feminist geographer Doreen Massey calls "power geometries," that gives locals crusading for LGBT recognition a fighting chance (Massey 1994, 22).

I use the following thick description of how one local organization brought the discussion of gay teens to the center of their small town to illustrate how "family" can be used to counter the alienation of being considered a queer stranger. It also exposes the tensions between a poli- tics of visibility and strategies of familiarity when taken to the rural town square rather than the State Capitol. A strategy of familiarity can only carry LGBT visibility so far in places with limited venues and resources on hand to sustain the work of transforming strangers into familiar locals. With the exception of Berea, the majority of rural youth I met lived in communities that had no progressive college campuses and few venues available to campaign publicly for the transformation of queer strangers into familiar locals. They worked against a media backdrop and an urban- focused social movement that represented them as strangers in a strange land. Most importantly, powerful local moral entrepreneurs blocked their passage out of this narrow field of representation.

Bringing Strangers Home: Grayson County Homemakers Advocate for Queer Youth

After several e-mail exchanges, I met Mary Bird in May 2002 at Ryan's Family Steakhouse, an all-you-can-eat buffet restaurant in Elizabethtown, Kentucky. You can't miss Elizabethtown if you're driving east from Lou- isville. It's the only sizable town with more than one interstate exit for 80 miles. Yet Ryan's seemed so empty. The endless rows of green, faux-leather booths only added to the restaurant's air of inordinate size. There were a handful of elderly customers taking advantage of the early-bird dinner dis- count, but the place obviously didn't rely on this meager late lunch or early dinner crowd. Ryan's made its money on the weekends from after-church- goers and working families from neighboring towns in the county. It was the destination of choice for large family gatherings in need of an inexpensive place to host birthdays, anniversaries, and other special occasions.

I was there to meet Mary Bird, president of the Grayson County Homemakers Club, to discuss presenting on a panel that her club was organizing. Typically, Homemakers Clubs sponsor toy drives and bake sales for school supplies. The Grayson County Homemakers Club planned to host a community forum on gay teens. When Mary and I talked on the phone about where to meet for lunch, one of the first things she said was, "As you . . . you can see, I stutter . . . but, after I . . . I calm down, I do better. Have done this all my life. As a child, it was hell. I think that gives me some . . . some insight into how cruel people can be because you are different."

Indeed, when we met in person, Mary's head nodded and her hands gestured as though she were using her body to coax her thoughts from her mind. Despite the meter of her delivery, her words had a striking eloquence. When I asked about her motivation for getting the Grayson County Homemakers Club to host this one-day informational session on the needs of gay teens, Mary smiled and said:

> You have to understand, this is my . . . my passion, reaching out, trying to help parents—anyone—to understand the process of acceptance. My daughter is a lesbian. She is the most precious gift I was given, and she's wonderful just the way she is. When the church nuts get too close to me or my heart, I tell them, "Look, God has given us many mysteries that have no answers." I don't question how or why my daughter is who she is; I just feel very blessed that my daughter is a lesbian, as she has opened a path I may have never seen or walked or experienced in my lifetime.

When we met, Mary was 60 years old and had been married for 31 years. After a lifetime working as assemblers at the General Electric plant in Louisville, Kentucky, Mary and her husband retired and moved back to his hometown of Leitchfield, Kentucky, for "family and a slower pace of life," as Mary put it. They live on a 35-acre farm a little more than an hour's drive from Louisville and only 30 minutes from Elizabethtown, the seat of neighboring Hardin County. Mary has been a member of PFLAG since 1989, and she held the president's seat in the Metro Louisville PFLAG chapter for more than three years. "I am the PFLAG contact person here," Mary informed me. "We have no chapter anywhere in or near Grayson County."

When Mary first moved to Leitchfield, she wondered how she would be able to continue her PFLAG work. She said she felt "lost" until the day she talked with a woman at the Grayson County Extension Office about clubs for area residents interested in charity or social-service work:

> She asked what I did in Louisville before I retired. Well, to say the least, I had no idea what to tell her, but I felt I didn't have anything to lose since I knew very few people. My husband knows more of these people, as he was raised here. I told her about PFLAG, my daughter being a lesbian, and fighting for civil and human rights with our gay community. Well, she pointed out one club that would be liberal enough for me and what I'd shared about my interests. She was right. They are the most under-standing group of women I could ever have hoped to meet.

That group was Grayson County's Kentucky Extension Homemakers Association (KEHA). All 120 counties in Kentucky have University of Kentucky Cooperative Extension Service offices. These Extension offices are a networked system of outreach to "take the University to the people in their local communities," housed in the College of Agriculture at the University of Kentucky. The University of Kentucky and its land-grant partner, Kentucky State University, jointly administer the Kentucky Cooperative Extension Service. It offers educational programs in agricultural and natural resources, family and consumer sciences, 4-H and youth development, and community and economic development. It bills itself as the "local front door" to the University of Kentucky campus—the Commonwealth's flagship public research institution. One or more agents work as full-time Extension Service employees in each of the Commonwealth's 120 county cooperative offices.

The Extension Service model began nationally in 1914 when county, state, and federal governments organized to provide citizens direct and local access to the knowledge public universities generated. The collaboration partners the U.S. Department of Agriculture with county governments and a national web of land-grant universities. University of Kentucky Cooperative Extension Service county agents serve as the link between local communities and faculty, staff, and resource specialists on the Lexington campus at the University of Kentucky and in all the university's colleges, and with faculty and staff located at the Western Kentucky Research and Education Center. These local county agents coordinate and provide educational programs for their constituents through meetings, workshops, field trips, consulting, and web or satellite broadcasts of University of Kentucky–based events. They also provide publications, newsletters, computer programs, videotapes, and other educational materials to county residents and Extension organizations and associations.

The Extension Service's stated values are: valuing diversity and capitalizing on its potential to strengthen programs; being locally driven, flexible, and responsive; identifying and supporting high-priority statewide programming thrusts; educating people to solve problems, make decisions, and embrace change; applying knowledge and research-based information; accomplishing work through collaboration, volunteerism, and leadership development; fostering an empowered and contributing people; developing youth, adults, families, and communities; and fostering effective lifelong use of personal and natural resources. Woven within the above goals are implicit tensions. So, for example, these extralocal service agencies must negotiate moral and market values for "diversity" in fairly homogenous places that put a premium on familiarity. The state's investment in "diversity" can register as a dismissal of local valuing of familiarity and an indictment of relying on it in response to deep-set poverty and economic disenfranchisement. Calls for "diversity" look suspiciously like glossy marketing campaigns meant to soften Kentucky's image as a racist, backwater state. Locally, these efforts have been part of a wider sales pitch to open rural communities' raw materials to global capital flows and capital expansion projects like the North American Free Trade Agreement (NAFTA) that have, by most measures, been devastating to all but a few local elites.[16]

So how do Extension Services motivate communities to "embrace change" that pushes against rural structures of familiarity and often privileges statewide "high-priority programming thrusts" perceived to benefit few in the community? They draft off of the rhetoric of familiarity and create jobs that establish their agency's legitimate presence as a "locally driven" community-based organization. These agencies provide stable jobs to locals in communities where only 63% of community residents have full-time year-round employment opportunities and the median household income is $25,861.[17] The entrepreneurial individuals who land these positions circulate state resources made available through Extension offices and work to creatively mitigate tensions between local and state interests. As important resource distribution points and bridges between local and extralocal concerns, local office agents operate as moral entrepreneurs occupying a somewhat unique position in the social relations of rural power geometries.

Mary wasted little time in joining the Clarkson Club, Grayson County's local Kentucky Extension Homemakers Association, and making it her base for LGBT youth advocacy. The Grayson County Homemakers Club had nine members when she joined. "Three or four of them are very religious and believe being gay is a sin but understand the education part of what we are trying to do," Mary said in characterizing her fellow homemakers. "We have been giving out information and slowly doing 'back door' work here. We won two awards [from the Lincoln Area Homemakers Association] in the last two years for things we have done for our community.... Some of it was gay-relative [about gay issues]." As Mary noted:

> These Homemakers Clubs do crafts, help with the county fair and education on all sort of things, but nothing about being gay. Our club went to them with the idea of a project on this topic [gay youth] when I first came down here. It was at a counselor [Kentucky Cooperative Extension agent employee] meeting, I got up and very briefly explained. None of them wanted to be a part of our project, which came as no surprise.

Mary's club had so successfully managed events that leaders from the Homemakers Association for the Lincoln Trail Area encouraged them to apply for grants at the statewide County Extension level. Mary Bird believed that, with the right mixture of residents and educational resources, she could transform the Homemakers Club from a local support group into a vehicle for collective action toward LGBT visibility. Mary was still optimistic as she told me, in 2002, how it all began.

> I knew a little about grants from my work with the [Louisville] Metro PFLAG, so we went ahead and submitted a proposal. We got one right off the bat from the KEHA. Our project won First Place. I think it was the first Homemakers Club award for this county, and now we have the first grant. We're using that grant money for the Fall 2002 event we are having—a gay teen informational forum. We will have a doctor, a minister, a teacher, a gay youth and some parents. I'm trying to line up my speakers now.

It was Mary's search for additional speakers able to add to the event's authoritative, informational, and educational appearance that led to our meeting. The club had asked me to talk about my research on young people questioning their sexuality and gender and how they find support and information living in rural Kentucky. Mary had heard about me through one of the other speakers she had already recruited, Natalie Reteneller, director of the Louisville Youth Group (LYG). Before planning the gay youth informational event, Mary had made some inroads into providing LGBT-specific information to area teens and social-service providers, but not enough to leave her feeling that there was adequate support for local youth. "I have been e-mailed by a few students at the school. Most are OK, or at least they think they are," she mentioned. "One guy's family didn't understand much. The healthcare service here did understand and took the information and my card, but I have yet to get a call from them for more resources."

Mary was provoked to go to all of this trouble to set up a forum not by any specific local incident but because it frustrated her that the negative views of a couple of loud conservative religious leaders seemed to be the only ones heard in her community. She wanted to create an alternative for her small town and make it a better place for young people she imagined must be living in her midst, even if they weren't reaching out to her in large numbers. I asked Mary why she felt such a pressing need to get information out in her newly adopted community, and she replied:

> Well, what I do know about rural life is that there are many here not educated enough to understand [gay issues]. Many are very poor . . . and I'm not sure they'd know what gay was if it hit them in the face! Many think, after all my letters to the editor, that I'm "the gay lady." See what I mean? They don't get it. I have had to write a few church ministers for their articles in the paper about homosexuals. One of them kept on writing to me, and, finally, I had to pull out all the stops. I told him it looked like hate letters to me. After this he stopped for a while.... I'm living in a community where people are fighting and being sued by the ACLU for having the Ten Commandments on the courthouse wall! There are so many churches that moral views are the rule. When we get ready to do this forum, I'm sure I will get run out of town or no one will show up. Either way, they will have something to talk about for a few days.

For Mary and the Homemakers Club, this was as much a fight for the right to publicly advocate for recognition of rural LGBT and questioning young people as it was an effort to use the Homemakers Club, as a representative body of community mothers, to protect the young people of their county. As sociologist K. L. Broad and her colleagues found in their studies of PFLAG, activists like Mary Bird and her fellow Homemakers can use their symbolic roles as moms to appropriate and redefine the rhetoric of "family" and regain territory once thought lost to conservatives in the "family values" culture wars (Broad, Crawley, and Foley 2004, 510–13). Rural communities, however, must contend with a different kind of terrain and conditions for such a battle where "family" carries more than symbolic weight.

Countering Indoctrination and Stereotypes

Mary worked tirelessly on the invitation to the informational panel about and for gay teens. At first, it was a one-page flyer that said "Grayson County Homemakers Club invites you to An Hour of Personal Conversation with Gay Teens and other Professionals on What it's like to be gay." "I really need it to be clear," Mary said, "but, also, it must not sound like it is promoting. These people here don't know the difference between that and education."

The presentation was scheduled to take place Saturday, September 14, 2002, from 1 to 3 P.M., on the third floor of the Grayson County Courthouse at 10 Public Square, in Leitchfield, Kentucky. The end of the announcement listed Mary Bird's cell phone and home phone numbers and her e-mail address. Mary proudly placed these words in bold along the bottom of the flyer: "Program funded in part by a Development Grant from the Kentucky Extension Homemakers Association." After sending out the invitation and immediately getting "three hits [e-mail messages] wanting flyers," Mary debated spicing up the ad with some catchy phrases that might draw attention, like "1. Are you curious? 2. Everything you ever wanted to know! 3. Help others understand. 4. Stop Homophobic remarks, come and learn firsthand. 5 Examine your own biases. 6. What is Sexual Orientation?" But as the day of the presentation drew near, Mary expressed her growing concern that the event would be poorly received if it did not seem "neutral" enough. "I guess I'm getting nervous," she said in one of our e-mail exchanges. "We need to keep this educational, and

maybe tiptoe into all the other stuff. If you give them too much information, will it be only [gay] rights they hear?" She added:

> This isn't Louisville, and I've seen people get up and leave over nothing.
> My biggest fear is we will have preachers wanting to debate the Bible,
> and some of my friends coming from Metro [Louisville] PFLAG like to
> get into this. There's nothing wrong with that, but not here. They will go
> home, and I have to stay and live here. We need to keep it as peaceful as
> possible.

Mary Bird's strategy of remaining "neutral" and keeping it as "educational"
as possible to avoid engaging "preachers wanting to debate" on the surface
may seem similar to the normalizing strategies sociologist Jessica Fields
insightfully notes in her study of PFLAG's political work. Fields found
that parents of lesbians and gays often advocate for LGBT social justice
by arguing that their gay sons and lesbian daughters are just like anyone
else.[18] Parents also use these appeals to sameness to minimize their own
residual stigma and recoup their family's reputation as "normal." In doing so, PFLAG activists invoke and reinforce gender and sexual norms.[19]
Fields raises the critical question of whether "looking like everyone else"
is an accomplishment or a derailment for progressive LGBT social movement and identities and, ultimately, decides it is a setback (Fields 2001,
166).

To be sure, Mary's efforts to tone down the presentation narrow the
discussion of LGBT experience. However, the conversation in rural communities hinges not on whether LGBT youth look like everyone else as
much as do they live here at all. What these youth looked like mattered
much less if Mary could convince her rural community that they were
its own children. Mary's anxieties about the need to keep the discussion
"neutral" and "as peaceful as possible" came from a different concern. She
knew that the subtle power geometries of familiarity in her small town
might raise the question of her standing as a local, and therefore her
right to raise the question of LGBT young people's place in the community. Opinions voiced publicly in small towns, even those from a pulpit,
spotlighted individuals, not organizations. Much as Arlene Stein found in
her study of a small, economically troubled Oregon logging town, "Taking a stand on a divisive issue can . . . be a scary prospect, threatening
the pervasive belief in small-town solidarity" (Stein 2001, 192–93). One

strategy Mary felt she could use to "keep it peaceful" and therefore manage her own arguably tenuous status as a local-in-solidarity was to build
a focus on information rather than debate into the event's structure. "So,
right before we start," Mary recited to me over the phone, as she practiced
her opening remarks, "it's going to be made clear this is not a debate, so
please don't try and make it one. Then I close things up and ask people
to talk to our guests and have refreshments. We will give everyone in the
audience a packet of information when they come in with an evaluation
sheet to fill out, and have them give it to us before leaving."

Press coverage was also going to be a strategy for making sure that
the presentation's "official story," as Mary put it, was as accurate and clear
as possible. The *News-Enterprise,* a paper in neighboring Elizabethtown,
contacted Mary about covering the event and profiling some of the panel
speakers. The extensive cover story they published was a favorable and
sympathetic piece on the importance of the Homemakers Club's efforts in
Grayson County. Between the lines, the article distinguished Elizabethtown as a more sophisticated place, with less need for such programming
efforts. Elizabethtown did, after all, have a gay-affirming Metropolitan
Community Church congregation. Moral crusaders in other small towns
used the Homemakers' gay teen forum to mark their sophistication and
modernity, playing out the power dynamics of rivalry and hierarchy that
pit neighboring rural communities against one another in an economy of
scarcity.

The *Grayson County News Gazette* also contacted Mary for information
about reporting on the presentation. Mary was far from surprised when
she later learned from the *News-Enterprise* reporter that people were calling the paper, threatening to picket the Homemakers Club presentation.
Mary dismissed the picketing threat as "a scare tactic," adding, "I really
don't think anyone will do anything, but I'm going to go talk to the sheriff and chief of police to remind them about what we are doing. I expect
they'll do their jobs if there's any trouble."

On September 8, only six days before the Homemakers Club event,
Mary Bird e-mailed an urgent call for help. It began, "We were booted out
of the space [for the presentation] we have had for months at the Grayson County Courthouse! After going around and around with a clerk (the
judge was not there), they wouldn't budge." Mary explained in the e-mail
why the Homemakers were being blocked from using the courthouse
facilities:

We know he [the judge] has been pressured to do this. The clerk never really gave me an answer as to why our reservation for the space had been cancelled, but she gave me her opinion why we shouldn't be allowed in—which I didn't ask for. But this room is used by lots of groups, from music on Friday, to Saturday/Sunday fundraisers and church singing. I have cried, but understood this could happen, but it makes me feel alone. We have had three members quit our club so now we're down to six from pressure from their families and them not being able to speak up.... We now are going to meet at the Grayson County Public Library.... Please pass this on to anyone who might have been coming.... Peace to all.— From one fighting Mama, Mary Bird.

After pushing Grayson County Courthouse staff to explain the cancellation of the Homemakers Club reservation, Mary received a letter from the courthouse clerk saying that the room had been "reserved under false pre-tenses [sic]." The letter further asserted that Mary had misrepresented the program as a collaborative event of the Grayson County Extension Office and the Homemakers Club. Mary was outraged by both the implication that she had misled the clerk and by the suggestion that the Extension Office was involved in any way.

Indeed, when Mary originally approached the Extension Office requesting use of their logos and other support typically provided by the "local door" to the University of Kentucky Cooperative Extension Service, she was told that she would not be allowed to bill the program as officially connected to the Extension Office. As Mary explained the Extension Office's intentional distance from this Homemakers Club event, I came to understand why, early on, it was important to Mary for the club to appear as neutral on the topic of gay teens as possible. As she explained it:

The Extension Office in Grayson County has given us no support. We put in for the statewide Extension grant as a single club because this agent here wanted to change the program where it wasn't all about gays but was, more generally, a diversity program. Or, she said, we could have a debate on the gay issue. When she said this, I knew she had no idea what she was talking about. You can't debate this safely. On a state level, when we pleaded to use the University of Kentucky Extension logos, we were denied. The reason they gave us was because it was not a program they approved, since it didn't come out of the Extension Office at the county level.

Moving away from her initial praise for the University of Kentucky's fore-sight in supporting the need for this programming, Mary cynically specu-lated that they only gave the Homemakers the grant because she called relentlessly. She said, "I think they gave it to us to cover themselves, so we could not yell, 'Discrimination!' That doesn't say much about how they feel about what we're doing. Does it?"

Mary ended her e-mail lamenting the absence of her supportive "cho-sen family" of fellow PFLAG members and LGBT activists she left behind in Louisville. But she was buoyed by her characteristic optimism that the event would overcome the obstacles it faced:

> I cried all day yesterday, even though I knew this might happen. Made me think of all I had experienced in Louisville . . . plenty of bad stuff like this, but I had a community there. When I lived in Louisville, there was a large family all over the city. We did have nine members of this club do-ing this, and we now have only six. I thought for a while I was going to have to clear out my den and have it [the program] here. But you know, I am a spirited person, and when the judge said "No," another door opened for us, from the library. So it will all work out.

Mary does not position the urban scene of Louisville as a place where such "bad stuff" doesn't happen. What makes the city a refuge for Mary Bird is the presence of an extended "chosen family" of activists. Through sheer numbers, she and a network of LGBT activists could collectively mitigate the institutionalized discrimination exacted by moral crusaders with the power to lock them out of the county courthouse. They could also likely mobilize quickly to rent another (probably more fabulous) lo-cation than a public library. But the lack of population and finances left Mary few places to turn in Leitchfield. As anthropologist Kath Weston noted in her study of gays and lesbians living in the San Francisco Bay Area, "To the extent that gay men and lesbians mapped 'biology' and 'choice' onto identities already opposed to one another (straight and gay, respectively), they polarized these two types of family" (Weston 1991, 28). Mary Bird lived some of this identity polarization as a PFLAG mom and LGBT ally in Louisville and drew strength from it. But she and the LGBT-identifying teens in her rural community arguably do not have the op-tion to draw political energy or resources from this polarization. In many ways, Mary mourned the reality that she now lived in a place that required the politics of LGBT visibility to contend with a structural need to build on ties between families of choice and families one does not want or cannot afford to leave. Nurturing such a family in Leitchfield—for herself and others—continued to drive her determination to make the Homemakers Club presentation a success.

Public Library Hosts the Homemakers Club Forum on Gay Teens

Mary advertised the presentation in both of the local area papers. The Homemakers Club sent press releases to eleven papers in and around the area. They used the local radio's community news program to broadcast a public service announcement. They contacted and sent flyers to all the regional colleges.

On the morning of the presentation, the Homemakers Club stapled bright-yellow construction paper signs, announcing the "Gay Teen Talk," to the telephone poles that lined the route from Main Street to the Grayson County Public Library. A caravan of Mary Bird's family of supporters—mostly members of the Louisville Youth Group and Metro Louisville PFLAG—had made their way to the 6,100-person community of Leitchfield, the county seat. The small library parking lot was completely filled thirty minutes before the start of the program, so people parked in the unpaved lot next door, too.

The event program listed the guest speakers and their brief biographies to indicate their areas of expertise. The panel included myself, described as "a Ph.D. candidate in the Communication Department at the University of California, San Diego" doing a "study on how rural LGBT youth access social services in KY and how the Internet plays a role in their lives." Mary added that I had "written a book on some of these findings," although I had published only on past research dealing with urban youth experiences.

Dr. Stuart Urbach, M.D., Associate Professor of Medicine at the University of Louisville School of Medicine and a member of Louisville's Metro PFLAG, was also a speaker. He planned to address the science and contemporary medical teachings on homosexuality. He was also the expert on hand for "basic human sexual information." Natalie Reteneller, director of the Louisville Youth Group, addressed how her organization helps and supports young people by "providing resources and a safe social place for gay, lesbian, bisexual, and transgender [youth] under the age of 21."

Natalie encouraged Mary Bird to add two LYG youth leaders, Jakob and Michael. The program listed them together as "gay teens" slated to share their experiences dealing with family and the importance of family support in the process of "coming out."

The Reverend Cathy Porter, pastor of the Metropolitan Community Church (MCC) in Elizabethtown, also served as a panelist. With both a bachelor's and master's in social work, Reverend Porter joined the Southern Baptist Theological Seminary in Louisville before leaving to become an MCC minister. As an ordained minister and a licensed clinical social worker, Porter was brought on to field "the Bible questions" that Mary expected would fill most of the question-and-answer session. Mrs. Carita Warner, vice president of Metro Louisville's chapter of PFLAG, was also present to describe the support group in Louisville and provide information about the PFLAG national organization.

Mary Bird herself rounded out the guest list, billed as both the "contact for PFLAG in this area" and "the mother of a lesbian daughter and member of PFLAG since 1989." Mrs. Judy Weimer, a Metro Louisville PFLAG member, served as the program's moderator, introducing the speakers and keeping the question-and-answer session civil. Although conspicuously absent from the speaker's list, the remaining Homemakers Club members stood at the back of the room with brightly colored name tags, handing out information packets and slips of paper for the program evaluation as people filed into the room. Their absence from the event program but physical presence in the space marked them clearly as distinctly not experts from elsewhere but local surrogate parents there for support.

An overflow crowd piled into the Grayson County Public Library's Children's Reading Room for more than two hours of discussion. Forty-three people attended. As is the case with many controversies, the event itself was relatively unremarkable compared to the incidents leading up to it. The forum drew more than a dozen supporters from out of town and a larger group of local community supporters. The Homemakers Club members had heard rumors from the reporters covering the talk that conservative Christians protesting the forum would overwhelm the event. The audience identified itself on the evaluation forms as counselors, families with gay or lesbian relatives, teens, and community leaders interested in learning more about lesbian and gay young people. By the forum's end, it was clear that only four members of the county's Independent Baptist Church had decided to attend the talk. Two men and two women stood along the back wall of the room with their arms folded, listening to the panelists and scanning the crowd occasionally to gauge the audience's reactions to what was being said.

After the presentations, Mrs. Weimer invited questions from the audience. Most people just wanted publicly to express thanks to the Homemakers Club for sponsoring the event. As predicted, though, the majority quizzed Reverend Porter on the finer details of Old Testament references to homosexuality and the ins and outs of Leviticus, the only biblical text that directly speaks to the "abomination" of homosexual acts. Until then, the Independent Baptist Church's minister had been quietly standing against the wall, hemmed in by children's crayon scrawls of handprints made out to look like Thanksgiving turkeys and autumn leaves. With only a few minutes remaining in the time allowed for the meeting, he humbly asked for his "chance to be heard."

Mary Bird was visibly upset by his interruption of the scheduled program but, after consulting her fellow homemakers, decided to let him speak. She prefaced turning over the floor to him with a brief reiteration that the event was not to be a debate over whether being gay is right or wrong, but merely about "informing people and giving support." With a shaky voice, the minister thanked Mary and proceeded to describe for the audience the deep burden he carried for all homosexuals. The audience politely listened to the minister's outpouring of grief for the souls of these sinners. He argued that God's compassion was as important a part of this debate as anything said earlier by the guest speakers. He bowed his head and shook his clasped hands of interlaced fingers for a moment, then rested his overlapping palms against his chest. The crowd clapped thinly and briefly, then quickly headed to the cookies and punch at the back of the room. Mary and the program facilitator called the meeting to a close.

I stood in the back waiting for the cookie line to thin while talking with Darrin, who referred to himself as "the only out gay person" at his high school. He was quick to add that he certainly was "not the only gay kid there." As Darrin and I talked, a taut, athletic woman in her late thirties, from the Baptist church, stepped to the young man's side and broke into our conversation, warmly inviting Darrin to their church. "You're friends with James, aren't you? He goes to our church. You should stop by some Sunday." Darrin was polite, nodded, then asked if the church was gay-affirming. "I don't really want to go somewhere that I can't just be who I am," he said. The woman responded, in a coy tone, "Well, just come by and see for yourself."

She then shifted her attention to me. "Are you from Kentucky?" she asked. When I responded, "No, I was born and raised in California," she gave me a knowing look and said, "Oh, I bet you'll be happy to go back there when you're finished with your project." I defensively answered that I wasn't sure when I'd be back to California because "I'm enjoying the time with my partner's family—our two nephews, her grandmother." She added, "And, promoting your lifestyle." With that, she turned back toward Darrin, smiled, and walked away. Witty retorts spooled through my mind, but I knew nothing I could say would justify or redeem my presence here. I was a stranger here brought to the event for my "expertise," validating queerness not only through my advocacy for LGBT and questioning youth, but by bringing attention to the fact that queerness was easy to find in her small town.

I later found out that several community members knew the Independent Baptist minister who spoke at the end of the question-and-answer session. They did not know him from his church. In fact, ministry was not his day job or full-time employment. One lesbian couple had bought a washer and dryer from his used-appliance shop, and a local gay man had sold groceries to him for years and gone to high school with his brother. I was somewhat used to vitriolic sermons shouted at me by anonymous preachers standing on the sidelines of Gay Pride parades, but this was the first time I had seen anti-queer and pro-queer positions embodied in neighbors who actually knew each other personally. As illustrated by my exchanges with the Baptist Church member, community members' familiarity with one another only marked me more clearly as an out-of-place stranger.

Aftermath of the Homemakers Club Presentation

At the beginning of the presentation, the Metro Louisville PFLAG had handed out packets of materials. The overstuffed folders included PFLAG pamphlets, a copy of the flyer for the event, and articles with titles such as "Homosexuality and Religion" and "How to Talk with Other Parents" about having an LGBT or questioning child, published by PFLAG's national offices. The evaluation sheets collected by the Homemakers Club at the end of the afternoon registered 100% support for the information presented. The Independent Baptist Church members declined to take the PFLAG packet, which included the event's evaluation sheets. Many who attended wanted more contact information for area resources.

The following week, both the *News-Enterprise* of Hardin County and Leitchfield's own *Grayson County News Gazette* ran full feature stories on the Homemakers Club and its educational programming. Mary Bird

received calls from several people unable to attend but interested in receiving copies of the packet the Homemakers Club handed out at the event.
She was also contacted by a few gay-identifying teens who had wanted to
come that day but whose parents would not allow them to attend.

As successful as the program was, Mary Bird and her fellow Homemakers Club members were exhausted by the end of it. After the program, Mary and the other Homemakers Club members debated disband-
ing their KEHA club. "Maybe we should just be a club of women," Mary
said in a sad, exasperated voice in our follow-up conversation. The next
day, she sent this e-mail:

> When this is over, I will write every person who is on the UK [University
> of Kentucky] Board of Advisors and top people of Kentucky Extension
> Homemakers Association, and then I am going to quit. I am 60 years old
> and will not spend the rest of my life with a bunch of people with such
> closed minds. I can fill my time another way. I'll never quit PFLAG or
> being the contact person here—that's for life. But I am going to write all
> of the UK Advisors and let them know about the word "discrimination"
> and how we have been treated from the top of the Kentucky Extension
> Homemakers Association . . . from logos to nonsupport from agents here.
> I then will resign from this club as a KEHA club. I did what I set out to
> do (a workshop), and now I have to wait and see if anyone reaches out. If
> no one does, at least they do know I am here.

Despite the positive feedback and public show of support, the event's
successes were not enough for Mary Bird. She and the Homemakers Club
created a moment of visibility, public affirmation, and local acceptance
for gay teens. Mary demonstrated locals' willingness to embrace LGBT-
identifying youth as their own. But the lack of institutional support from
the Extension Office and county courthouse discouraged Mary. Local rule
enforcers could too easily use their positions in the power geometries of
small towns to control the limited venues making the politics of visibility
Mary preferred an exhausting prospect. While Mary decided to continue
providing a presence for PFLAG in Leitchfield, she resigned from the
Homemakers Club not long after the presentation at the library.

The Homemakers Club presentation on gay teens illustrates how rural
LGBT advocacy or support networks see and project themselves as surrogate parents and extended family. Members of these local groups, through
the auspices of institutional infrastructures like the University of Kentucky

Cooperative Extension Service and other national nonprofit organizations such as PFLAG, are driven by concerns that local parents are not doing what needs to be done for young people. As Mary argued in her letter of complaint to the University of Kentucky Cooperative Extension Service directors:

> This education is needed. Families aren't father, mother, 2.5 children anymore. In counties all over Kentucky there are gay teens, and they have families and they need this education. These kids are killing themselves because no one understands or even will listen. As homemakers we are teachers, leaders in our community. This education is just as important if not more than some of the classes that have come down from UK to teach these clubs.

Groups like the Homemakers Club are positioned by the state and their relationship to the local moral economy as a community's internal response to local needs—an insider's efforts to improve or buffer the harsher conditions that affect the rural United States. For instance, in 2004 the Grayson County Homemakers Club started a new program called Books for Babies. To promote literacy, they donated a new book to each baby born to a county family. Statewide, the KEHA clubs across rural Kentucky focused on the effects of domestic violence. Club members donated toiletries and other comfort items to shelters across the state to support women seeking respite from abusive partners. But as the local Extension Office response to Mary Bird's program attests, community groups can just as easily be cast as bringing a disruptive outside influence into the community or, in this case, introducing topics that are out-of-bounds of local standards for sexuality and gender.

Ironically, "local standards" are implemented through the apparatus of extralocal institutions. The University Extension manages its mission to be "locally driven" by distancing itself from ownership and control of local happenings. It structurally appears as a neutral party by employing a county resident to serve as its representative. At the same time, the University Extension can advance its goals of "valuing diversity" and "educating people to . . . embrace change" through its funding opportunities. As this case of the Homemakers Club and the University Cooperative Extension Service shows, these negotiations of local values happen on a much broader scale than the local scene. This complicates drawing clean boundaries between what is rural/local and what is not.

Conclusion

Anthropologist Kath Weston argues, "If . . . kinship is something people use to act as well as to think, then its transformations should have unfolded . . . on the more modest stage of day-to-day life, where individuals have actively engaged novel ideological distinctions and contested representations that would exclude them from kinship" (Weston 1991, 29). Weston was commenting on gays and lesbians reworking kinship categories. In this case, however, true to Weston's broader assessment, the Homemakers Club members took the lead as moral entrepreneurs in their communities and used the powerful institution of the family to bridge the divide between queers as strangers and LGBT young people as local sons and daughters.

Despite earnest efforts by powerful community gatekeepers and popular representations to the contrary, rural LGBT people can come to be seen as locals to their communities. As the examples above illustrate, it takes brokering between familiarity and stranger status through the category of "family." It also requires individuals to mobilize interlocking local and extralocal organizational infrastructures—as the Berea College student lobbyists, PFLAG members, and the Homemakers Club did—to create LGBT visibility in rural communities. Ironically, rural activists and their allies, often stretched thin on resources because of a lack of queer critical mass, must carefully manage their image as "locals" to maintain their footing of familiarity in their own rural communities. This can be exhausting for an activist like Mary Bird who is driven by the logic of LGBT visibility to seek the same strides she made in an urban area with an already visible and sizable LGBT-identifying community fighting alongside her. More broadly, the dominance of a politics of visibility in popular representations of LGBT people and in national LGBT organizing makes it difficult for rural activists to see, let alone revel in, their accomplishments. By all accounts, for example, the Berea College students' postcard campaign discussed at the beginning of this chapter proved to be a successful strategy for creating positive dialogue and recognition on their campus. "I thought it was really cool that we not only got that much support, but that everyone at the tables said they met so many other gay kids, or kids with gay relatives, or just people who know gay people here who are tired of someone like Napier saying we don't exist," said Dale, an ebullient white, gay and more recently genderqueer-identifying Berea College senior. Dale grew up in a sparsely populated Kentucky county surrounded almost exclusively by an extended family uneasy with his love of home economics. Even though, at the age of 16, he came out to his family as gay and felt accepted by them, Dale had never before experienced such a public sense of affirmation like that generated by the Berea students' tabling efforts.

Yes, the postcard campaign gathered hard evidence that rural LGBT people existed and therefore had a right to legislative representation. But, like the Homemakers Club forum on gay teens at the local library, it also created a venue, albeit contingent and temporary, for youth to experience a scale of public recognition and local belonging that they would likely not receive through legislative action in Kentucky any time soon. Arguably, directing political and social energy at legislative action misses the mark altogether. Political theorist Wendy Brown, for example, contends that "legally and politically codifying justice as matters of protection, prosecution, and regulation tends to turn us away from 'practicing' freedom" (Brown 1995, 21 n. 38). Beyond the steps of the State Capitol, strategies of LGBT visibility face tough competition in places unified by conditions of poverty and disenfranchisement that leave them structurally reliant on a myth of familiarity. Appeals for recognition and prioritization of queer difference can only take rural LGBT activists so far and come at a cost. The Homemakers Club experience of hosting an informational event about gay youth shows that the notion of family can help LGBT and questioning young people navigate and suture their familiar-stranger status. A family structure grafted onto community-based and nongovernmental organizations can also ameliorate tensions between national nonprofit-driven LGBT political agendas and local models of community organizing.

The Homemakers Club story illustrates the struggle to make LGBT identities fit in rural places and how important families are to this work. Families have legitimacy as "real locals" and the imagined progenitors carrying forward the myth of continuity and familiarity so central to rural life. Families can transform or diminish the stranger status assigned to LGBT-identifying young people by popular media and moral crusaders hostile to their cause more than politicians ever have or will. But familiarity can only take the politics of LGBT visibility so far, depending deeply on the local venues available for that work. This chapter focused on the family as a strategic metaphor to turn inside out the idea that youth lay claim to LGBT identities or find queer visibility alone, in the privacy of their homes among family. To the contrary, the cases discussed above illustrate how public youth negotiations of the politics of LGBT visibility are. This work does demand "family" in rural communities. It draws on the very public uses of a rhetoric of family that already circulates and dominates in rural settings. The remaining chapters turn to the public nature of such visibility projects and the landscapes they traverse.

3

School Fight!

Local Struggles over
National Advocacy Strategies

Boyd County sits along the border that stitches West Virginia, Ohio, and Kentucky together. While Ashland, Kentucky, Boyd County's largest town, has more than 20,000 residents, Boyd County High School draws most of its 900 students from surrounding towns with populations smaller than that of the high school itself. In Spring 2001 a Boyd County High School graduating senior submitted a petition to his school's Site-Based Decision Making (SBDM) Council requesting a new nonacademic student club—a Gay-Straight Alliance (GSA). At the time there were only four clubs in Kentucky listed on the national, chapter-based non-profit Gay, Lesbian and Straight Education Network's (GLSEN) registry of GSAs.[1] In Kentucky, Boyd County High's GSA would be the first formed in a school outside of a metropolitan area like Louisville or Lexington. The six-member SBDM Council—three teachers, two parents, and school principal Jerry Johnson—rejected the student's request for the group on the grounds that it was too late in the school year to form a club. Under Kentucky state laws, the SBDM Council has the right to make such curricular decisions and, in theory, has the final say.

Undeterred, but not permitted to meet on school property, the GSA met informally at a church 12 miles outside of town. Then, early in 2002, junior Tyler McClelland from the unincorporated township of Summit Kentucky submitted a second application to form a GSA. He argued that students and community members should be aware that "there are people from diverse sexual orientations here . . . [y]ou can't assume everyone is straight." Other supportive students suggested GSAs could address animosity toward gay students in a manner similar to how school environments dealt with racism. "It's become mostly uncool to be a racist, so now we're trying to make it mostly uncool to be a homophobe," a 15-year-old

Boyd County High student explained.[2] But, for a second time, the Council rejected the application, arguing that the school's active Human Rights Club already promoted respect for all people and therefore there was no need for a GSA. Kathy Felty, a teacher on the Council, thought the Human Rights Club could address sexual orientation and suggested teachers felt a GSA would be too disruptive and polarizing. Repeatedly, local citizens and students opposed to the GSA argued that there was a "time and place" for discussions of sexuality and school wasn't it.

Schools have extensive histories as contentious public spaces that certainly predate discussions of homosexuality. Schools were central to the debate at the turn of the last century over where, when, and how to train "good citizens"; key sites of struggle in the civil rights era; and important battlegrounds in the history of anti-war protest in the United States.[3] Educational settings are flashpoints and important battlegrounds in public debates about youth sexuality and, in this case, young people's rights to participate in lesbian, gay, bisexual, and transgender (LGBT) social movements. As sociologist Janice Irvine persuasively argues, advocating for gay issues in schools "constitute[s] a version of citizen politics" in which "battles [are] not simply about homosexuality, but over . . . which citizens are valued as legitimate" (Irvine 2002, 167). Boyd County citizens' call to keep GSAs and, by extension, talk of sexuality out of the schools echoes these broader cultural debates over the time and place of sexual education in school settings. But there is more going on here than conservative or liberal views on the role of sex education in schools or a blanket hatred of queer difference. When advocates organize in small towns for or against Gay-Straight Alliances, they also haggle with each other and with advocates beyond their communities over the legitimacy and right of LGBT people to count not just as citizens but also as "locals." Debates about GSAs are contentious enough as sites for the recognition of belonging, as Irvine suggests. But they are further complicated by two other factors: the heightened valence and value of familiarity that structures rural communities and the presence of ongoing struggles around class and racial divides that frame the terms of debate when rural communities fight over who has a right to speak for their town's ideals and who should be branded foreign agents of change.

With these entwined histories of racial and class division framing school-based fights over LGBT rights in mind, this chapter examines how student-driven organizations like Ashland, Kentucky's Boyd County High School GSA and local members of chapter-based national advocacy organizations like the GLSEN engage the politics of LGBT visibility in rural communities. Along the way, they complicate what readers might expect their progress and alliances to look like. Power geometries among local advocates, local officials, and extralocal powers that be, like those discussed in the case of the Homemakers Club gay teen presentation, contest more than the place of LGBT-identifying youth in rural communities. They circle back to long-standing battles over economic disparities between rural and urban areas. They also re-open old scars about a different intractable yet invisible "other" that shames these rural communities, namely the legacies of regional racism that endure through the persistence of white homogeneity. The alignments of community locals and assignments to the category of "other," however, dynamically shift as parties vie for meager resources that trickle down to small towns, including community autonomy and pride. One cannot read the story of LGBT visibility strategies in rural educational settings without considering the pivotal roles class and racial tensions play in these efforts.[4] As anthropologist David Valentine eloquently argues, the "contours of racial or class experiences can shape and reshape what gender and sexuality themselves can mean" (Valentine 2007, 18). While Valentine is particularly concerned with the experiences of gender-variant people of color in the heart of Manhattan, this is no less true a statement for rural white folks of Eastern Kentucky.[5] The cases of GLSEN-KY and Boyd County High School's GSA highlight how rural community leaders, educators, and youth manage these tensions enmeshed in the politics of LGBT visibility as well as the different roles students and adult advocates play on all sides of the debate. But before turning to the specific stories of GLSEN-KY and Boyd County's GSA, let me lay out some of the racial and class politics that seem most pressing to their stories.

Mapping Kentucky's Racial Divide

To understand how race and class inform the politics of visibility for rural LGBT youth, one must look at the history of each as it relates to rural educational environments. Kentucky provides a clear example of the backdrop against which rural Gay-Straight Alliances and national LGBT advocacy organizations attempt to establish visibility in settings embroiled in long-standing struggles over access to basic resources and recognition from extralocal powers that be.

If, as argued in this book's introduction, the rural places in which I worked are less clearly defined by where they start and end, one characteristic visibly delineates them: they are racially homogenous. Although this characterization flattens the racial histories as well as the more recent flows of Mexican and Central American immigrant labor in these areas, the regions of Kentucky discussed in this chapter are arguably the least racially diverse of the mid-Southern Atlantic region.[6] As James W. Loewen and Elliot Jaspin document, this is no coincidence. They reflect what these authors describe as the legacy of "Sundown Towns."[7] Historically, white townspeople policed racial lines with casual practices or more formal "Sundown" laws meant to snap racial divides back in place at the end of the business day. For example, shopkeepers posted threats of violence in their windows addressed to African-American residents who dared to linger downtown after dusk or into the evening, further deepening segregation between white and African-American communities that lived literally next door to each other. These rural areas of Eastern Kentucky where I worked are part of the regional "Sundown Town" legacy of ethnic cleansing that took place at the turn of the 20th century. Around this time, as masses of poor whites and African Americans migrated between and within regions across the United States in response to the industrial boom, mobs of rural white citizens ran African-American neighbors and newcomers out of small towns and seized their property. In the aftermath of regional racial violence and mob rule, all-white towns formed that have remained racially homogenous ever since. Kentucky bears clear marks of this past. According to the 2000 U.S. Census, 89.5% of the state's 4.2 million residents are white, compared to the national average of 73.9%. But in many of its rural counties, 96% or more of the residents are white. Although African Americans make up the largest racial group other than whites, they represent only 7.4% of the state's population, compared to 12.4% of the population nationally. The cities with the highest concentrations of African-American residents are Louisville, 13.2%; Lexington, 10.5%; Elizabethtown, 10.5%; and Bowling Green, 7.9%. Yet several smaller communities have significant numbers of African-American residents. The largest concentration of African-American residents can be found in Christian County, where 21.1% of the 67,000 county population identify as African American; nearly 31% of the 30,000 people living in the Christian County town of Hopkinsville are African American; 25% of Harlan County's coal town of Lynch, Kentucky, population 900, are African American; and in Fulton County's two towns, Fulton, population 2,775, and Hickman, population 2,560, African Americans make up 29% and 34% of residents, respectively. Still, the racial heterogeneity of Kentucky is contained to 3.1% of its overall population. In other words, racial politics are still set in black and white and, with the exceptions noted above, map onto urban and rural geographies. Class politics play out against and within school districts shaped by this racialized landscape.

Legacies of Division: Class and Racial Politics in Kentucky Education

In 1985 66 of the Commonwealth of Kentucky's poorest school districts, most from rural Appalachian towns, formed the nonprofit organization Council for Better Education.[8] The Council hired Bert Combs, a past governor and retired federal judge, to argue its case. The Council filed a class-action lawsuit against Kentucky on behalf of poor school districts across the Commonwealth joined by 22 public school students, their parents, and the Boards of Education from counties best known for their coal-mines and labor organizing. They charged that the financing and management of Kentucky's educational system was broken beyond repair. The Council for Better Education and its fellow plaintiffs wanted the Commonwealth's educational system deemed unconstitutional and Kentucky's General Assembly held responsible for overhauling it. Four years later, in 1989, the Council for Better Education won its case in the Kentucky Supreme Court. The decision led to unprecedented educational reform.[9]

The Council for Better Education's case underscored the dismal state of Kentucky's public education. The case cited a 1986 study that found Kentucky ranked in the lower 20% to 25% in nearly every category used to measure educational performance nationally. Thirty-five percent of Kentucky's adult population dropped out of school before completing the 12th grade. The suit also highlighted deep-rooted antipathy between the wealthy elites in the affluent suburbs of larger cities, like Louisville and Lexington, and the vast patchwork of impoverished rural counties struggling to run the majority of Kentucky's public schools. At the time, the wealthiest school districts outspent their poorest country cousins by nearly $1,200 per student annually. Only 20% of Kentucky's school districts—all in the Commonwealth's wealthiest communities—provided an education that met national benchmarks. In comparison, 80% of Kentucky's public school students were, by every evaluative criterion, receiving a substandard education.[10]

But Kentucky's public education was a melancholy two-step between the haves and have-nots long before 1989. Legislation crafted after World War II to keep state educational spending low reversed strides made in the 1930s and 1940s by scuttling extra funding earmarked for the poorest districts. The state's leaders seemed bent on thwarting equitable public education funding just as landmark civil rights cases sought to challenge inequalities wrought by Jim Crow. For example, in 1952 Kentucky eliminated mandatory per-capita spending on students and gave the state's General Assembly the right to fund schools based solely on local property values and tax revenues. Arguably, this hampered the 1954 *Brown v. Board of Education* decision's ability to redress racial discrimination in public education funding. After all, the most property-poor communities were found not only in rural school districts but also in the few African-American enclaves left in the shadow of Kentucky's "Sundown Town" legacy. Maybe it was class bias or perhaps a desire to undercut desegregation; either way, Kentucky's decision to dole out school funding based on property taxes hit the state's poorest rural school districts and those in African-American communities the hardest.

One might say it was poetic justice that when Bert Combs, the Council for Better Education's lawyer, was Kentucky's governor (from 1959–1963), he ordered the desegregation of public accommodations and opened the first Human Rights Commission office to ensure counties followed his orders. When he won the 1989 case that found Kentucky's public education system unconstitutional, Combs ushered in an era of educational reform that called not only for fairness in school financing but also for equality in educational opportunity. This history sets the stage for how rural communities scrutinize who speaks for their families and interrogate who counts as a "local" alongside appeals for fairness that invoke race and class differences. All these factors shape the roles of schools as public spaces for coping with the expectations of LGBT visibility in rural communities.

From Angry Mother to National Advocate

Three and a half hours south of Boyd County and two years before students' efforts to form a Gay-Straight Alliance at the local high school, Gina Cooper helped her son sue the Somerset Independent School District in 1999 over the daily harassment he faced at school because students thought he was gay. No matter where I traveled to find participants for my research, the people I met told me, "You've got to meet Gina Cooper."

Her story and her willingness to walk young people and parents through the same legal quagmire to defend students against harassment based on sexual orientation or gender identity made her an invaluable resource not just regionally but statewide. I met Gina not long after my Lobby Day experience with the Berea contingent (who also asked, "Have you met Gina Cooper?"). I drove to Somerset's small county library to introduce myself to Gina before a meeting of the Kentucky chapter of the GLSEN she had founded. It was freezing outside, a typical gray February afternoon when the steep hills that surround the area seem to trap the damp weather, blocking out any warmth that might attempt to sneak between them. I found out later that before each monthly GLSEN-KY meeting, Gina and her husband park their 1997 silver Chevy pickup truck in a prominent spot behind the library where they usually gather and drape a plastic banner across the vehicle's side displaying the national organization's apple and books logo and block fonts spelling out "GLSEN." It made it easy to find the meeting and, as I drove into the lot, it was clear from Gina's smile she enjoyed the ceremony of planting GLSEN-KY's flag for all to see. "Isn't this banner great?!" she exclaimed as she pulled me toward her and gave me a hug. I could smell the cigarette smoke in her jacket and black curly hair, but until I stepped away I had not noticed that she was pinching the butt of a recently extinguished lipstick-stained cigarette between her fingers. "I'm trying to quit," she said guiltily as she waved already dissipating smoke wafts away from us. I came to quickly recognize that familiar gravelly voice and smoker's cough as we settled into a routine of talking on the phone or meeting a couple of times a month for the duration of my research.

Gina's family had moved to Somerset, Kentucky (population 11,000), in January 1997 to be near her elderly parents. Because they lived inside the Somerset city limits, all three of Gina's children enrolled in schools in the Somerset Independent School District. Almost immediately, Brad was singled out and taunted by his fellow classmates. Gina took it as "new kid on the block stuff." Even though Somerset High School enrolled more than 400 students, most of them had known each other, quite literally, all their lives because they all came from the same lone elementary and middle school that fed the high school. Gina assumed things would get better after students got to know Brad. But by the end of Brad's first school year, matters did not improve; in fact, they grew far worse. Brad's status as an unfamiliar newcomer made him an easy target at his high school.

Within three days of his second year at Somerset High, Brad came home distraught. Several students had followed him around asking if he was gay, throwing spit wads at him, and yelling out "AIDS spreader" as he walked to his classes. Gina told her parents what was happening at Brad's school, despite fearing rejection from her father, a retired fundamentalist Baptist minister. "My dad warned me that we would be stepping on some big toes if we started legal action against the school," she said, adding, "he told us to be ready to leave town and to be prepared for our house to be burned—you mess with the powers that control the school and you mess with the families who pretty much own the town."

When Gina met with school officials, the district superintendent told her that he "just did not know what to do" and that he had "never seen anything like 'this' before." When the district chose not to investigate three death threats left for Brad at school, Gina delivered the handwritten notes to the police herself. They laughed at her for wanting to investigate what they called "schoolyard taunts." Gina and her family decided to follow the last directive in Somerset High's grievance policy handbook. They contacted the U.S. Department of Education's Office for Civil Rights (OCR) and sent copies of everything they had documenting Brad's harassment.

Within two weeks of filing a complaint, the school district offered the OCR and Gina Cooper's family a "Commitment to Resolve" Brad's harassment.[11] The agreement stopped short of acknowledging any wrongdoing on the part of Somerset High but held the school district to mandatory, schoolwide diversity trainings and offered counseling for Brad for as long as he needed it.[12]

When Gina learned the OCR agreement would expire in the next two years and held no other parties responsible, her disappointment and desire to protect other students from potential harassment motivated them to start looking for lawyers. "Some lawyers laughed at us, some told us we didn't have a prayer. David Buckel, senior attorney for Lambda Legal in New York, was a godsend. I could not have survived without David and WebTV [a service that lets users surf the Internet from a television set rather than a computer] to search for information that might help us fight our case." In March 1999 Brad filed his case against the Somerset Independent School District in Federal Court in London, Kentucky.

To keep the case from going to court, Somerset Independent School District agreed to a tougher anti-harassment policy that included sexual harassment based on "actual or perceived sexual orientation," teacher trainings, and a small settlement for Brad.[13] Gina Cooper started a GLSEN chapter in Kentucky in August 2000.[14] She knew from Lambda Legal and conversations with other education advocates that GLSEN wanted to build its presence beyond cities, particularly in the southeast. Gina had the experience of taking on a rural school's inaction in the face of discrimination, and she felt it was important to bring that expertise to a national network of organizations and legal efforts to address the kind of harassment her son experienced. GLSEN seemed like a perfect organization with which to partner.

GLSEN-KY tried to expand its efforts to other parts of the state but was stymied by how to cut through the perception that it was a national advocacy group coming in to push local school authorities around rather than the mobile translocal support organization it had become. Even though GLSEN was called in by and worked with individual students and families, these communities did not have pools of resources or broader local circles of support with clout to counter the asymmetry of schools' overwhelming authority as moral entrepreneurs in these small towns. As Gina noted, "Helping students can sometimes be tricky if you are not the parent giving the help, and, many times, if a student is GLBT and getting harassed, they may not feel they can 'come out' to parents and get help with what is happening at school. That just makes it hard to seem like we're not just some crazy radicals from the outside pushing a gay agenda on schools, telling them what they should do—although, you know, I work with what I've got."

Sociologist Melinda Miceli's thorough study of Gay-Straight Alliances' impact on educational policy and the school-based advocacy efforts that predated GSAs offers some telling clues researchers have perhaps overlooked as to why groups like GLSEN-KY might face unique obstacles as chapters of national gay and lesbian educational advocacy groups organizing in rural communities. Miceli's study focuses almost exclusively on city-based advocacy efforts, and understandably so as cities have been central to the birth and development of these movements. Miceli asserts that general community intolerance explains the spotty record of GSAs in rural areas and certain states (Miceli 2005, 101). But this assertion ignores many of the power struggles to form city-based advocacy groups that she documents. These efforts certainly involved virulent expressions of community and statewide intolerance of LGBT advocacy in school settings. The gay and lesbian support service called Project 10 of Los Angeles, for example, founded in 1984 by school counselor Virginia Uribe and sustained by her inexhaustible efforts, faced organized letter campaigns by

Lou Sheldon's Traditional Values Coalition, a then powerful conservative Religious Right organization, and threats from the California State Assembly's education committee to cut all Los Angeles school district funds if her high school did not dismantle Project 10.[15] Project 10 managed to survive because of the support of a majority of school board members and Uribe's principal. But, despite keeping Project 10 on the books, the district allocated almost no funds to support its work for a district of more than 800,000 students. As Project 10's public profile rose with press accounts of attempts to dissolve the program, private and corporate donations began to roll in. A nonprofit organization, Friends of Project 10, formed to take in the donations used to support everything from its college scholarship fund to diversity trainings for teachers and its telephone hotline and detailed website (Miceli 2005, 98–99). The P.E.R.S.O.N. (Public Education Regarding Sexual Orientation Nationally) Project managed to sustain itself not by stamping out community intolerance but by building a strong coalition with powerful leaders in Los Angeles' LGBT Community Center, city government, Human Rights Commission, and large Parents and Friends of Lesbians and Gays (PFLAG), GLSEN, and Anti-Defamation League chapters to insulate itself from those opposed to its mission. In other words, city-based education advocates like the Person Project contend with similar forces of community intolerance that confront Gina Cooper, but they overcome them by tapping into and building on a base of financial capital and political power able to maintain public dissent and visibility as local advocates on a scale simply unfathomable in a rural area.

Although it did not have anything close to the amassing of power and wealth to challenge unsupportive schools, Gina could use her knowledge of the law and the weight of GLSEN-KY's national affiliations to her advantage when advocating for students facing harassment. Gina recalled one strategy she took to help Michael, a young gay man at a rural school several counties away, who had called her for help:

> I sent two faxes. One to the high school principal and one to the superintendent. I told them that I had been made aware of a young man who had been forced to deal with terrible harassment. I quoted a couple of statistics in the letter. Then I said that I was willing to help them work this issue out. I ended it with saying that I expected a response and corrective action (meaning policy changes or revisions) to be taken. I sent it on our GLSEN-KY letterhead. The next day they called Michael into the office and asked him if he realized who I was. He told them he was aware

and they told him they would do something to stop the harassment. He isn't really sure what was done, but he still tells me that he is the happiest gay guy in the world. The rest of his one and a half years at the school were great for him.

Unfortunately, GLSEN's national strategy for success worked against the climate of poverty and underemployment that permeates Somerset and its surrounding towns. This strategy—building a core base of $100–$500 regular, local donors—depended on a visible, available, and sizable donor base to augment funds raised from basic membership fees. A significant portion of the basic membership fees goes back to the national organization, but donations over the membership amount can be kept locally. For larger urban areas like Boston and New York, this fundraising model has produced incredibly strong and visible GLSEN chapters. In other words, it is a great model if you have wealthy queer folks in your midst. Gina Cooper and other GLSEN-KY members believed in the educational lobbying by the GLSEN national office. But GLSEN-KY was unable to sustain itself as a local chapter in an economically depressed area using the national organization's model of fundraising. But for most rural community members, particularly the majority youth members of the GLSEN-KY chapter, the basic membership alone (at the time $35) was a stretch for some and a financial hardship for many. GLSEN-KY was also not allowed to accept funds from certain sources, such as Lexington-based bars willing to run ads in its local homespun newsletter, which further limited its fundraising options in rural communities. Any funds the chapter received from state sources or grants it would also need to share with the national office. What GLSEN-KY's rural chapter members felt they needed most was funding to purchase a van that could shuttle members to and from meetings and events like the ones held in support of Boyd County High's GSA.

The story of GLSEN-KY shows the importance of family in organizing LGBT youth advocacy and identity negotiation. There is a family structure built into this community-based organization (CBO) as many of GLSEN-KY's members are also members of Gina's extended family and other active members regularly bring cousins, siblings, and parents along with them to GLSEN-KY functions. The concerns of this CBO were far more personal—caring for sick members, finding legal aid for each other, sharing downloaded and forwarded e-mail alerts with one another—than the more policy-driven advocacy efforts of GLSEN's urban-based chapters.

Urban-based chapters' members could enter principals' offices and school board meetings as social equals with the same, if not greater, class status and with the influential presence of a few powerful financial backers and civic leaders in their corner. GLSEN-KY, on the other hand, was more concerned with the individual needs of its members. It had less to gain by working at the level of school board meetings because its communities had neither the allied CBOs nor the friendly gay neighborhoods or lesbian and gay business associations to stand with it and take part in (or financially support) such a public fight. In early June 2002 GLSEN-KY voted to disband. Members were frustrated that GLSEN-KY had not managed to bring more local adult allies and resources into their work. They felt that GLSEN's national focus on advocacy for policy change rather individual LGBT students' needs did not fit their realities and community priorities. In the end, their goals were not compatible with those of the national organizations and the expectations of chapters because the constraints they faced in the fight for visibility had never been considered important enough to recast national agendas. The core members of GLSEN-KY who had kept it alive from early 2000 to June 2002 decided to reconstitute the group and raise money to address their own local agenda. They changed their name to Kentucky Advocates for Equality, opened a new Hotmail account, and changed their mission. They still planned to help Kentucky students and staff in public schools, but they also broadened their vision to make HIV testing more readily available to rural young people. They stepped up their efforts to find grants for legal funds to help people who, like Gina, struggled to fight individual discrimination and harassment cases based on sexual orientation and gender identity that were too mundane to yield the high-profile, impact litigation that drew the interest and aid of Lambda Legal or the American Civil Liberties Union (ACLU). Rural Gay-Straight Alliances struggle with similar limits due to the socioeconomic conditions of their communities. But in the case of Boyd County, tensions around LGBT-identifying students' claims to queer difference seemed the more pressing concern.

Genealogy of a Rural Gay-Straight Alliance

In the early 1970s, paralleling the growth of the gay liberation movement, college-based gay student organizations blossomed across the United States. In response, opponents (usually from the camps of the nascent Religious Right movement) charged gay student groups with exposing young people to deviant lifestyles and argued that schools should not endorse homosexuality by allowing it to be discussed (Miceli 2005, 18).

The breakthrough for public schools came when the Massachusetts Board of Education adopted a "Safe Schools Program for Gay and Lesbian Students" in 1993 that included recommendations for support groups (Miceli 2005, 31). Kevin Jennings, who went on to found GLSEN in 1995, was part of this landmark decision. He testified at the hearings, describing the successes of the high school Gay-Straight Alliance he helped start at a private boarding school where he worked as a history teacher. The unanimous decision to pass the Safe Schools initiative came on the heels of a 1989 U.S. Department of Health and Human Services study that reported alarmingly disproportionate suicide rates among gay and lesbian youth.[16] Over the next decade, several states adopted similar programs and a handful codified protection of sexual orientation in their state nondiscrimination clauses. But case law establishing GSAs' access to school property combined with state and national advocacy have solidified the place of GSAs in schools (Miceli 2005). Ironically, high school students' legal right to sue schools that block Gay-Straight Alliances is rooted in the Equal Access Act (EAA) signed into law by President Ronald Reagan in 1984. Religious conservatives rallied behind the legislation, which they hoped would protect the rights of Bible study groups to meet on school grounds. Warnings that the same law could open doors to protect gay and lesbian student groups meeting on school property were dismissed as either too unlikely or worth the risk (Miceli 2005, 39).

Back in Boyd County, students contacted Kentucky's ACLU for help. They knew from consulting GLSEN National's website and through e-mail exchanges with Gina Cooper that the ACLU had sued on behalf of students elsewhere to establish GSAs. In September 2002 the ACLU office in Louisville, Kentucky, sent a letter to Boyd County High School explaining it would be violating the federal Equal Access Act if it denied students' request for a GSA. The letter forced the Council to reopen the discussion. Students like Sarah, a 17-year-old at BCHS, worried that approval of the GSA would only lead to further tensions at the school. "The people who don't want it very adamantly don't want it here…. It'll take a lot to get it accepted by those people."[17]

One month later, Boyd County High's SBDM Council bent to the ACLU's pressure and, in a divisive 3–2 vote, approved the formation of the GSA. At the Council meeting, 30 members of the GSA and their allies faced off against 50 opponents. A former BCHS student from Rush,

Kentucky, an unincorporated town of 2,700 in Boyd County, put his support of the GSA in very personal terms: "I don't think anybody should have to walk out of their door and into school and be in survival mode." His support stemmed from the harassment he endured even as a closeted gay student at BCHS. He left before graduating and felt a Gay-Straight Alliance could have given him the support he needed to make it through school.[18] Lena, a BCHS sophomore and GSA member from Catlettsburg, Kentucky (population 1,960), was elated by the decision. She hoped their victory would make "more people in the area and the state speak up and try and get chapters in their areas.... Maybe we'll set the pace," she mused.[19]

While Boyd County High School GSA members hoped their home-grown activism might inspire others, some local residents felt it was another example of how schools overstep their bounds and tell parents what their children should learn. Tim York, the pastor at Heritage Temple Free Will Baptist Church and president of a county ministers association, even suggested that parents take their children out of school in protest and consider filing lawsuits of their own. Council members who had approved the GSA expressed a sense of being bullied by outside interests. As teacher and council member Joyce Wellman put it, "We didn't have a choice, no matter what we felt personally," citing the federal court rulings that put them at odds with the EAA and liable to a lawsuit if they barred the GSA.[20]

But two days after the vote, on Wednesday, October 30, 100 students walked out of school in protest of the decision to allow the GSA. Although most students returned before the end of the day, one was arrested and suspended indefinitely after harassing a teacher during the action.[21] Despite the ruckus, the GSA held its first meeting on campus that Friday. More than nineteen students attended without incident, and the group's faculty adviser, Kaye King, along with the GSA's student co-founders felt the mood had calmed considerably since that Wednesday's walkout.[22]

Then, to the community's shock, the following Monday 435 of the high school's 974 students stayed home to protest the Council's approval of the GSA. No one claimed to have organized the action. Students reported that the idea spawned from discussions among students who walked out the week before and wanted a nonviolent means to continue protesting the GSA. Others acknowledged in press accounts that some students stayed home to get an additional day off from school. (Classes were dismissed on Tuesday, November 5, for Election Day.)[23] In other words, it was impossible to gauge whether the more than 400 students who boycotted school strongly opposed the GSA or saw an opportunity to cut class without much guff.

Nevertheless, local, regional, and national groups following the case took the boycott at face value. Area pastors called the students' actions a clear sign of just how upset students were by the GSA. Andrea Hildebran, executive director of the statewide gay and lesbian rights advocacy coalition, the Kentucky Fairness Alliance, thought the boycott was a "dramatic reaction to what in most schools isn't an earth-shattering development," suggesting Ashland's community was far from typical in voicing its discomfort with a GSA.[24] James Esseks, national director of ACLU's lesbian and gay rights project, said this was the first time he had seen a student reaction like this on such a scale. He argued that it "illustrates the need for a safe place for these kids to meet," adding, "Can you imagine being a gay or lesbian student in a community where people feel so free in expressing their intolerance? That must be a difficult place to be."[25]

Just six days after the BCHS student protest, on Sunday, November 10, 2002, local pastors in Cannonsburg and Catlettsburg organized a community rally to protest the GSA. More than 1,000 people attended the demonstration held in the parking lot of Cannonsburg's Church of the Nazarene.[26] Some participants reported driving from neighboring counties to "stand up for our godly rights" and defined the rally as a way "to protect our children at all costs."[27] Guest speakers included Scott Lively, from the California-based Pro-Family Law Center, and David Miller, vice president of Citizens for Community Values, a Cincinnati-based "pro-family" group. Rally organizers encouraged the crowd to continue voicing their opposition to the GSA and to form a legal fund to fight its continuation at BCHS. The Pro-Family Law Center's Scott Lively urged school officials to replace the GSA with a classroom curriculum (like the one his center developed) that opposed "the legitimization of homosexuality" by teaching the immorality of homosexual acts while underscoring the importance of tolerating gay people.[28]

Some BCHS students who attended the rally debated whether the turnout really represented their community. Lena Reese, a GSA member, argued that most of the opposition came from organizations outside the school. Fellow BCHS students, however, said the gathering and the student boycott reflected their resistance to a "small group of students run[ning] [BCHS]" and "homosexuals get[ting] more rights" in their school than they.[29]

Sociologist Arlene Stein found similar organizational strategies among the Religious Right in her ethnographic study of "Timbertown," a small logging community in rural Oregon (Stein 2001). Stein analyzed the organizing efforts for Measure 9, legislation that would have barred inclusion of sexual orientation from all state and local nondiscrimination clauses. Although the measure failed because of overwhelming opposition in urban areas like Portland, Stein found that widespread rural support for Measure 9 was often driven by a grassroots coalition of a few local conservative Christian ministers and the powerful Oregon Citizen's Alliance (OCA), a Portland-based statewide conservative organization. The OCA used the now familiar "culture wars" rhetoric that positions homosexuality as a symptom of a world heading to hell in a handbasket. The OCA argued that working-class, small-town Oregonians were the victims of the "special rights" homosexuals and racial minorities supposedly gained through nondiscrimination laws and the like (Stein 2001, 110). Stein found that support for Measure 9 resonated with rural community members for reasons that had less to do with a blind hatred of gay people than a strong belief in self-reliance and a deep suspicion of anyone seeking redress from the government. Arguments that gays and lesbians might get a leg up through "special rights" proved persuasive because they tapped into a palpable stress over status loss and a sense of disenfranchisement locals experienced across much of the economically depressed rural communities exemplified by "Timbertown" (Stein 2001, 117).

On the national stage, reactions to the Cannonsburg Church in the LGBT press echoed responses to the earlier student boycott. The Boyd County GSA's struggle came to stand in for Kentucky writ large. PlanetOut.com's website coverage framed the incident as yet another case of a backward state guided by conservative interests keeping gay kids from their right to form a student group.[30] The ACLU reiterated how these shows of opposition demonstrated the need for a "safe space" to counter the "hostility and fear" on display at the rally. The GLSEN national office also weighed in for the first time as Eliza Byard, GLSEN's deputy executive director, speaking to a Gay.com/PlanetOut.com reporter, observed that GLSEN National had begun "seeing focused efforts by right-wing groups to scare school districts away from providing support to GLBT students in their community." She added that GLSEN hoped community members "will try and learn more about why this GSA was necessary and understand that some of their fellow classmates need the kind of support that a GSA can provide."[31]

Despite petitions and appeals from the churches behind the Cannons-burg protest, Bill Capehart, Boyd County's school superintendent, upheld the SBDM Council's approval of the GSA. He argued that based on state and federal law brought to their attention by the ACLU, the school had no choice but to accept the GSA. In an interview, he made a point of saying that the GSA did not recruit members and that the meetings did not discuss sexual practices, but this did not quell the debate.[32]

The next month, however, the Boyd County school board delivered a stunning reversal: they unanimously voted to overturn the SBDM Council's stand and ban the GSA, along with the four other nonacademic clubs—Human Rights Club, Pep Club, Bible Club, and Fellowship of Christian Athletes—from meeting at the school. But the legality of the board's move remained unresolved. The Kentucky Education Reform Act (KERA) of 1990 gave SBDM Councils, not school boards, jurisdiction over curricular issues like school clubs, and the SBDM Council did not, in fact, back the board's decision. Ironically, the Kentucky General Assembly created SBDM Councils as part of KERA in response to the *Rose v. Council for Better Education* landmark case discussed earlier. That lawsuit successfully argued that rural schools were disenfranchised from decisions about how to spend state and federal educational dollars and, as a result, were at a severe financial disadvantage compared to urban Kentucky schools. KERA was enacted to answer the demand for more rural community control over their schools and address the economic disparities between rural and urban communities. The legislation has had limited success in narrowing the spending gap between rich and poor school districts. Its initiatives, like wiring 95% of Kentucky's classrooms to the Internet and establishing Site-Based Decision Making Councils to bring locals into the thick of curricular and hiring decisions, have been popular but difficult to evaluate as direct responses to KERA's stated mission.[33] The state law's critics, for example, note that spending still favors rich over poor, metro over rural, and white over black students. Even with Internet access, which makes the state a national leader in education technology, dropout rates haven't changed significantly since KERA's introduction. And the Site-Based Decision Making Councils give the appearance of local control, but, as the Boyd County case illustrated, it remains unclear whether SBDM Councils have any real legal power.[34]

Unable to scout out any common ground between the GSA supporters and opponents, Boyd County High School Superintendent Bill Capehart upheld the proposed ban. At least one of the school board members who approved the ban on nonacademic clubs argued that this had less to do with the GSA and more to do with a battle waging for years in the district over the appropriateness of nonacademic clubs.[35]

In one last odd twist, just as schools closed for winter break, the Boyd County school board met again and decided to sidestep the issue entirely by banning all student clubs, academic and nonacademic alike. Although unprecedented in Kentucky, this was not the first time a school board had blocked the formation of a GSA by eliminating all school groups. In 1996 Salt Lake City's East High school board banned all student clubs knowing that, under the EAA, it was the only way to keep the GSA from meeting on school grounds. The school eventually lost a legal battle waged by the GSA, represented by the ACLU and supported by amicus briefs from GLSEN, Lambda Legal, and a host of other social justice and education advocacy groups. What is most striking about the ban in Kentucky is that the Boyd County school board's actions also violated Kentucky state law directives that SBDM Councils hold the power to authorize school clubs. The Council, although not unanimously supportive of the GSA, did want to retain its right to serve as the legal voice of the community as much as it wanted to avoid an ACLU lawsuit and further characterizations in the state and national press that they were a small-minded town opposed to students' rights to assemble.

Kentucky's Department of Education responded immediately by siding with the SBDM Council, claiming that the school board didn't have the right to ban academic clubs during school hours. Boyd County school board member Theresa Jackson countered that her fellow school board members felt tensions were running so high they just wanted a "halt of conversation about anything that has to do with clubs" in the schools.[36] Jeff Vessels, ACLU Kentucky's executive director, likened the school board's decision to the days "when communities used to close down public swimming pools instead of allowing minorities to come to those pools," equating it with the kind of aberrant racism supposedly a part of Kentucky's past. Local pastor Tim York said, "They [the school board] had to do what they had to do," suggesting the ban came not from a xenophobic impulse or discrimination reminiscent of Jim Crow racism but from pressures leveled by a meddlesome legal system and ultra-radical special-interests groups from outside the community like the ACLU, KFA, and GLSEN. Alignments of who spoke for locals versus outside interests and the connections between the banning of all student clubs and legacies of communitywide discrimination came to the forefront in the ensuing debate over the school board's challenge to the SBDM Council's approval of the BCHS GSA. Nothing would twist, strain, and realign Boyd County community members' alliances to either side of the debate around the GSA like a counterprotest.

Rallying for Unity

No single event reflects the interweaving of local, regional, statewide, and national advocacy efforts like the Unity Rally held Sunday, January 12, 2003, in Ashland, just as the Boyd County GSA issue was at its height of national publicity. The Boyd County Human Rights Commission (the body established by Governor Bert Combs in the 1960s to investigate race-based discrimination) organized the rally. Carol Jackson, chairperson of the Ashland Human Rights Commission and one of the organizers of what was billed as the "CommUNITY" rally, said the event was not in support of the GSA or homosexuality but of diversity and equality more broadly. They hoped it would demonstrate the town's tolerance, something they felt had been lost in the coverage of the GSA. A few members of the Kentucky Advocates for Equality (formerly GLSEN-KY chapter) drove up together to take part in the event. Gina Cooper could not make it that weekend because of family obligations. As so often happens in ethnographic fieldwork, I had overbooked myself and scheduled other interviews elsewhere in the state that I did not feel I could cancel. I would only find out after the event, from news coverage and personal accounts from the youth I knew who did attend, just how significant this rally would become for the area and my research.

The Unity Rally proved more solidifying than anyone anticipated, thanks in no small part to notorious Kansas-based Westboro Baptist Church minister Fred Phelps. For those unfamiliar with Phelps and his church congregants (reported to be made up entirely of his extended family), they have made a name for themselves toting "God Hates Fags" signs around the country to protest events ranging from Matthew Shepard's memorial service to funerals of soldiers killed in Iraq.[37] Boyd County locals, both for and against the GSA, galvanized against outsiders like Phelps condemning their own. Ironically, the presence of Phelps and his kin is what ultimately united the community.

Between two hundred and three hundred people participated in the Unity Rally held in the restored Paramount Arts Center.[38] Across the street, eleven of Fred Phelps' church members (Phelps himself was not present) picketed while standing on the American flag and waving signs bearing messages like "God Hates Fag Enablers," "Fag Church," and "Thank God for Sept. 11."[39] They had come to protest local churches, not the Unity Rally, because they believed the community's clergy were not strident enough in their condemnations of homosexuality. "It's a rather remarkable thing that in this place, which would be considered rather conservative and religious, you'd find a Gay-Straight Alliance…. The churches have failed," Phelps said.[40] Local police maintained the peace and distance between Phelps' small contingent and local counterprotesters.

Sixteen-year-old Uriah said he came to the rally because he worried that Phelps' Westboro Baptist Church made other Christians look intolerant and hateful. He noted that, while he was "personally opposed to homosexual activity," as a black person he understood discrimination and wanted to publicly stand against it.[41] Gary Adkins, a middle-aged assistant attorney for the Commonwealth from Morehead, Kentucky, said, "I thought it was important to show these folks from Kansas that a message of hate and intolerance is not something that people in Eastern Kentucky believe."[42]

Inside the theater, David Welch, Ashland's former mayor, spoke to the audience about the test their community faced. Alluding to, though not speaking directly about, the Boyd County GSA controversy, Welch expressed hope that matters would be resolved peacefully through the legal system, adding, "Unity does not mean we always agree, but we can be united against bigoted views."[43] While the speakers acknowledged the presence of students from Boyd County High's Gay-Straight Alliance, no one representing the group was allowed to speak at the event. Later, at an ACLU press conference, GSA student members said they appreciated the support but expressed disappointment that they were not allowed to speak. Alliance leader and Boyd County senior Tyler M. said most speakers at the rally skirted the issue of sexual orientation. "It seemed like they weren't really sure who they were supporting. The people standing outside espousing messages of hate had more of a chance to express themselves than we did sitting inside."[44]

Former Mayor Welch's hope that the GSA matter would work its way peacefully through the courts came true. Ten days after the Unity Rally, the ACLU sued the school superintendent, the school board, and BCHS' principal on behalf of seven members of the BCHS GSA, their parents, and the student group's adviser. At issue was the unfair application of

BCHS' policy barring school groups. There were reports that some student clubs continued to meet on school property despite the school board's ban. And there was ongoing dispute over whether the school board had the right to set curriculum policies when that is the jurisdiction of Site-Based Decision Making Councils under the 1990 Kentucky Education Reform Act.

Once again, GSA students vented frustration that they were "provoked into taking . . . drastic steps."[45] The GSA's school adviser lamented, "We have exhausted every avenue to have this solved and unfortunately we are forced to go to court."[46] Jeff Vessels, executive director of the ACLU of Kentucky, said they had given the school "every opportunity to do the right thing," and added "[the lawsuit] puts Kentucky schools on notice that the ACLU stands firmly with Gay-Straight Alliances, and we will not hesitate to go to court to preserve their constitutional freedoms."[47]

On April 19, 2003, after overwhelming evidence proved BCHS allowed the Bible Club, the Drama Club, and the Beta Club (a service organization) to meet at school but not the GSA, District Judge David Bunning issued an injunction against the school ordering it to permit the GSA to meet while the ACLU's lawsuit wound through the court system.[48] Bunning also noted examples of anti-gay harassment at BCHS that suggested the GSA was sorely needed.[49] Kayla, a 15-year-old at BCHS, said, "I don't really care. They don't bother me," when asked by a reporter what she thought about allowing the GSA back. Luke Lyons, 18, a BCHS senior and member of the Future Farmers of America Club, wasn't a GSA supporter but said if the court injunction allowed his group to meet, he was okay with having it at his school. He didn't think other students would care that much either. Principal Jerry Johnson agreed with Lyons: "I think the kids are way past this."[50] David Friedman, ACLU of Kentucky's general counsel, said in praise of Bunning's decision, "He rightfully recognized that the GSA serves the public interest by working to foster tolerance in a community that clearly needs it."[51]

Finally, after several revisions of its ban on school clubs and hints from Bunning that it would be difficult to prove they were not just trying to block the GSA, the Boyd County Board of Education dropped its ban on student clubs in early 2004. The ACLU and GSA members settled their lawsuit out of court and in exchange the board agreed to do anti-harassment trainings for the entire district, with particular attention on discrimination based on sexual orientation.

Conclusion

GSAs, such as the one formed at Boyd County High School, are success-ful not because of a clear consolidation of local support but rather be-cause of the incongruent convergence of federal laws, state educational reforms, and pressures from and between familiar locals and strangers to these communities. "Intolerance" in and of itself cannot explain the lim-ited presence of GSAs in rural areas and certain states (Miceli 2005, 101). Missing are the community-based organizations and allies with clout that can fiscally champion the existence of a GSA and sustain the fight for ed-ucational reform.

The political organizing of Boyd County High's GSA and GLSEN's Ken-tucky chapter challenge the presumption that resistance to LGBT youth in rural communities is simply an expression of "Red state" homophobia endemic in small(-minded) towns. The situation called attention to the complicated intersections of racial and class tensions that structure ru-ral life. These tensions simultaneously buttress and undermine strategies for LGBT visibility in rural places. Entrenched antagonisms between state and rural communities and the tectonics of class and racial discrimination make rural schools particularly contentious cauldrons for debates about homosexuality. Small towns manage their differences through rhetorics of fairness and justice as they struggle over representations and resources and make space for a politics of visibility driven by rural queer youth. GSAs are unparalleled political strategies for this work as they register as both local and national movements. This gives them access to a range of resources and a built-in defense to charges that they are the product of meddlesome outsiders because they can only be formed and led by stu-dents. GSAs powerfully counter the claim that there are no local LGBT youth or straight allies who care about LGBT social justice issues (Miceli 2005, 110–11). At the same time, information and models of success found online have proven crucial to GSA formations (Miceli 2005, 135). Miceli argues that the GLSEN website acts as a clearinghouse of information on how to advocate for rights in schools and form GSAs (Miceli 2005, 111). Boyd County gathered most of the information for how to start a GSA from web-based "GSA Frequently Asked Questions" like the ones archived on the GLSEN website, conversations with regional community advocates, like Gina Cooper, and e-mail exchanges with national organi-zations like the ACLU that support young people's efforts to claim free speech in their schools.

In contrast, national gay and lesbian education advocacy groups like GLSEN have had meager success beyond urban centers not because of a lack of community interest, but because of class assumptions built into the foundations and political strategies of their national advocacy organizations. GLSEN's chapter-based model presumes, I think correctly, that locals know best how to fight locally (Miceli 2005, 108). However, this strategy also assumes a local power base that is (or imagines itself to be) on equal footing with its schools and has the financial muscle to fight for policy changes. It also assumes a local GLSEN chapter is necessarily and unequivocally understood as local.

Rural communities reproduce a sense of familiarity and localness through their schools. As was the case for Berea's PFLAG lobbyists and Mary Bird's Homemakers, metaphors of family and the rights of locals to control their own affairs echo through the hallways of rural schools like Boyd County High. Citizens for and against recognizing LGBT-identifying students lean on the myth of familiarity to retain their rights to speak as locals on LGBT issues. But associating with national organizations compromises this familiarity. Power brokers, like the GLSEN and ACLU, are read as outside lobbying agencies steamrolling over the will of locals, raising the specters of other times federal and state laws have intervened in rural schools' affairs.

Local schools have long been sites for national struggles over material resources and social boundaries. State and national laws that tap the roots of deeply entrenched class and racial politics are particularly vexing minefields. Rural communities in KenTennesse and the Central Appalachian Region more broadly still struggle with racial difference and making racial others familiar components of rural communities. This continues to intensify as more Latino families move to rural areas for manufacturing and agricultural jobs.[52] GSAs and national nonprofits like GLSEN-KY advocating for LGBT youth in educational settings must navigate a history of opposition to anything perceived as originating from outside the community. These politics contextualize visibility for LGBT youth in rural schools. As such, GSAs and LGBT education advocates fight for space on a crowded agenda of concerns in rural communities. They can make advances, but along the way they must contend with the thorniness that familiarity and rural anxieties about claims to difference introduce. They must carefully balance the priorities of public recognition demanded by a politics of LGBT visibility with the poverty, lack of access to higher education, ongoing structural racism, and other disadvantages that rural schools struggle to address.[53] One resource LGBT youth can turn to is a history of rural communities translating issues of class disparity and, albeit less successfully, racial divide into local concerns, transforming them into community issues to be given political priority.

The Unity Rally is an example of one rural community's attempt to grapple with local young people's demands for recognition of queer difference and translate that desire for LGBT visibility into a community-wide concern. In some ways, as sociologist Arlene Stein found in her work among rural whites in Oregon, for those opposed to the GSA, queer difference may stand in for their tense relationships with other strangers (whether racial others or urban elites), barely visible but always looming. Queers are perhaps viewed as the newest "other" on the block seeking "special rights" while poor rural whites continue to struggle to find jobs and make ends meet (Stein 2001, 110). But this expression of stress over the potential loss of status to new "others" in town is complicated by the GSA students' indisputable claims to being local. These may be queer kids, but they are our queer kids. The presence of Fred Phelps was just what the town needed to sort out who was the more abhorrent stranger. And, as important, the Unity Rally was an opportunity to redeem the town's reputation as a tolerant and accepting place. While uncomfortable recognizing and naming queer or racial difference in the room, the event's organizers used the logic of familiarity to demonstrate the community's embrace of all locals and repudiate any stranger coming to condemn their own. The GSA's engagements with a politics of visibility cannot be understood without considering how deeply it is steeped in a regional history of racial homogeneity (and collective shame) rooted in violence toward racial difference. At the same time, these rural communities fortify themselves in their own brand of shared queer difference. They have historically taken comfort and found solidarity in the familiarity that binds them—their rural sameness that marks them as different and less than in the eyes of their wealthy, urban counterparts.

Because schools play a vital role as public spaces for citizenship claims, community skirmishes over GSAs serve as transformative moments when the boundaries of queerness further sharpen and define LGBT citizenship. Just as important, particularly for LGBT-identifying youth advocates beyond the city limits, these struggles index how dynamic recognition of local citizenship can be and how vulnerable, tentative, and disenfranchised rural communities view their citizenship vis-à-vis the nation-state. And, as the next chapter illustrates, schools are not the only sites of contestation drawn into the work of LGBT youth and their allies. Building analogies are strained in places still struggling with the meaning and limited visible presence of difference, racial or otherwise, and the limits of analogies among social justice for class, race, and queerness more broadly.

4

From Wal-Mart to Websites
Out in Public

The Highland Pride Alliance (HPA), a community-based so-
cial support group for area lesbian, gay, bisexual, and transgender (LGBT)
people and their straight allies, usually met at a member's house or in
the basement of a local public county library. Only a few members had
homes with the space and welcoming families to accommodate the six to
ten regular attendees. No one could host this particular week and another
community group had booked the library's meeting room. So, the HPA
gathered at Dolly's House, the Christian bookstore across the county line.

Recently, the owner had decided to put some green plastic lawn chairs
around carafes of flavored coffee in the store's entryway and call it a café.
Dolly's House quickly became a popular youth hangout. Take a few steps
past the coffee and you were in the bookstore—a room with several racks
of greeting cards, books on tape, and "ready-to-order personalized Bibles."
Because this was one of the Wednesday evenings when Dolly's owner
closed up early to attend church, the members of the HPA shuffled their
meeting to the Gas-n'-Go farther down the highway that cut through the
deep river valley they routinely traversed. It was the only place open after
9 P.M. on this stretch of road where the closest town was a mile off the
highway exit and had less than 3,000 people.

When I first began participating in Berea's Parents and Friends of Lesbians and Gays (PFLAG) monthly meetings, one of the group's members,
a white, gay-identifying man in his early twenties attending Berea College,
told me about the HPA. While he did not belong to the HPA, "it was just
too much drama," he said, he had known most of the group's members all
his life and offered to introduce me to them. He grew up where the HPA
was based, an eastern area of Kentucky known for its beautiful state parks
and seasonal tourism. He called the group's co-chair, told him about my
project, and the next day I got an e-mail from him inviting me to join

the HPA at a Ponderosa Steakhouse restaurant in a larger town a county over from where most of the group's members lived. I drove four and half hours from my apartment in Louisville to meet the HPA's core members: six gay-identifying white men, a white lesbian couple, one white bisexual woman and one white trans-identifying man all in their mid-teens to early twenties. At different times, male and female white straight-identifying friends around the same age, an older gay male couple, and the trans-identifying man's mom joined them. I made the drive almost every other week to hang out with them ever since.

This time, Shaun, HPA's co-chair and my main contact, was the first of his friends to arrive at the donut shop attached to the Gas-n'-Go. Shaun called to let me know that the meeting had moved and invited me to join them at the new rendezvous point. The talk of next month's HPA Halloween fundraiser turned to casual gossip and chatter regarding this evening's after-meeting plans. They could go back to Tim's place and watch some movies. That was quickly rejected. They spent hours at Tim's last night watching the then recently released (U.S. version of) *Queer as Folk* First Season collection on DVD. Other possibilities were bandied and then dismissed as "too boring" or "too far away." Joe tossed out the idea of heading over to neighboring Springhaven—20 minutes due south—to do some drag at the Wal-Mart. He was dying to try out the fake eyelashes he had bought at the Dollar Tree last weekend. The group's collective uproar of affirming whoops and laughter drew the eyes of two bleached-blond-haired women in their mid-twenties listlessly tending to the donut display case and coffee hot plates. Shaun met their tentative smiles with a large grin and a small princess-atop-a-float wave. Turning back to the group, he giggled and said softly, "Now, settle it down, y'all."

This would not be the group's first foray to the Wal-Mart Supercenter located in the county seat, population just more than 10,000. Within a few months of the Supercenter's grand opening, the HPA had reappropriated Wal-Mart, turning it into a regular gathering spot for their post-meeting social activities. At one point, the HPA website even featured photos snapped of members posing in their most memorable outfits amid Wal-Mart's aisles. The HPA had turned Wal-Mart into a meeting space, drag revue, and shopping excursion all rolled into one.

That these boisterous LGBT-identifying rural young people and their allies move among house parties, public libraries, Christian bookstores, gas stations, Wal-Mart, and websites may seem surprising. I will admit, it surprised me. I had assumed they met exclusively in friends' houses to avoid trouble or hostility from locals. But as I would learn again and again, the everyday lives of rural youth I met complicate simple dichotomies of rural and urban experience or private versus public experiences of queer visibility. I hope that by detailing the work of responding to the expectations a politics of LGBT visibility poses, particularly in an era saturated by gay visibility in the media and via the Internet, I can show that, for the people who live in them, rural communities are more than backdrops or landscapes to late-modern queer subjectivities. If, as feminist geographer Doreen Massey argues, "the social is inexorably also spatial" (Massey 1994, 265), we cannot examine the social relations of power that produce the meaning of LGBT identities without a careful consideration of how locations, rural locales in this case, matter to those relations.

Most strikingly, rural queer and questioning youth entangle their broader surroundings in integral ways, blurring, as Mary Bird and the Boyd County Gay-Straight Alliance advocates did, clear boundaries of what constitutes "the local." These young people live in communities that lack the human, social, and financial capital to maintain the gay neighborhoods, bookstores, and coffeehouses found in urban settings such as the Castro in San Francisco, New York City's Christopher Street, Chicago's Boystown, or Dupont Circle in Washington, D.C. Nearly all of them live in "dry counties" where alcohol cannot even be sold let alone served in a gay bar. These youth can (and regularly do) travel to gay enclaves in Louisville, Lexington, and Nashville. But they cannot produce in their rural daily lives the sustained infrastructure of visibility that defines urban LGBT communities. Instead, they travel to each other's houses and caravan roundtrip to a larger city with a gay bar or gay-affirming church several hours away. In other words, much as historian John Howard found in his history of queer community formation in rural Mississippi of the 1940s–1980s, rural queer and questioning youth make up for their lack of local numbers and gay-owned spaces by using a strategy of circulation rather than congregation (Howard 1999, 78).

Imagining Rural Queerness

The image of rural spaces as inhospitable to public displays of queer difference is nearly monolithic. As British rural geographer Paul Cloke aptly noted in his own studies of representations of the rural, "Many people are likely to 'know' rural areas more through watching popular television programmes than through personal experience" (Cloke 1997, 372). Even though I had grown up in a small California town, my years living in West Coast cities left me as likely to assume the worst about rural Kentucky as anyone who had been brought up on *The Beverly Hillbillies* and *The Dukes of Hazzard*. In the United States, popular representations, such as John Boorman's classic 1972 film adaptation of James Dickey's popular novel *Deliverance*, marked rural spaces as endemically hostile, plagued by the rawness and cruelty of inbreeding and poverty. The film's brutal male-on-male rape scene of Bobby, played by Ned Beatty, by a toothless maniacal local evoked an animalism that lurked beyond the civility of urban society; the heart of America's darkness ran rampant in the wilds of backwater Appalachia.[1]

More recently *Brokeback Mountain* has eroticized and, certainly for me, redeemed what unquenchable queer desire looks like (no offense to Ned Beatty fans) out in the country. The desolate rural landscape, however, remains pitted against the purity of Jack and Ennis' private romantic love. Still, they must monitor their passions closely in this enemy territory.[2] Ultimately, gay cowboy love is treated as the tragic victim of rurality's paradoxical beautiful ugliness. Director Ang Lee's sweeping vistas become characters in the film that fail to publicly recognize and respect love's universal qualities as any decent city would.

Even historical accounts of the recent rural past paint private house parties as the primary location of queer possibility and community—if any community is imagined possible at all.[3] Drawing on popular documentaries screened at LGBT film festivals in the first few years of the 21st century, historian John Howard argues that rural LGBT lives are marked not by violence or isolation, but by "mundane, everyday trade-offs" such as "fewer public displays of affection, a greater feeling of rootedness, less pride in outness, more of a sense of safety" (Howard 2006, 101–102). As Howard notes, hate crimes directed at LGBT people are more often perpetrated by groups of men who use the safety of their numbers to single out victims living in dense urban areas (Howard 2006, 101–102). Although LGBT-related hate crimes are not nationally recorded and systematically tracked, studies of rural crime patterns suggest that violence directed at queer difference in rural spaces (an issue I will return to at the end of this chapter) is different from, though statistically no greater than, the violence cities exact.[4] Contrary to popular representations and presumptions drawn from historical accounts, today's rural youth do not (arguably cannot) privately suffer an endemic estrangement or isolation from queer subjectivities. The trickle of denigrating national press accounts of "the homosexual lifestyle" that began in the mid-1960s presaged a veritable flood of gay visibility.[5] Rural youth in the United States have unprecedented access to national media markets. These markets saturate them in a politics of LGBT visibility that demands public recognition. Seeking acknowledgment as lesbian, gay, bisexual, or transgender means grappling with these demands no matter where one lives. Rural youth must respond to the call for LGBT visibility that structures their feelings of authenticity amid vastly underfunded, rural public spaces that prioritize allegiance to familiarity and solidarity over public claims to difference of any kind.

If rural LGBT-identifying youth are at times hard to see, it is as much because researchers rarely look for them as they have so few places to be seen. They must also be strategic about how they use their communities for queer recognition if they are not to wear out their welcome as locals. And, in some cases, they are rendered invisible because urban-based models of LGBT visibility refuse to recognize rural queerness as anything of value. Rural queer youth, therefore, challenge us to meander through small towns and rethink where and how a public sense of queerness might transpire.

Working Identity

Youth in the United States have a unique relationship to modern constructions of sexual and gendered subjects. Young people's pronouncements of identity are easily dismissed as products of adolescent confusion. Their legal status as minors effectively bars them from directly representing their needs. In short, their position as "youth" complicates their access to the kinds of queer citizenship projects imagined by feminist and queer scholars. Rather than assume queer-youth sexualities and genders are aberrations or signs of mental health crises, this study works from the premise that sexual and gender identities are cultural expressions of collective interaction negotiated among youth through public spaces, peer networks, media engagements, and service-provider environments.

Often, young people who challenge sexual and gender norms of propriety and abstinence are dismissed as promiscuous, playing with fire but playing nonetheless. Youth expressing same-sex desires or questioning heteronormative sexualities and genders are often characterized as confused, as though sexuality and gender identity naturally "clear up" once you reach adulthood. This dismissive gesture is one way to manage social anxieties that the majority of children and young adults are, in fact, active sexual and, I would argue, gendered beings. By asserting that most young people are simply playing with, rather than working very (very) hard at, creating sexual and gendered meaning, we partially recover the story of sexual innocence so central to Western narratives of modern childhood.[6] Certainly the Religious Right attributes LGBT-identifying youth with some agency, characterizing this population as particularly licentious. But, more often, they are depicted as hapless victims of gay adults' immorality, expressing what Janice Irvine refers to as the Right's "conversion anxiety" (Irvine 2002, 172).

The politics of LGBT visibility draw on a similar logic of sexual innocence. Whether through popular media like *Dawson's Creek* or national LGBT social-movement rhetoric produced by the Human Rights Campaign, LGBT-identifying youth are offered as visible proof that gay, lesbian, bisexual, or transgender identities are essential, inner states of being just under the surface waiting to be discovered. The work of identity formation is contained to individuals scaling the ladders out of their foggy, suppressed subconscious and opening their closet doors, heavy lifting for some kids and a mere flick of the wrist for others, depending on where one lives. To suggest that queer youth must work arduously *to achieve*, not discover, LGBT identities and the sense of authenticity they confer is to approach the concept of identity as an ideal embedded in and constructed through the politics of social interactions rather than the expression of fixed traits. In the words of sociologist Wayne Brekhus, who studied the taxonomic subtlety of suburban gay men's identities, it is to see the "self as changing and shifting across time and across social contexts" (Brekhus 2003, 21). Ultimately, from this vantage point, the politics of visibility are part of social systems of identification and stratification that purchase the privilege of recognition for some at a cost to others.

Drawing on the broader research approach reflected in Brekhus' examination of the social rather than psychological underpinnings of identity, I define queer-identity work as the collective labor of crafting, articulating, and performing LGBT identities.[7]

Mapping Boundaries

The experiences of the HPA and other rural LGBT-identifying youth in this study suggest that a variety of public spaces serve as key landscapes for queer-identity work. I define these landscapes not as specific, bound places but as *boundary publics*: iterative, ephemeral experiences of belonging that circulate across the outskirts and through the center(s) of a more recognized and validated public sphere. Such experiences of place and connection can register to onlookers and participants as repetitious— seemingly the same meeting happening in the same friends' homes or library basement. However, these experiences of boundary publics transform the superstores, churches, and other de facto public spaces of the rural United States. Boundary publics therefore should not be seen so much as places but as moments in which we glimpse a complex web of relations that is always playing out the politics and negotiations of identity.

Before discussing specific examples of the kinds of boundary publics produced by the queer-identity work of rural youth, let me begin with some grounding in the traditional notions of "the public sphere" as outlined by Jürgen Habermas.[8] I use this foundation and critiques of it to refine my notion of boundary publics. Habermas' landmark analytical model of a bourgeois public sphere theorized spaces with clear separation among economic, state, and private interests (first English translation, 1989). Habermas' public sphere featured autonomy from state and corporate power; exchange and critique of criticizable validity claims, notably those grounded in something other than personal standpoint; reflexivity; explicit examination of personal and social interests; good-faith efforts to understand other perspectives; and discursive inclusion and the social equality of peers.[9]

Key critics of Habermas' model note that it neglects the importance of the "plebeian" public sphere (trade unions, working-class organizing) and idealizes the "bourgeois public sphere" as exclusively invested in Enlightenment projects rather than more mundane interests like gossip or backbiting. Feminist scholars, such as Nancy Fraser, have pointedly critiqued the model because it labels both the household and the economy as private matters. Therefore gendered work (not to mention domestic and other forms of "invisible" labor) by definition becomes excluded from the public sphere. Indeed, such an analytic or literal separation of these interests shortchanges the very possibility for those marginalized by the public sphere to bring their grievances, read as private matters, to public attention. Ultimately, there is common agreement among feminists, as political theorist Debra Morris points out, that the "private and public evolve together" (Morris 2000, 324).

Nancy Fraser challenged the notion that separating the private from the public was in practice maintainable. Her main focus of critique, however—and contribution to the discussion here—was her argument that "subaltern counterpublics" have always been a part of the making of the public sphere.[10] Fraser defined these counterpublics as "parallel discursive arenas where members of subordinated social groups invent and circulate counter discourses to formulate oppositional interpretations of their identities, interests, and needs" (Fraser 1992, 123). Fraser uses counterpublics of second-wave feminists to her illustrate her point. Specifically, she argued that feminist women's bookstores, publishers, music, child care, and other resources were exemplars of alternative spheres. Fraser casts subaltern counterpublics as "discursive arenas . . . (that) recast needs and identities, thereby reducing disadvantage in official public spheres" (Fraser 1992, 124).

Michael Warner carries forward counterpublics with particular attention to how "participation in such a public is one of the ways by which its members' identities are formed and transformed" (Warner 2002, 57). Participation in counterpublics then becomes constitutive to the identities of the individuals involved. As Warner states, "Homosexuals can exist in isolation; but gay people or queers exist by virtue of the world they elaborate together" (Warner 2002, 59). Warner notes the outpouring of queer culture that circulates in the streets of New York's Westside, particularly on Christopher Street. He offers that the "street becomes queer and develops a dense, publicly accessible sexual culture . . . a base for non-porn businesses, and a political base from which to pressure politicians with a gay voting bloc. No group is more dependent on this kind of pattern in urban spaces than queers" (Warner 2002, 204).

The counterpublics Fraser and Warner imagine call for conspicuous, though never accounted for, critical mass and urban buttressing. This is reflected, for example, in Warner's contention that "if we [queers] could not concentrate a publicly accessible culture somewhere, we would always be outnumbered and overwhelmed" (Warner 2002, 204). Rural queer- and LGBT-identifying young people cannot achieve the kind of critical mass or amassing of capital described above. As such, their assertions of visibility challenge the urban bias that undergirds these theories of counterpublics. The independent entrepreneurship of feminist cultural production and the thriving commercialism of Christopher Street are features hard to come by in rural places where the public domain is one step away from foreclosure. Fraser and Warner both imagine urban spaces as the ideal environment for the visibility, and invisibility, necessary to the nurturing of alternative subaltern counterpublics. However, rural queer young people's authorized access to public space is fragile. These youth are entangled in broader economic and social conditions of rural public spheres quite different from the ones Habermas, Fraser, or Warner imagined. There is no economic base to spawn a strong bourgeois public or from which alternative bookstores can be built. Nor can youth, as minors, directly address the public sphere as private citizens in a "shared world of equals" (Warner 2002, 59). Finally, counterpublics cannot account for the power geometries that shape rural public spaces or the asymmetries and inequalities these geometries produce when confronted with youth queering the familiarity that organizes these spaces.

To better address the conditions and experiences of rural youth, their queer-identity work, and the publics they enact, I suggest framing these moments of public engagement as boundary publics. This move acknowledges the practices of rationing, regulation, and integration that delineate discursive public spaces in rural communities. I bring a spatial-temporal dimension to the notion of boundary objects developed by sociologist Susan Leigh Star. For Star, boundary objects are not fences or lines dividing separate social worlds.[11] Rather, boundary objects are entities that meet the distinct expectations of different social groups "both plastic enough to adapt to local needs . . . yet robust enough to maintain a common identity" (Star and Griesemer 1989, 393). Treating public spaces as boundary objects emphasizes their nuances as points of access to and moments of social recognition "plastic enough" to convey queerness "yet robust enough" to provide familiarity. Additionally, the incorporation of new media into young people's local space-making projects defies the argument that these technologies simply provide escape from tormenting or bleak offline worlds. In this sense, new media qua boundary publics are vantage points from which to observe the dialectic between media use and media's meaning in people's lives. There is a permeable and malleable consistency to boundary publics that makes them simultaneously recognizable and elusive to onlookers and constituents, a quality of foggy familiarity tinged with ambiguity that proves critical to queer-identity work in rural communities.

Rural LGBT-identifying young people illustrate the very public nature of queer-identity work and the importance of considering where this work takes place. The boundary publics described below mark their engagements on the margins as they negotiate and articulate their own kind of belonging without the help of adult allies. These locations of collective practice constantly shift because of the broader lack of historical or economic mooring in their communities. They do not stay put. So, in my discussion of rural youth and their uses of publics for queer-identity work, I point out uses of space that go unrecognized or fly under the radar of the formal public sphere. In fact, it is the lack of formal notice or public recognition that makes these spaces viable. By skirting notice—just barely—they also manage the risk of being recognized or recognizable as queer. They are at once within and just beyond the reach of conservative elites' attempts to control structures of familiarity in rural communities. The irony here is that most of the youth I spoke with talked about their unacknowledged status as the "town gay kid." As one 15-year-old from a township of 3,000 noted, "What do I have to be afraid of? Someone finding out? They all know." This youth's comment speaks to the tensions among familiarity, visibility, and knowability that shape public recognition in rural settings. As the quote above suggests, there is an ongoing accommodation and adjustment to the presence of queer youth, a "counterfeit secrecy" in which sexual and gender nonconformity are widely known but treated as open secrets inappropriate for, or just too obvious to warrant, public conversation.[12] Referring to these skirmishes and concessions as boundary publics here demarcates the spaces that rural young people are shaped by and shape. This particular phrasing gives weight and representation to the imbalance that constitutes both formal public spheres and the boundary publics I attempt to map.

Rural young people make space for themselves through acts of occupation. They work to "be themselves." They do so by inhabiting corporate bodies—from Wal-Mart to 501(c)3 nonprofits and commercial websites. They also temporarily commandeer and recast rural environments where "everyone knows about them," but they are expected to remain functionally invisible. These occupations are dangerous, though perhaps not as much as the urban-generated depictions of rural places lead us to believe. I turn now to examples of these boundary publics followed by a discussion of their fragilities and strengths. As productive as boundary publics are to rural queer-youth identity work, as a strategy to address the expectations of LGBT visibility they pose limits.

Dragging It Up at Wal-Mart

A bright, neon archway flickering "always low prices, always food center"— hovers above the entrance to the Springhaven, Kentucky, Wal-Mart Supercenter. The blue-trimmed, one-story building starts at stoplight 14 and spans an eroding stretch of state highway that bisects the town. On this

Sunday evening, young men and women hold hands and roam through the aisles. Aside from a few young Latino families, most customers are white and speak with the low, slow drawl of Southern accents.

The Supercenter has nearly 100 aisles, from a full grocery on one end to pet supplies and beauty products on the other. Rows of fabric bolts spill out of their display bins. A range of household appliances, an electronic wedding registry kiosk, floor rugs, and an extensive work-boot collection crowd the West Entrance. Monitors above the aisles blare advertisements from the DisneyHealth Network produced for Wal-Mart hawking products in between snippets of music videos. University of Kentucky logo-wear easily fills a 9-foot-by-12-foot space. There's an eatery to the right of the automated superstore double doors. Smokers fill the red and white tables, savoring their last cigarette drags before entering the smoke-free discount merchandiser that has been in this strip mall for 18 months.

The Springhaven Wal-Mart is the only business open 24 hours within an 80-mile radius. I found out about the popularity of this Wal-Mart when I asked Clay, a local teen, what he and his friends did for fun. "Most gay people around the county, we all go to Hardee's or the new Backyard Burgers." He added casually, "And then most people all haul up together in big carloads, put on some drag, runway walk the Super Wal-Mart in Springhaven and walk around for about five hours with people almost having heart attacks and conniption fits cause we're running around.... We take pictures of us all, post them to the website, and have fun with our little getaway from living in rural Kentucky."

When I asked other area youth about their experiences at Wal-Mart, they confirmed that performing drag in the superstore's aisles was a rite of passage for those entering the local gay scene. Joe recalled his initiation this way: "The first time I was with them, we all put on these furry jackets and we was walking through the aisles. That was fun. Me and all my friends, we all gather up several cars all the time, and now we go once or twice a month. We all just huddle up together and run up there." With the exception of a few young people working night shifts at factories or fast-food chains, Highland Pride Alliance members attended drag nights at Wal-Mart as regularly as they attended the group's more formal organizational meetings.

When asked to describe why they chose Wal-Mart, most of the young people couldn't remember, nor did they understand my surprise. To them, the Wal-Mart Supercenter seemed an obvious place to hang out. As Shaun put it, "Why wouldn't we go there?! It's the best place to find stuff to do drag. They've got all the wigs and makeup and tight clothes and stuff." Then he added, "Besides, no matter how much we bug people doing what we're doing, we're still customers too. And we have friends who work there who won't let nothing happen to us if they see any trouble start." Contrary to the anonymity Wal-Mart and other so-called big box stores might provide in the suburbs of metropolitan areas, HPA members do not experience this space as anonymous. It is their own backyard after all, and there are few options this close to where they live.

Beyond the makeshift runways and basic drag gear found in Wal-Mart's aisles, the mega-chain's national guidelines that situate its customers as "guests" also facilitate youth doing drag in its stores. As long as these young people are still readable as consumer citizens, the logic of capital cannot bar them from this queer twist on the public square. Plus, Wal-Mart's (then recent) instatement of domestic-partner benefits for employees signaled that Wal-Mart was, as Clay put it, "a tolerant place where they could expect to be accepted." Unlike their public school experiences, which where described by many as a "living hell," Wal-Mart stood out as a safe public space where they would be protected.

Part of Something Bigger

Gay rights organizations dot the rural landscape. One finds chapters of nationally organized nonprofits, like PFLAG and the Gay, Lesbian and Straight Education Network, discussed earlier. One also finds statewide and regionally based groups, such as the Kentucky Fairness Alliance (KFA) and the Highland Pride Alliance. Each organization draws capital investments from donors and then circulates resources in time, training, and visibility to local residents—including youth in this study—interested in connecting to a broader community of organizers.

Rural youth seeking terrain for their queer-identity work can find fertile ground in not-for-profit organizations. These corporate structures provide the integrative yet ephemeral experiences of publicness that characterize the boundary public model I proposed at the beginning of this chapter. As one 17-year-old gay-identifying man put it, "Going to PFLAG or KFA's Lobby Days in [the State Capitol in] Frankfort and meetings and stuff like that makes me feel like I've got a whole big gay extended family out there . . . like I'm part of something bigger even when nothing's really happening in my own town." For many youth this means taking advantage of a ready-made structure that includes things like banners, e-mail addresses, listings on national websites and directories, and an imagined network of like-minded allies and friends.

Locally grown groups with overlapping membership in these offshoots and branches of national or regional organizations are equally important. The Highland Pride Alliance, for example, has existed for nearly a decade.[13] Most members are white, gay or nonidentifying and range in age from late teens to forty-something men. All of them come from four surrounding counties. Some members found out about the group from someone they met while hanging out (or cruising) at the local state park. Others were clued in by the group's reputation or, increasingly, the group's website.

When I met Shaun, he was the driving force behind the group. When he joined the HPA two years earlier, it consisted mostly of local white men interested in quiet social gatherings. Period. They met at each other's homes and did their best to keep out of the public eye. But Shaun was 17 and stinging from harassment in public high school. He wasn't about to "go back to meeting secretly." "What was the point?" he said. In his town of 2,100, everyone knew he was gay. If they didn't know it from the common gossip of the schoolyard, they heard it from a popular Baptist minister who was once a close friend of Shaun's:

> I was the youth minister for some time at my church. I was so filled with the Spirit, you know? I grew up in that church and my family all attended—my Maema [grandmother] was a deacon there. Well, when I started having these feelings for other boys and went to my preacher . . . some response! He wanted to cure me, but when I decided I didn't need curing—or at least didn't think that's what God wanted from me—he told the entire congregation and asked them to pray over me! At first, I was willing to try this . . . prayer can't hurt. But it was clear to me and everyone else that this was who I was, there wasn't anything to change it. So, when I got involved in HPA, I told them I was going to blow the barn door off this town, honey!

Shaun instigated many of HPA's activities, such as meetings at the public library, involvement in rallies supporting a distant, rural high school's efforts to form a Gay-Straight Alliance, and plans to bring the first "Meals on Wheels" service for people with AIDS to the region with support from AIDS Volunteers of Lexington. Shaun saw the building up of the HPA and its relationships to statewide groups as vital to creating opportunities for all local LGBT people.

Queercore at the Methodist Skate Park

Rural queer youth also used local churches as boundary publics. To use the facilities associated with these institutions—from using a church meeting room to attending a church-sponsored event—was more than a matter of signing an individual's or group's name to a form. Gatekeepers and bureaucratic structures govern these types of space, making them publics of a different order from the home offices of nonprofit volunteers or the privatized commercial spaces of businesses like Wal-Mart. In principle, these spaces are open to all on a first-come, first-serve basis. In practice, however, there is a local reckoning for allocating affordable or free gathering space, a limited resource. At the same time, conventions of public access and acceptance opened these sites to queer possibility.

Tension between the limits and prospects of these churches made them particularly useful as boundary publics and therefore ideal sites for queer-youth identity work. Local churches offered a way to work around the economic and infrastructural limits of rural communities. They also afforded ambiguity, leaving room for youth to question sexual and gender identities without risking particular recognition or declarations. A permanent structure (e.g., a nonprofit office building or gay storefront) ostensibly readable as "gay" faced scrutiny and policing by local elites, not to mention overhead costs. So, rural youth blurred the boundaries between the centers of formal public spheres and the margins of their queer social worlds by taking advantage of local church recreation facilities.

The First United Methodist Church of Coal County, Kentucky, saw a way to draw young people to its Outreach Ministry Program. There were no local facilities for youth in this county of 6,000 to go to if they were into skateboarding. The town council and local sheriff were tired of trying to keep kids from destroying the elementary school's benches and cement curbs. So, Eileen, First United's youth minister, proposed to the church elders that they build a skate park connected to the 150-year-old church building to accommodate a half pipe, skate shop, and performance stage for area young people to use under the youth ministry's supervision. There was some resistance. The church had limited funds for youth outreach and this would exceed its budget for the year. There was also some concern that drawing youth to the church grounds may not put them in the pews. Certainly there was nothing in the Methodist tradition that made skating "evil" or "uncivilized." The Primitive Baptist minister had characterized skating as such a few years ago during a prayer breakfast of area preachers when "Godly youth activities" was the discussion topic. Eileen thought that if First United Methodist offered the skate park, they could further distinguish themselves among the county young people as a more hospitable—or downright cool—place to worship Christ. She suggested seeking funding from the town council's youth recreation budget to help with the construction of the skate park. It didn't hurt that Eileen's great aunt was in charge of the county park and recreation maintenance. The town council approved money for the electrical hookup and water service to the skate park and arranged volunteers to donate building materials and labor.

Within a year, Eileen had the FireXcape, a full-service skatepro shop and skating facility, open six hours a day, six days a week, and closed only on Sunday. The FireXcape included a performance stage where popular local "straight edge" punk bands and Christian alternative rock music groups played. Although a smaller county, Coal's neighboring county to the northwest had a thriving underground punk music audience thanks to funding for the arts brought in during the Johnson administration's War on Poverty. Eileen's husband, Jake, an avid skater, volunteered to take charge of operations and did additional fundraising to create a small salary for himself. The church's existing insurance covered the skate park. This saved First United Methodist a substantial amount of the startup costs that otherwise would have come with the venture.

Among the bands to play the FireXcape was a group called Jarvis Avenue, a self-described queercore punk band based in Pulaski County, Kentucky. The band's members all attend Pulaski County High School. The bassist, Tommy, is a slight wisp at 14. He is shy but likes to wear glitter on his face and in his hair. He said his family was closely monitoring his activities, fearful that he might turn or already be gay, but they encouraged his participation in the band, particularly when they played the FireXcape, as they thought it would keep Tommy "out of trouble." The band's lead singer, Amanda, wore a black leather fedora, black vest and pants, and strategically torn fishnet mesh the length of each arm. The 16-year-old's bobbed hair, tucked underneath her hat, was the deep black of a recent home dye-job. Tasha, Amanda's 14-year-old cousin, played drums and second guitar to replace Amanda's now ex-girlfriend. On the June evening I saw them perform, their sets were strained and intense. A punk edge was there, but an "I want to go pop/be popular" thread hummed through their songs.

The audience was mostly teenagers, fellow PCHS students, a few neighbors of the band members, and other members of local punk bands showing their support. The young people present signaled the kind of queer crowd you might expect to see at any city gig of a politically progressive, alternative music group that billed itself as a cross between the feminist queercore riot grrlband Bikini Kill and the sexually fluid Ani DiFranco. The only older couple in the crowd turned out to be Tasha's mother and her mom's new boyfriend, both in their late thirties.

Once the music started, everyone moved toward the FireXcape stage. Head-bopping made it clear people enjoyed the show. During several of the numbers, audience members belted out lyrics along with Tommy, Amanda, and Tasha. The end of each song brought a frenzy of hollering and applause. Focused on their music, the Jarvis Avenue members appeared oblivious to the audience's affection. When I asked them about their following and whether they worried the First United Methodist Church might frown on the explicitly gay-friendly variety of music and crowd they represented, shy Tommy uncharacteristically spoke up first:

> Well, aside from my family, I think everyone knows about me [being gay]. I don't really have to say it. So, if I wear glitter and sing about wanting to date, and love, stuff everyone sings about, who's going to really to feel like I'm cramming anything down their throats?! I mean, I'm just playing my bass . . . and I don't think the church really gets our lyrics, so I'm not too worried about that.

Amanda followed Tommy's comments with some clarification:

> We don't make a point of saying, "Hey, we're a queer band." Unless you're looking at our website, I don't know that you'd know that that's what we're about. But the church minister booking the shows does know we draw the punk kids they really want coming to church rather than out sniffing glue or splitting oxy or something. So, I don't know if they care that we're queer. They're just looking to use us to draw kids and we just want a place to play.

Tasha, who identifies as straight "but not narrow" adds, "I think punk music is one of those things that can make it easier for kids to just be together and not think about who they can't or don't date . . . it's really about coming for the music regardless of what you think about gay people." I did not ask the First United Methodist youth minister whether she knew about Jarvis Avenue's music and queer-youth following because I did not want to inadvertently disrupt the boundary public this band had created for itself and its fans. However, the band members' pragmatic approach to using the FireXcape speaks to how effectively rural youth can put even church skate parks to queer use.

The First United Methodist FireXcape skate park illustrates the boundary publics available to queer and questioning rural youth. The space is not definably or definitely queer, but its open-endedness allows for queer definitions and understandings to be written into the space.

New Media

Visible, engaged counterpublics that sustain the queer-identity work that claims difference or dissents from the structures of rural familiarity are in short supply out in the country. In addition to occupying Wal-Marts, nonprofit organizations, and church skate parks, they also use new media to carve out boundary publics in their work to articulate sexualities and genders that disrupt mainstream expectations. These senses of place ricochet among computer desktops, cell phones, and peers as news posted to one locale immediately circulates to others. Resisting the move to solidify new media as a particular location, I examine new media as sets of social relations—metaphorical landscapes of social interaction—rather than any given, particular place. These landscapes offer a momentary glimpse of pivotal relations that make up our understandings of ourselves, our surroundings, and of others. But new media do not offer stable sites with literal clear entrances and exits to social worlds. I consider two examples of such media landscapes and how rural youth experienced them: the Highland Pride Alliance website, discussed earlier in this chapter, and the personal web-based journal of AJ, a young female-to-male transsexual living in rural South Central Kentucky. In both cases, the producers and users of these new media transform them into boundary publics that address the economic shortcomings of their local environments and stretch their sense of connection to others imagined to be like them. Through the HPA web presence and what AJ called his web journal, but what is now more commonly referred to as a web log or blog, queerness is both extended outward and brought back home.

The Highland Pride Alliance group greets you as you click on its website and invites you to enter with the following clarification: "The Contents of this page are of a Homosexual Nature (not sexually explicit) so if you find Gays, Bisexuals, Lesbians and Transgender people gross and against your beliefs or if your [sic] not interested in helping or supporting the Gay, Bisexual, Lesbian, and Transgender Community Please Click Exit, and Have a Nice Day!" If you click on Enter, another entry page pops up. This one states HPA's mission: "Highland Pride Alliance is a Social Group for Gays and Lesbians and Their Friends. We Strive to Make a Strong, Clean, Safe, and PROUD! Gay Lesbian Bisexual and Transgendered Community.... HPA has several fun and exciting events and we Invite Anyone and Everyone to come, Gay Str8, Bi, Lesbian! Come have some fun and meet new people!" Below is a set of links to a "Questions or comments" form, the group's "Links" page, or an invitation to "Join the e-mail list." Further down are advertisements for the commercial service providing the free web space, along with links created by the HPA to the search engine portal Gayscape.com. Below that is a link to Lethimstay.com, a website supporting the adoption of three African-American children by two gay fathers in Florida—a hotly contested story in the news at the time.

Follow the Links page and the browser arrives at yet another text list of "Area Organizations and Links," "Kentucky Organizations and Web sites," and a "Submit your site!" link that takes you to another form-generated page. At the very top of the page, a bright-red hyperlink reads, "HPA Warning Page." This takes the reader back to a page that restates the warning on the initial splash page.

The HPA website features a prominent link to local and statewide sites, but the most dominant link is to national LGBT groups without representation in the area. Buttons, selected by the site's creator because they were groups familiar to him, take the viewer to Dignity USA (a Catholic support group for LGBT people), the Human Rights Campaign (a national LGBT rights organization), and the Green Party's statewide and national political website, reflecting an interest in doing political work and a sense that such political work lays elsewhere.

When I asked HPA members about their local political ambitions, they expressed an interest in expanding support to LGBT youth in schools and raising funds for people waging lawsuits for job discrimination. But there wasn't a clear sense of how to achieve those goals by organizing locally. As one member put it, "We can't go door-to-door asking for money. People don't have an extra five dollars, even if they would spend it on gay causes." Instead, the group poured its energy into connecting locals. Their MSN-based discussion list is a venue for posting photos of social gatherings and plans for future events. In this way, they shape this new media to document the queer-identity work that occupies them locally.

While organizational websites may bring communities of young people together virtually, personal websites are also a means to both produce and document queer-identity work. Although more of AJ's story is presented later in this book, how AJ's personal website serves as an important boundary public is pertinent here. His journaling and detailed, online documentation of his physical transition from a female-born lesbian-identifying teen to a self-identifying asexual transman extends his sexual and gender transformation both into and beyond his rural town. His website features monthly, journal-style updates on his mental and emotional well-being; an "about me" section with a brief introduction to AJ and his feelings about his gender identity and its origins; a "Gallery of T-effects" documenting AJ's use of testosterone hormone therapies from detailed pictures of his top (double mastectomy) surgery; photos of his growing hair organized by body area; MP3 files of his voice recorded at monthly intervals to demonstrate the deepening effects of testosterone; essays about asexuality as a sexual identity; a complete listing of his doctors and surgery prices; a "Links" page with hyperlinks to friends' websites and various transgender resource sites; and a third-party commercial form-generated guestbook feature with entries from the last two years of the website's existence.

AJ's mother wrote the first entry in his viewable guestbook: "Great work on your site especially the educational part and family part. Remember we love you, kid. Mom!" AJ's guestbook is filled with similar remarks from his local friends in the HPA and aunts on his mother's side of the family living in Ohio. But there are also comments from an international network of acquaintances met in trans-friendly, Internet-based chat rooms, through organizational web-based mailing lists such as FTM International, and at transgender support groups closer to home based in the city where he sought out sexual reassignment surgery in the Kentuckiana region.[14]

AJ's voice rarely rises above a whisper during our interview, but his voice booms on the website he created to chronicle his hormone therapy and sexual reassignment surgery. The minute he turned 18 (one month after we met), AJ started physically transforming his body to match his gender identity. "I've known I was different for a long time. I thought I was a lesbian when I was about 13 because I liked girls. But I didn't know how to talk about how much I hated my own female parts." From watching a television documentary, he learned it was possible to change from a female to a male. Now AJ and his mother drive to a city, 230 miles away, to recast his gender identity.

When asked why he feels the need to document his own transition, AJ responded, "The main purpose of my website was to help other transmen like myself, because there are some websites with either not enough information or the information/pictures are not free and I wanted to give people all the free info and pictures that I could." At different times in our conversations, AJ also spoke of the central role his web-journaling played as a personal resource. It allowed him to, as he put it, "think out loud" to himself and mull through his own anxieties about gender reassignment surgery and what it would mean to become the boy he felt he had always been.

As AJ's website illustrates, Internet technologies can be both a private experience and a suspended moment of public engagement. When rural youth browse websites, they may sneak off to locations unimaginable to their offline peers. But when they create and post to their own websites, as AJ does, they create a sense of public through the expression of their experiences. AJ's detailed website offers the visitor access to photos of his leg hair, recordings of his changing voice, and, at one point, photos of his genitals as they grew with testosterone. AJ's self-disclosure comes from a desire to help others like himself who want to know "how it's done" but also his need to create a forum for local recognition that he is doing this work in his hometown. The personal is political for AJ in a way that could not be expressed locally without creating a forum fraught with complexities for his family and his personal safety. The website became a way for AJ to locally embody the transperson he was becoming in the absence of locations in his town for expressing or sharing the intimacy of that process. The site also became a way for him to circulate the knowledge he was accumulating about what it meant to be transsexual.

For rural youth especially, new media technologies can be both a private and public encounter. These youth live in conditions that afford little sense of rights to privacy. Additionally, they are engulfed by public spaces that offer little sense of anonymity or status as a stranger. In fact, rural young people's experiences vis-à-vis these technologies can model not only the dialectic of boundary publics and broader public spheres but also the dismantling of private/public spatial dualities.

The HPA homepage and AJ's website demonstrate that rural LGBTQ young people understand new media, particularly the Internet, as technologies that craft and expand their access to and the boundaries of their local and extralocal public spheres. The publicness sought and established online is a response to strongly controlled access to public space in rural communities rather than the often-presumed need or desire to mask queerness from an imagined inherently more hostile social world. Rural young people's conditions for expressing their queer desires or genders are limited by the oppressive heterosexism that shapes all our lives. Its expression is organized by the solidarity and structures of familiarity of rural spaces and their deep investments in gender and sexual norms.

For youth who choose or have no choice but to stay in their communities, the conservative values of family, faith, basketball, and country living affixed to their rural towns are both backdrop and foil to queer praxis. These popular imaginings of the rural shape what it means to "live out in the state"—both locally and in more urban locales. Queer and questioning rural youth, in turn, accommodate and adjust to these depictions and continue on with their queer-identity work. What they lack are meeting places that provide affirming adults and peers supportive of their sexual and gender exploration and/or reidentification. They scale this barrier by going online. But Wal-Marts, churches, and new media are by no means a panacea. Boundary publics are constitutionally fragile, meant to be struck like a tent when the weather calls for one to move on.

Fragility of Boundary Publics

Boundary publics are fragile not simply because of some blanket conservatism that enshrouds rural landscapes. In fact, conservatism's most prominent power centers and media conglomerates pitch their battles from the affluent suburbs and urban areas of places like Orange County, California, and Colorado Springs.[15] The ease with which boundary publics can be disrupted, pushed out of reach, or blocked has more to do with the infrastructural poverty that typifies rural publics. Schools and churches dominate as the only brick-and-mortar publicly accessible spaces. Local elites invested in an image of community solidarity and familiarity tightly regulate these spaces and squelch publics that compete for recognition and legitimacy. Mainstream print or mass media can provide some alternative boundary publics, threaded through privatized zones and new media, but do not offer refuge from these instabilities. Instead, they deal squarely with the tensions between these publics and dominating rural public spheres. Looking at these delicacies, particularly the interweaving of new media with other publics, can be a productive counter to seeing new media as an escape or denial of local realities. I return now to the examples given above of boundary publics as scenes of queer-identity work and their complex relationships with publics that simultaneously produce and constrain their production. This reassessment complicates the presumption that new media liberate our bodies from locations and highlights what rural queer-youth identity work can teach us about the politics and conditions of sexual- and gender-identity formation and their indissoluble entanglement of the "public" and the "private." Importantly, some genders, classes, and ethnicities are more successful at navigating boundary publics than others.

Bashing at the Wal-Mart

What follows is an account of drag gone awry in Springhaven. HPA members noted that turning the aisles of a regional Wal-Mart Supercenter into a boundary public for drag performance was fun and, to them, safe. They felt their status as "guests" could shield them from any direct harassment. They also presumed that friends who worked at Wal-Mart would intervene and protect them by asserting their positions as the default authority of this milieu. But there was also a sense of belonging that permeated their temporary occupations of these privatized zones. "This is my hometown," Clay commented. "I know a lot of the folks coming in and out of the store already.... I know who to steer clear of." But, as the incident below suggests, knowing whom to avoid does not always guarantee safety when boundary publics interlock with the broader social worlds of rural queer youth.

"Maybe they thought my lipstick was too loud," Shaun giggled. "I mean really, why should they care? I wasn't hurting anyone." A month earlier, a dozen or more HPA members and their friends—ranging from 16-year-old Chris to Phillip, who had just celebrated his twenty-third birthday—sashayed through the Wal-Mart like they had on so many nights before. Typically, HPA drag nights elicited no more than occasional stares, but this time things were different.

After trying on a tight girl's T-shirt glittered with the words "Star Gazer" across the chest, Shaun walked out of the men's fitting room to find himself face-to-face with a boy from his old high school. Sneering, the boy growled, "What are you doing in the wrong dressing room, faggot?" Shaun pushed past the boy, as he had so many times before in the school hallways, rolling his eyes and clicking his tongue, "Tisst! Whaaat . . . evverr!" while nervously scanning the aisle for his friend, Clay, whom he found in the makeup section "trying on 'Shades of Passion' for the umpteenth time." Shaun and Clay gathered up as many HPA folks as they could find and headed for the checkout counter. They assumed one of their friends was working her usual shift but were informed by the young man staffing her register that she had unexpectedly taken the night off.

Shaun and Clay's voices filled with frustration and exhaustion as they recalled what happened next. "He was just a big ol' redneck with nothing better to do than give us a hard time, that's all," Clay said. Shaun added, "It wasn't anything that wouldn't or didn't happen at school . . . difference was, I thought my friend was working that night . . . she would've put him in his place." Instead, the 17-year-old boy followed the HPA youth out to the parking lot and yelled every epithet he could conjure. An older man exiting the store told the harasser to settle down, but the young man paid no attention. No one from the store intervened. Shaun yelled, "We're not hurting no one!" and then saw two more of his old high school nemeses approaching. Rather than continue the exchange, Shaun and his friends sauntered to their cars and piled in to them for the drive home.

The next day, Shaun took down the photos of HPA's Wal-Mart drag extravaganzas, as well as pictures of equally fabulous outings to the town square, from the group's website. When I asked him why he no longer wanted the photos of his friends in their tight minis and platinum wigs on the HPA homepage, he paused and said, "I just don't know if it's safe to have those up there. Someone we don't know could see them.... I guess I don't want anyone getting bashed because some narrow-minded homophobe from out of town saw a picture of us up there and thought we had taken things too far."

Some could read the HPA members' initial feelings of entitlement to their surroundings as an implicit assertion of their racial privilege as white young men. They anticipate moving through their surroundings without the scrutinizing that might, say, be cast on the one Latino youth who was new to the HPA. Members of the HPA see their harassment as a response to the ways they trouble expectations and norms of their male privilege. They categorically liken it to the chiding young women receive for walking through the stores: "I know I've seen girls given a hard way because they don't dress all proper and they might be having fun, being loud. If someone's mad at me, it's because I'm being too girly—that's what being gay means to them anyways . . . that I'm being a girl." The notion of homosexuality as gender inversion persists in these communities much as it does in popular culture despite generations of gay and lesbian organizing to distance itself from the intersectionality of sexuality and gender.[16]

Publicly disrupting normative gender expectations arguably remains as, if not more, contentious than homoerotic desires.

HPA youth threaten an unspoken agreement to "live and let live" when they visibly assert themselves as readable gay subjects. But they seem to break tentative, unspoken rules of occupying the boundaries of public spaces when they visibly stray too far afield from their status as familiar gay locals and become ambiguous queer objects that undo expectations of what it means to be a young man in the community. Their tentative feelings of safety are rattled more by how they challenge gender norms than by the implicitness of their sexual identities.

The mixed-class backgrounds of these youth, which range from white collar to working poor, also complicate access to a presumed privilege. The youth felt dragging it up at the Wal-Mart was more of a right than a risk. But several youth were aware that their status as "gay" would be compromised if they actually admitted to shopping for clothes at Wal-Mart, even though it's what they could afford. As Dale, a 21-year-old from Eastern Kentucky, put it, shopping at Wal-Mart is "just not gay enough." He is a student at a small Christian college. He is on financial aid and works part-time to help support his mother and younger sister. He can only afford to buy clothes at Wal-Mart. "Sometimes it's such a burden to be gay nowadays," he lamented:

> … because you're expected to know everything. They [his straight-iden-tifying college friends] come to you. Well, you're gay, what do you think about this outfit? I'm, like, "I'm not that kind of gay! I may sound like I'm that kind of gay." I'm, like, "Look at me! I'm wearing Wal-Mart clothes! My entire outfit comes from Wal-Mart! Everything! I did not spend 40 bucks on this entire thing, and you're asking me about fashion!" They're, like, "But you're gay!" I'm, like, "So?! I'm a badly dressed gay man. I admit it. I embrace it. Leave me alone. Let me do my clearance aisles at Wal-Mart."

Dale's exasperation at navigating the "gay standard" of high fashion on a Wal-Mart budget shows the encroachment of a very different main-stream into his boundary public. Not being able to afford the consump-tive markers of gay identity left Dale and his working-class peers shaken in their sense of self-identity. Alongside vicious verbal attacks lobbed in store parking lots or in school classrooms, LGBT visibility's commodifi-cation and its demanding consumer pressures posed considerable chal-lenges to the queer-identity work of working poor kids like Dale.

Shutting Down The Amp Space:
The Productive Destruction of Boundary Publics

One of the Jarvis Avenue shows I attended took place at the Pirate House, a makeshift performance venue in the basement of James's house. How James's basement became a music scene is a contentious issue in Pulaski County. James was once part-owner of The Amp Space, the town's only alternative music venue. The music was loud, and most of the club's audience was made up of students from the county's high school. The problem was that on weekend nights youth filtered out of The Amp Space and loitered in the dilapidated town square until well past midnight. A downtown renovations committee, commissioned by the town council, approached James and his co-owner about temporarily closing The Amp Space. They said the building would be inspected and restored as part of a downtown revitalization project. But when the town council took control of the building, it soon became clear it had other plans. Within five short months of The Amp Space's closure, the circa 1923 brick building was demolished.

What troubled James more than the ease and speed with which the town council destroyed the venue was the First United Methodist Church's involvement in the scheme. James comments:

> I'm Christian. I was even part of the group supporting the building of the church's skate park. But they didn't like the fact that we could compete, that kids would want to come to a place not connected to the church to hear good, local music. They have church members on their town council and I know they must have asked them if they thought they could handle the kids coming to them if The Amp Space was shut down . . . it wouldn't have hurt them for us to stay open. I don't know why they'd want to lose a place for kids to hang out when there are so few places out here.

Although the First United Methodist Church's role in closing The Amp Space cannot be confirmed, James and others had their suspicions. After all, the success of the church's skate park—as an underground, queer punk music venue—hinged on the absence of competing venues. Then there's the fact that the popular youth hangout was summarily shut down just in time for the church's FireXcape skate park to open. Undoubtedly, the absence of alternative music venues bolstered the church's dominance as a de facto public sphere.

That's how James, a member of a local punk band and an alumnus of the well-respected Berea College arts program, came to host small shows in his mother's unfinished basement. He christened the space the Pirate House to recognize its outlaw sensibility. James meticulously sets up and records all the shows he produces. The space can only hold thirty people. Usually around twenty-five people crowd the space, oblivious to the exposed insulation between the wooden beams and the washer/dryer crammed in the corner. James advertises with small handbills, notices on his website, and through the websites of the bands booked to perform. The Pirate House can't provide as large a space for young music enthusiasts as the old Amp Space or First United Methodist's FireXcape, but it does offer itself as a boundary public with its own possibilities for queer-identity work. The Pirate House is different in valence from what can be extended through the auspices of the church skate park. While the skate park may supply a cover to kids in need of an alibi for time spent in a queercore music scene, the Pirate House (like its predecessor The Amp Space) imparts an unabashedly queer visibility just as compelling and provocative for rural queer-youth identity work.

New Media Landscapes Revisited: HPA's Hate Mail and the Fragility of New Media as Boundary Publics

In the examples above, boundary publics and the fragility accompanying them structure young people's sense of publicness. It is tempting to assume that the Internet and other digital media offer something entirely new to rural queer and questioning youth. But the experiences of rural youth indicate a different direction for such analyses. For these young people, new media were imagined as both a supplement to local queer-identity work and an integrated part of this local occupation. Youth didn't use new media as hideouts from the real world. Indeed, nothing illustrates their integration into their immediate surroundings more substantially than new media boundary publics' own fragility—these digital boundary publics entangle social worlds as deeply as any other.

As discussed earlier, Shaun quickly took down photos chronicling HPA's drag excursions after what members referred to as "the bashing at Wal-Mart." He was sad and reluctant to remove the pictures at first. Shaun was proud that he had not only taken the snapshots but also learned how to crop the images and post them to the HPA website. But after the HPA received hate e-mail through the website's interactive guestbook a few days after the heated exchange in the Wal-Mart parking lot, he thought it needed to be done.

As the person responsible for sifting through e-mail coming in from the website, Shaun bore the brunt of these comments. One was the ALL CAPS standard, "I HATE FAGGOTS. KISS MY STRAIGHT ASS." The other told the HPA that they "were welcome to have their sexuality but it was disrespectful to hang all over each other and put pictures up on the website of this" (referring to photos on the HPA website of the group dragging it up at the Springhaven Wal-Mart and around the town square a different weekend). The e-mail went on to say "they should have some respect for the county."

Although there was no need for more than one person to monitor the HPA account, Shaun wished someone else would have read the e-mails first. "It just made me so mad and sad all over again! . . . I know these people are probably the same ones we ran into—and that means it's my fault that we're getting these hate mails." Both e-mail messages referenced Rust Falls—Shaun's hometown—building his suspicion that they were likely connected to the young men from high school he confronted that night. The irony is perhaps that the author/s of these e-mails saw the HPA website as reflective of their community and a kind of public that needs monitoring. The e-mails also suggest there is room for the HPA's sexuality, indicating the quiet, if begrudging, acceptance Shaun and his friends felt in their communities. But when this boundary public of queerness seems to hostilely expand and take over straight space, its fragility is revealed.

The HPA website as a boundary public is a conspicuous site of revelation in this case. It can extend and repeat the displays of queer-youth identity work beyond the moments they happen at the Wal-Mart or any other boundary public. But the website can also become the target and focus of a neighborhood watch that shifts inward for Shaun. Removing the photos makes him complicit in keeping local queer youth's boundary publics from expanding too far into and thereby threatening an imagined public sphere.

Conclusion

Media coverage of the 1993 New Year's Eve murder of Brandon Teena, a young female-to-male transperson, in rural Nebraska and the even greater swell of reporting and public outrage that followed the 1998 killing of a young gay man named Matthew Shepard in Wyoming emphasized the brutality of their deaths against a backdrop of the rural communities in which they were killed.[17] As Judith Halberstam observes, "The varied responses to the tragic murders of these two young white, rural queers have much to tell us about selective memorialization and political activism, space and sexual identity, and the mobilization of trauma" (Halberstam 2005, 17). There is much to unpack regarding the different treatments and degrees of culpability placed on these young people's bodies, most notably the relative political silence in 1993 around Brandon Teena's rape and murder compared to national vigils and outcries for gay-inclusive hate crime reforms that immediately followed Shepard's brutal murder. However, in both cases, news and film narratives placed Brandon and Matthew as young queers in the wrong place at the wrong time. Small-town, working-poor America was put on trial as horrific scenes of intolerance.[18]

Samuel Delany has argued that small towns are indeed more hostile, their contempt for difference the driving force behind New York City's moral cleansing and Disney makeover of Times Square.[19] While Delany's arguments regarding the sanitation of Times Square for tourists invested in small-town family values is compelling, it displaces this fear of difference on rurality. Rather than keeping a sharp eye on how fear works in and through urban residents, business investors, and those with the capital to gentrify urban spaces, Delany's ire falls on small-town tourists being sold a squeaky-clean urban theme park. Examining urban fears of difference would be a more productive way of teasing out how residents of rural and urban areas deal with the fear of "otherness" differently instead of perpetuating the myth that cities are indifferent to or unquestionably celebratory of difference. For white middle-class urbanites, negotiating the dense presence of visible difference may simply be a matter of grabbing a taxi instead of riding a bus line through an "edgy" part of town.

Ethnographic studies of queerness in rural communities suggest that cities and rural areas are differently (incomparably perhaps) intolerant toward queer difference. Shaun and other HPA members are constant reminders to their fellow rural residents that structures of familiarity are vulnerable as much from locals as from strangers. Rural communities manage the perceived threats of difference in myriad ways. They may attempt to excise queer difference, as in the case of threats of violence to HPA members outside Wal-Mart, the efforts to close down venues for local queercore, or the bombardment of the HPA website with hate e-mail. Alternatively, community members might make appeals to the local status of their queerly different neighbors in an effort to maintain the fragile structures that organize the mythos of familiarity in rural life.

Lest I seem to offer a rosy picture of the oppression of queer difference in rural areas, let me reiterate: the examples of harassment explored above reflect the realities of violence in rural communities. But this violence is notably most often experienced as intimate, exacted by those these youth presume they know rather than the random acts of property destruction or "stranger danger" that pervades the psyches of most queer urban dwellers bashed outside populous city nightclubs.[20] The one critical advantage Shaun saw to the distinct quality of violence that permeates his community was that, as he put it, "I know who I need to avoid. I've been working to steer clear of those people all my life." Years later, Shaun underscored this point in a conversation with me about media representations of gay people living in rural places and, specifically, the movie *Brokeback Mountain*.

Shaun felt a certain dissonance watching Hollywood depictions of foreboding rural communities and their hapless queer inhabitants. He found Ang Lee's Academy Award–winning 2005 film about rural Wyoming cowboy lovers (Jack and Ennis) in particular "just ridiculous." When I asked him why, he seemed exasperated that he had to explain what seemed so obvious to him. "It just didn't make any sense! People in small towns don't go around killing people who have lived there all their lives [referring to the plotline that connects Ennis' fear of living with Jack to childhood memories of the brutal murder of male lovers in his hometown and, later, Jack's murder by a faceless mob]." Shaun then added, "Jack and Ennis could have lived together quietly . . . anyone who lives in a small town knows about couples or relatives like that. You know how to avoid trouble if you've lived in a place long enough." Ultimately, it was *Brokeback Mountain*'s representation of isolation and unpredictable mob violence lurking around the bend that seemed most at odds with Shaun's own sense of conditional safety traveling around the boundaries of his community. It wasn't that violence couldn't happen. Indeed, Shaun had experienced persistent verbal and sometimes physical harassment through much of his high school years at the hands of longtime, childhood friends. But for Shaun, it seemed unfathomable that such extreme violence would be exacted by a mob of people you considered neighbors. Violence inflicted by loved ones was a much more familiar scenario but, through its familiarity, seemed easier to predict and circumvent. Violence wrought by strangers in rural communities would not go unnoticed or unchecked and therefore seemed more out of place.

In the end, Shaun decided to remove HPA's photos of drag at the Wal-Mart not because he feared retribution from local "troublemakers." In fact, much like the folk belief that the most vehement homophobes are queers in disguise, Shaun assumed anyone he knew "making hay was probably gay." His greater concern was that strangers might happen to find the photos and zero in on the HPA as an easy target.

The fragility of boundary publics indexes how ensnared rural youth's queer-identity work is with more formal public spheres. New media are an effective lens through which to view these entanglements. Studying boundary publics created by rural youth more broadly illustrates that divisions between "public" and "private" need to be reimagined not as particular or literal spaces but as varying conditions for the possibility of political or sociocultural work. Public spheres conceptually come up short because they cannot account for the presence of youth or the economic realities of rural public spaces. It is necessary to account for public spheres precisely because of the exclusions they manufacture. In turn, those exclusions help construct the social worlds of queer youth. These worlds nest and intersect, but they also layer and enmesh multiple publics in indissoluble ways. Rural queer youth recycle the spaces around them, then occupy them for as long as they can. It is temp work at best.

New media, conceptualized as digital boundary publics, are a productive disruption to the divisions historically made between "private and public." The study of how rural youth put new media technologies to use illustrates that what counts as public and private is evolving and shifting. In looking at this disruption, we also see the politicization of what is relegated to the realm of the public sphere and what is considered the domain of private matters. When sexualities and gender identities are framed as matters of privacy, we are prone to overlook the realities of how people use public spaces for the expressions of their private selves. Publics are vital to our experiences of the private. Rural places send up the realities of this intermixture because there is so little public infrastructure to work with, so little raw material with which to parse out the private from the public.

But what kind of real estate is the interstitial world of websites? Can information also serve as a location? Locations are experienced as places through the discourses that animate their meanings. Places have certainty to them not because of their outright existence but through the conversations that happen in, around, and because of them. Because places, particularly public places, carry this kind of informational currency, discussions of the public sphere cannot be separated from debates about the private/ public divide. New media underscore that privacy is not found in a place. My aim in this chapter was to unravel the publicness of queer-identity work and engage the dialectics of privacy stirred up by young people's use of new media.

New media signal rather than create the fluidity between public and private. They showcase the intermingling of a sense of publicness with privatized space that increasingly defines this late-modern, deregulated, liberalized world in which we all live. Rural nonprofits designed to provide public space and for-profits that provide de facto public space exemplify this fusion. Rural youth put new media technologies and other boundary publics to work to provide social spaces for those "quiet believers" who feel queerness has a right to flourish locally but lack the comfort or ability to collectively voice their objections to its suppression in an undernourished public sphere (Stein 2001, 37). As someone Stein met during her analysis of a small Oregon town's response to statewide anti-gay legislation pointed out, "Anytime you voice your opinion, you become an activist" (Stein 2001, 192–93). As Stein keenly observes, "Taking a stand on a divisive issue can therefore be a scary prospect, threatening the pervasive belief in small-town solidarity" (Stein 2001, 193).

How do new media make identity work different? What sort of resource is it? Despite its name, it is not the newness of the media that matters. New media's role as a tool and site for identity work must be understood as a response to the dwindling or compromised resources for community organizing less available to all of us but particularly noticeable in the impoverishment that defines rural areas. New media don't create new ways of being; rather new media allow rural queer youth to respond to the hyper-commodification of LGBT identities and politics of visibility that showcase them. They search online to determine what's "expected" of queer boys and girls. They look to fit identifiable codes. They aspire to be readable to those "in the know." But their only option is to recraft these codes using what is at hand. So, in the end, they display their own queer sensibilities.

Youth have very different access to publics and therefore relationships to privacy. Queer youth do make space for themselves. Doing so is a necessary part of their identity work as they attempt to meet the expectations of the politics of visibility that demand public recognition. This work can and does happen in surprising places in rural communities. The above examples illustrate how rural youth who identify as lesbian, gay, bisexual, and transgender or question sexual and gender norms craft a tentative yet often vibrant sense of visibility. They occupy boundary publics that challenge and incorporate more mainstream aspects of the public sphere to construct a sense of shared, visible space or publicity. Their move to create these boundary publics is a complicated response to an overall lack of public spaces in rural communities that cannot be flattened into a more personal, psychological need or desire to "be closeted" or to some imagined sense that rural communities are inherently more hostile to queer identities. Yes, they accomplish this through the use of websites and other new media technologies, but they also commandeer publics available to them. Websites, Wal-Mart, punk music, listservs, public library meeting rooms, and church skate parks are the resources available to them. They make do. They get by.

Considering how rural queer youth get by allows activists and scholars alike to critically reexamine the significance and meaning of queer public space in infrastructurally impoverished communities and the conditions in nonurban environments for community-building that unsettles the status quo. These alternative community-building models challenge divisions or dualities between "public" and "private" evoked by references to "offline" as opposed to "online" experience. They also suggest the limits of assuming new media bridge a resource gap or provide a route of escape for rural queer-youth work. Seeing websites not as particular places or unlimited space in any tangible way but as metaphors for expanding a sense of public presence, as seen in the cases of the HPA's and AJ's websites, further grounds a more complicated case of the interlocking of privacy and being out in public.

PART II

Queering Realness

5

Online Profiles
Remediating the Coming-Out Story

I first started noticing that I was attracted to other girls when I
was about 12 or 13. Before then, I can't even say that I knew gay
people existed. But even when I was young I watched girls on TV
and was amazed by them. I was over at my friend's house one
night joking that I only watched "Baywatch" (my favorite show
at the time) for the girls. After I said this, I realized it was true.
It wasn't until about a year later, when I got on the Internet and
found other people like me, that I actually said to myself that I was
bisexual. I've always been attracted to both sexes, but I found my
true identity on the Internet.

—Amy, age 15

Amy, a white teenager living in Central Kentucky, cited the
discovery of lesbian, gay, bisexual, and transgender (LGBT) identities on
the Internet as a defining moment in understanding her identity. Similar
to many of her rural peers, she found that online representations of LGBT
lives seemed more pivotal to this shift in her identity than fictionalized
LGBT narratives, such as *Baywatch*'s campy queer subtexts or *Queer as
Folk* and *Will and Grace*'s out and proud gay and lesbian characters. Fictional representations of LGBT people in popular media have long been
theorized as a potential remedy to LGBT cultural marginalization and
a cause for LGBT people to celebrate (Gross 2001; Gamson 1998; Doty
2000). The numerous *Ellen* parties that occurred when the character Ellen, played by lesbian comedian Ellen DeGeneres, came out were hailed as
milestones, moments of visibility for the show and the LGBT community.
Media visibility seemed a natural step in the progression for full rights

and equal citizenship. Sociologist and feminist scholar Suzanna Walters convincingly argues, however, that LGBT visibility in the media means we are more widely seen but not necessarily better known. While more images of LGBT people certainly stream into Americans' lives through television, films, and the Internet, the increase in visibility has not translated into pro-gay stances at the voting booth or in the halls of Congress. Accordingly, youth, many of whom are fleshing out the boundaries and meanings of their identity, are no more likely to know themselves through these fictional images, particularly given how rarely they depict rural places, than a straight person looking to fictionalized characters to make sense of LGBT people's lives (Walters 2001). That is not to say that images of LGBT characters in popular media didn't inform (and fuel) the queering of Amy's desires. But the narratives of authenticity, of queer realness, that she found online reading coming-out stories from teens both in her state and living worlds away, following news bulletins posted to the National Gay and Lesbian Task Force and PlanetOut websites, and discovering outlets for buying rainbow flags, jewelry, pride rings, and stickers provided the grammar for a bisexual identity she eventually claimed as her own.

Of the youth I spoke with, many shared the belief that their identities expressed inherent desires that they were born with but that remained buried under the baggage of community norms and expectations of "having a family and settling down" in traditional heterosexual fashion. Their narratives of having been "born this way" echoed popular cultural understandings of sexualities and genders as expressions of one's core being (Lancaster 2003). Yet Amy's identity didn't coalesce through isolated introspection and self-discovery. She described the year or so she spent online making sense of her love for *Baywatch* as a busy one "reading everything I could about gay people" and "hanging out in chat rooms talking with other kids about how they first knew they were gay and whether they thought I was gay or what words even made sense." Her processing of self-exploration, making sense of "what words even made sense," is in practice highly social. Amy's sense of what it means to be bisexual is collectively organized through her interactions with what Bruno Latour calls "social actors"—from watching television shows to talking with friends and surfing the Internet (Latour 1996). From this perspective, rural youth sexualities and genders are best understood not as an unfolding state of biological fact confirmed in a moment of visually and textually mediated recognition but as residues of complicated dialogues—recirculations of coming-out narratives, most notably—that increasingly involve digitally mediated renderings of LGBT identities complete with particular ways to dress, look, and speak. Urban and suburban youth might come across commercially or subversively produced LGBT images posted along public transit routes, pinned to community boards at local coffeehouses, or embodied in the presence of Gay-Straight Alliances and other LGBT-advocacy organizations with offices around town. Rural youth, however, are unlikely to run across these images in their rural public spaces. As a result they are more reliant on venturing out of town and exploring media to find the words and practices culturally saturated with queer realness.

A blend of fictional television characters and conversations with friends served as critical materials for Amy's queer-identity work. However, as her insights suggest, she found confirmation and a sense of "authentic" identity online. In this sense authenticity does not reside in Amy. It is a "manufactured" moment when "a place or event . . . conform[s] to an idealized representation of reality . . . a set of expectations regarding how such a thing ought to look, sound, and feel." Amy does not discover or possess her queer realness as much as she, like all of us, pursues a credible and sincere performance of that idealized representation in hopes that it will "come off as natural and effortless."¹ She notes that the absence of locally visible LGBT communities made it harder for her to precisely name—let alone act on—her attraction to both sexes. In the end, Amy's bisexual identity coalesced from watching *Baywatch,* being teased by friends, and reading the Internet-based musings of other young people.

Young people like Amy spoke about representations they found online as both resonances of their own experiences and evidence that others like them existed beyond their small communities. This chapter explores how rural young people weave media-generated source materials into their identity work, particularly as they master the politics of visibility's master narrative event: "coming out." I argue that these online representations, from noncommercial, youth-spun websites to subscription-based personal ads on for-profit media properties like PlanetOut and Gay.com, provide rural young people with materials for crafting what it means to "come out" as LGBT or questioning in rural contexts.

If there are any consistencies to the online sites rural youth such as Amy turned to, it would be that Mogenic, a nonprofit website produced in Australia by and for youth, was one of the more commonly cited destinations beyond Gay.com and PlanetOut.com. Mogenic's collections of

coming-out stories, found on its message boards, were particularly popular. Other sites mentioned were Oasis Magazine Online, the Advocates
for Youth website, the Advocates for Youth LGBT youth project, and
the website for Parents and Friends of Lesbians and Gays. This is by no
means a comprehensive listing of the sites of queer realness rural youth
plumbed. In fact, the list is too disparate to be of much use. Youth were
just as likely to mention cruising the gay and lesbian sections of Yahoo as
any LGBT-specific site. The meaning and use rural young people found
in these sites are not easily discernible from the content of the sites
themselves.

Youth must continually search for these representations, as the Internet is always changing, constantly displacing reliable locations for
the kinds of reflections of realness they seek. But even though at times
difficult to track down, realness found in online narratives as compared
to fictional accounts in film and television indexes the limits of mass
culture's ability to bring visibility to LGBT-identifying people in rural communities. They find comfort and familiarity in the narratives
of realness circulating online because, more so than fictional characters situated in urban scenes where a critical mass of LGBT visibility
is taken for granted, these stories resonate with the complex negotiation of visibility and maintaining family ties that consume rural young
people's everyday lives. These digitally circulated representations of
LGBT identity categories interpellate rural queer youth by laying down
a basic narrative for the articulation of identity. At the same time, the
amount rural youth absorb or rework these categories has everything to
do with each young person's capacity to enact and publicly assert these
categories. This approach to studies of media's effects calls for a deeply
situated understanding of media engagements beyond the reception of
particular media texts.

Media Genres

Engaging these online representations as a genre infuses them with what
I call "queer realness." Here I draw on Jack Halberstam's prescient definition of realness, which he asserts is "not exactly performance, not exactly
an imitation; it is the way that people, minorities, excluded from the domain of the real, appropriate the real and its effects.... [T]he term realness
offsets any implications of authenticity. . . . [R]ealness actually describes
less of an act of will and more of a desire to flaunt the unpredictability of

social gathering" (Halberstam 2005, 51). Rural youth appropriate queerness as a possibility that is disparaged not only in representations of the rural, but also in mass-media depictions of LGBT people.

In referring to these representations of the real as a distinct genre, I am taking to heart media scholar Jason Mittell's call to examine media texts as "sites of discursive practice" (Mittell 2001, 9). Instead of focusing on the aesthetic codes or features of the new media texts that might generically hold together, I apply Mittell's practice of analyzing sets of themes and patterns that surface across media texts, the audience members' experiences of those texts, and industry practices that consistently produce and recycle these themes and patterns (Mittell 2001, 19).[2]

In rural contexts, Internet-based texts, found on commercial websites, other young people's homepages, and regional e-mail-based discussion lists, operate as a genre that queers realness. These texts circulate a hegemonic grammar for the articulation of identity and lend materials to the labor of parsing out and responding to the expectations of LGBT visibility so central to them. Rural LGBT-identifying youth come to see themselves in terms made familiar through the narrative repetitions of self-discovery and coming out found in this genre. How much rural youth absorb and rework these identity categories turns on each young person's material conditions, cultural context, and history. The accounts rural youth gave me of their reckoning with these genres highlight the recalcitrance of social categories like race, class, and kinship norms that trouble what we might uncritically attribute to the powers of the Internet.

Media are often assessed in terms of their benefits or malevolence. Popular discourses frame media as conduits of contagion to be contained or countered through traditional salves to vice and violence, such as the family, the church, or earlier (meaning more wholesome) forms of media consumption. This framing of the debate carried over into literatures of new media studies, particularly Internet studies of identity. Popular understandings of gayness and its social transference are also entangled in the ongoing debates around what the media "does" to kids (Levine 2002; Seiter 1993; Cassell and Jenkins 1998).

Why the lock-tight focus on media's effects? One possible explanation is that framing media as objects with measurable effects gives us the sense that our social anxieties have a detectable source. If we can trace what ails us back to its root, we can tackle the problem head on. For instance, if media representations scare us, then perhaps we can quell our fears by containing the representations. But this notion of media as a free-flowing force can oversimplify how media representations are understood and complicated by the practices of those doing the watching.

Queer Realness

Media engagements are one of many important discursive practices we integrate into our everyday lives. Media analysis cannot confine itself to an effects- or an impact-measuring project if it hopes to contribute to understanding media as part, rather than the center, of sociality. A rich examination of new media takes stock of how central it is, how it comes to be seen as meaningful, and when it seems less relevant. As new media scholar Nancy Baym argues, "Online spaces are constructed and the activities that people do online are intimately interwoven with the construction of the offline world and the activities and structures in which we participate, whether we are using the Internet or not" (Baym 2006, 86). The questions then become: What role do media engagements play in people's lives? When do they turn to media and when is it expendable background noise? When do media make a difference and what are the conditions that make these differences register as important or negligible? If we are to understand the relationship between media and young people's sense of their sexualities and genders, we need an approach that moves away from isolating media as conduits or contagions. Framing new media as conduits or contagions limits our ability to understand complicated individual and collective engagements with media. To address this need for a more relational method to understanding media, I suggest concentrating on studies of media "in situ." I borrow the notion of "in situ" from the archaeological study of material artifacts. The term literally means "in place." Archaeologists use this phrase to describe an artifact at the point of its unearthing or sighting, one that is still embedded in a deposit suggesting its age and cultural context. The concept of "in situ" embodies more than description of the artifact and its location, in this case, beyond the moment of reception. Although similar to media ethnographies of audience reception, my approach radically de-centers media as the focus of study. Instead of examining audiences' reactions to specific programs or websites, I attempt to map the relationship between rural young people's experiences of a cluster of media engagements and a milieu that is constitutive of its meaning. An in situ approach to media takes as the object of study the processes and understandings of new media among people

within the context of their use. This approach requires tracing the circulations and layers of socioeconomic status, race relations, and location in
the lives of the people I met that make their media engagements meaningful to them. A media in situ approach focuses on how media engagements fit into a larger mosaic of collective identity work. This approach
does not assume a singular message or effect is (or can be) conveyed or
transmitted.

A media in situ approach applied to this fieldwork shows rural queer
youth prioritizing particular genres of media engagement. Rural youth
used the Internet, particularly engagements with youth-spun websites
and personal ads on commercial media properties like Gay.com, to confirm the existence of queerness beyond their locales and strategize about
how to bring that queerness home to roost. These genres as "discursive
practices" are clearly experienced as sources of information and, to some
extent, unmediated truth about and for LGBT-identifying people (Friedman 2006; Mittell 2001; Hanks 1987; Bauman 1986). However, genres of
queer realness are not defined by the aesthetic codes they might share
as digital texts.[3] What distinguishes and clusters Internet-based personals, search engine results, coming-out stories, and chat rooms as genres of
queer realness is that they provide moments of storytelling that transform
how rural youth think and talk about their identities. As Richard Bauman
notes, "When one looks to the social practices by which social life is ac-
complished, one finds—with surprising frequency—people telling stories
to each other, as a means of giving cognitive and emotional coherence to
experience, constructing and negotiating social identity" (Bauman 1986,
113). Rural youth are in the thick of these negotiations.

Darrin, a gay-identifying 17-year-old from an agricultural town of
6,100 people, sees websites, like the commercial portal PlanetOut.com, as
"a place to feel at least somewhat at home." He adds, "But then I have to
figure out how to make that home here too, you know? Chat rooms give
me a place to go when I don't feel I can connect to others where I am."
Amanda, a 14-year-old from KenTennessee, describes her experiences online as "pretty much the only place I can Google stuff or say my true feelings and not have everyone know about it." Darrin and Amanda's mention of commercial LGBT portals and search engines suggests that these
genres offer a boundary public—a sense of place and the tools to find
more resources—for their identity work.[4] For example, Sarah, 17, from a
town of 12,000 along the Ohio River separating Indiana and Kentucky,
notes:

When I'm on these sites, I like to read others' stories and experiences. I use websites and search engines, like Google, most because they give the most info. I like personal stories, people's coming-out stories. How their family reacted. Going online and reading things from Betty DeGeneres [mother of lesbian comedian Ellen DeGeneres] on PlanetOut, where she does a little column. Trying to be as much of a sponge as I can when it comes to other people and their situations and how they handled themselves in those situations . . . using their experiences as possibilities for my own.

PlanetOut and its popular business partner, the Internet portal Gay.com, draw millions of visitors monthly.[5] PlanetOut, like other commercial sites that cater to community-specific niche markets, prominently promotes community areas and rotates spotlighted personal profiles along with designated message boards and chat rooms targeting youth, women, men, and a range of sexual and gender identities.[6] LGBT-specific news and entertainment refresh each time one brings up the site's main page. Sarah's perusing and information sifting is familiar to all of us. Sarah prioritized searching for coming-out stories and how-to's that could help her talk to family members about her queer identity. Sarah, like most of the youth I met, didn't want to escape from rural Kentucky. In part, her desire to stay put was because of her close ties with family, but she, like several other youth I interviewed, also had no funds to leave her hometown and no educational training or particularly marketable job skills to make moving anything but a frightening prospect. Instead, she wanted to refashion her local circumstances with the help of what she discovered online. As discussed in earlier chapters, "family" represents a social safety net that is otherwise absent from the public infrastructure of impoverished rural communities. Because I focused on youth who hadn't run away or been kicked out of their homes, what I learned about the conditions for queering identity and publics in rural communities came from young people who either did not want to leave their small towns or could not conjure a means to do so. Most were also minors and therefore had limited resources and legal rights to independence.[7]

Not surprisingly, most of these young people were financially dependent on their parents. More broadly, despite their queer-identity work, their communities embraced them because of their ties to local families. As such, families were primary sources of emotional and material support as well as social recognition and (albeit sometimes begrudged) acceptance. Narratives that conveyed how to handle family anger, disappointment, and potential rejection were particularly important to these young people. Youth, like Sarah, were heavily invested in finding the commensurability between the tangible social worlds of their families and the referential connections to online LGBT communities. Sociologist Tamotsu Shibutani called "audiences that are not obviously on the scene," like the ones Sarah encountered through her web surfing, "reference groups" (Shibutani 1961, 129). He argued that we orient and adjust our behaviors according to the reference group we envision. This process is complicated if one is at once learning about and seeking out markers of these reference groups. Rural youth needed to make their identities fit within the framework of "family."

The emphasis Shibutani puts on references to presumed but not present queer others is poetically illustrated among young people who use new media for what they refer to as "research." Joseph, for one, describes his early efforts to understand his attraction to boys this way: "When I was 11 or 12 years old, I started getting crushes on people, and I started going to search engines [on the Internet] and doing research about it.... I just started doing research, and I found out what everything meant and that I was gay."

Justin, another 15-year-old questioning youth from a small Kentucky town (4,500) on the Kentucky-Ohio border, describes his research this way:

> When I first got the Internet, my main goal was . . . I was about 13, I guess . . . of course, pornography, 'cause I heard boys at school talking about it. When I first started, I would go lookin' for main places and they would have lesbians and gays in separate categories. Finally, I realized they [lesbians and gays] had their own [websites]. I had to search. It really was work. It was really, really hard to get onto these websites 'cause some of them had a block, and you'd have to hunt around for the ones that were free. Sometimes, you'd wait for a picture to download for five minutes! I was risking getting caught, so I wanted to find something I really wanted to see!

The Internet presented both opportunities and challenges to Justin's research agenda. It required him to weigh his desires against the risk of exposure. He balanced the covertness and patience needed to find queer realness—primarily on personal listings on gay- and lesbian-specific web-sites—with his need to view something he could not see in his daily life.

Josh also talks about the Internet as a means to explore his new community:

> I was so uneducated about the gay life. I knew almost nothing. I mean, like, gay terminology. People on the Internet would use something and I'd be, like, "What is that?" I didn't know. I didn't have a computer at home. I mean, I knew about a few things from other friends, but most of them were, like, things, you know, like how to act in a bar. Well, this is a dry county and we don't have any bars. And I don't think there's much in the Western Kentucky area where I'm from for gay people.

Josh doesn't attribute his ignorance of gay life to his rural surroundings. Indeed, Josh is no more "ignorant" than any young person steeped in the heteronormative world that shapes our lives. He recognizes that local places and people can provide some of the references he craves, but he also knows his lack of Internet access limits his ability to connect with them. Josh continues:

> Online you're able to meet a lot more people than you are offline. You may get five people at a Tri-State meeting [regional LGBT advocacy agency] one day and they may know two other people, so there's, like, fifteen there. Online, I can talk to maybe twenty GLBT people in an hour! Since I live in a small town, where I know very few gay people, it gives me a sense that the gay community is small, but when you get on the Internet, you realize the gay community is everywhere and it's huge!

Rural youth use genres of queer realness to symbolize and actualize their connections to a larger network of gays, lesbians, bisexuals, and transpeople. They also use these media engagements with genres of queer realness to bring their performances home, anchor them locally, and transform them into experiences of self/senses of identity that can and do happen to youth "just like them."

Some young people seamlessly integrate genres of queer realness into their construction of identity, but this is not always the case. To incorporate genres of queer realness into an imagined sense of self, youth must traverse a dense terrain of other social realities. They must weigh how doable or desirable such realness is. As Shibutani notes,

"Each person performs for some kind of audience; in the drama of life, as in the theater, conduct is oriented toward certain people whose judgment is deemed important" (Shibutani 1961, 129). Our inevitable alignments with multiple audiences lead us, as Shibutani puts it, to "violate the norms of one reference group no matter what [we] do" (Shibutani 1961, 141). Disrupting (or queering) the norm stands out in rural communities where the audience is oriented toward presumptions of familiarity.

Negotiating Queer Realness and Rural Racism

Brandon and I e-mailed several times about his desire to share his story of growing up as an African American in rural Central Kentucky. Brandon is a self-effacing, yet confident, first-year student at a small college a few hours from his hometown. He contacted me after reading an online announcement about my research project forwarded to him by a friend involved with their campus LGBT student group. We met for the first time in an activities room tucked in the north wing of his campus student union. As Brandon waved effusively to people, everyone—from custodians to students and administrators—returned his greeting with a smile and a buoyant, "Hey there, B." After graduating from a Catholic high school in a town of 5,000, he had become a respected leader on campus and was particularly known for his work as the president of the campus's Black Student Caucus.

Brandon and I talked for nearly an hour about the organizing he did around race issues at his high school. He laughed loudly, but his voice evinced exasperation as he recalled those early leadership experiences: "Any black student at my high school knew that they were representing black with a capital 'B.' . . . We were coming from two or three counties from around the region, but when we got to school, we became an instant community.... I used to joke with my best friend, Lana, that we were the NAACP, BET, and NBA all rolled into one!"

Few people knew of Brandon's same-sex yearnings other than a young man on campus he had dated briefly and a smattering of friends he knew through online chat rooms and instant messaging. He had come out as bisexual to his friends in the Black Student Caucus only two weeks earlier. "I set them up, really. I suggested we play a game of Twenty Questions with the goal of sharing something with each other we'd never told anyone else. I've never been in a relationship with a girl here on campus, and it didn't take my friends long to ask the obvious, 'Are you gay?'" Brandon said he felt more "whole" since what he dubbed "the big reveal":

> It, well, I was just feeling so split. The pressure to tell someone just seemed there all the time. It really became an issue for me at the beginning of this semester when the LGBT [student] group needed some help doing an HIV awareness project and approached the [Black Student] Caucus, but the other members were, like, 'I don't want to work with the gay group!' . . . and I felt like such a fake pretending like I had nothing in common with these people [in the LGBT student group].... I didn't feel like I could ignore the political struggles of a group I basically belonged to—even if no one knew. What kind of civil rights leader would I be?

I asked Brandon how his student activism and political organizing affected his sexual feelings and identity. He gathered his thoughts and said:

> I've thought about this a lot lately. I've known for some time that I was attracted to both males and females . . . since probably sophomore year in high school . . . [long pause] . . . but, I guess . . . well, I felt like I had to choose between being black, I had to be either an African-American student leader or labeled the 'gay guy,' and I saw what happened to kids labeled 'gay.' . . . I don't think I could have handled being rejected by other black kids. Being black was more important to me.

Brandon wondered aloud whether the pressure he felt to appear heterosexual would have been tempered if he'd attended a more racially diverse high school. His high school was in one of the few nonurban areas of Kentucky with a sizable, visible, and well-established African-American middle class. The rural communities surrounding Brandon's are typical of the racial makeup of rural Kentucky more broadly with a 90% to 96% white populace. In a town of less than 3,000, this can mean literally one family of color keeps a town from registering as exclusively white. Similar to neighboring West Virginia, Kentucky has no adjacent townships of all or mostly black communities. Communities of color, predominantly African American but increasingly Latino families, live in relatively segregated neighborhoods in the metropoles of Louisville, Lexington, and Bowling Green. But there are a few towns often associated with military bases and factories with sizable African-American populations. To respect Brandon's request for confidentiality, I do not specify the town or region in which he grew up. However, he does live in one of several communities where race relations have long been addressed by a powerful though small community of African Americans in coalition with white civil rights and labor organizers.[8]

Brandon felt his white and black friends accepted him because of his middle-class upbringing, which as he said, "put them all in the same kinds of clothes, neighborhoods, and high school classes." He felt he quickly rose to assume a leadership position as class president in his high school because of the ease with which he moved between his circle of white and black friends. His high school had a history of welcoming discussions about race and social justice, so Brandon had room to advance projects like extensive Black History Month celebrations and forums on racially motivated hate crimes happening elsewhere in the state and across the border in Indiana. But when it came to opening up about his attraction to boys, he kept his feelings confined to a small circle of friends he talked to exclusively online:

> High school was a continuous battle between self-recognition or self-destruction…. It was a constant thing…. I realized that graduating from college, making achievements, all of that might not matter if people found out I was attracted to guys. So that was the sad part—why try to do good things if it wouldn't "count" 'cause I liked males? I think that was the reaction that most people in my life—family and friends—would have had. I wasn't courageous enough at that point to, like some of the people that I knew, to just go against the grain and come out. I think it was an ostracizing reaction for me to have, but it helped me survive this far.

One way to interpret Brandon's turmoil is that he sees his sexual desires as threatening to his closeness to family and friends and affirmation at school. Brandon does not possess the unequivocal self-acceptance and "sense of integrity and entitlement" that sociologist Steven Seidman defines as the "post-closeted gay sensibility" of today's gay youth identity (Seidman 2002, 75). Brandon's relationship to a bisexual identity is more complicated. Seidman does not suggest all gay people are "beyond the closet" but does claim that in this unprecedented age of gay visibility most gay Americans "live outside the social framework of the closet" (Seidman 2002, 9).

But as anthropologist Martin Manalansan argues in his ethnography of gay Filipino men's negotiation of sexual identity and diasporic life, gay identity in the United States is "founded on a kind of individuation that is separate from familial and kin bonds and obligations" and "predicated on the use of verbal language as the medium in which selfhood can be expressed" that do not have parallels or translate seamlessly in the social organization of Filipino life in the diaspora.[9] Brandon's struggle is as much with these generic expectations of distance between gay identity and family as with heterosexism. Brandon must reconcile the demands of distancing Manalansan describes as fundamental to U.S. gay identity and his need to maintain family ties and recognition as a local African-American leader. Seidman suggests that the identity negotiations Brandon confronts are exceptions to the rule attributable to the challenges individuals face when they must synthesize sexual identities and racial or other core identities (Seidman 2002, 43). But this is hardly a small number of individuals raising the question of why are those who privilege gay visibility valorized as "beyond the closet" and youth of color, rural young people, and other individuals with core identities vying for recognition seen as in denial? Seidman's liberationist approach configures the closet as the residue of a past "social system of heterosexual domination" that can be conquered through choosing recognition and coming out (Seidman 2002, 217–18 n. 10). For rural youth, particularly rural youth of color like Brandon, the politics of LGBT visibility do not provide greater access to unequivocal pleasures of acceptance and identification and put at risk the necessities of familiarity.

Brandon expressed ambivalence about coming out to his friends and family but did find solace and a way to negotiate the expectations of visibility through what he called his "gay outlet":

> The summer before my junior year, I got work as a station assistant at our local public radio station. I spent evenings stocking and entering things into a database in the basement of the station. The computer I worked on had Internet access, no filters like the computers at school, which I wouldn't have touched with a 10-foot pole! So one night, I don't even know what I typed in, I just found chat rooms with guys looking to hook up with other guys. But I also found websites about political stuff. . . . There was a whole world of people talking about being bisexual . . . well, not as many people talking about that, but at least I could see places that were for people like me.... This was my gay outlet. . . . I could read personals, stories about people my age telling their parents about their feelings. . . . I could even find rooms for chatting with people living near my hometown!

For Brandon, reading online personals and coming-out stories was a way to experience what coming out to his parents might feel like at a time when his ability to talk about his bisexuality seemed incompatible with his identity as a young, progressive African-American student leader in rural Kentucky. Ironically, his online explorations reinforced the racial reality of his daily life:

> You know, no matter how many times I went into the Kentucky chat rooms on Gay.com or looked at personals on places like PlanetOut, I never once saw another black kid my age living in my area. . . . I didn't find anything for black kids anywhere! Maybe that says more about my computer skills? [laughs]. I don't know if that means I'm the only one—I doubt it. . . . All of the personals I read either said they were white guys looking for white guys or race didn't matter . . . but it matters a lot to me!

Youth, like Brandon, use new media to temporarily patch the incongruence or alienation between their sexual desires and other social worlds. They must reckon this mending, however, with the resources locally available to continue their identity work. Brandon's "gay outlets" attended to parts of his experiences of identity. These engagements with genres of queer realness also reminded him that while "gay outlets" could offer the promise of connection with others "like him," these others would necessarily reproduce the segregation and racism of his surroundings.

The Case of John W.: Negotiating Gay Identity and Queer Desire

John W. generously made room for us to sit down by clearing away stacks of sheet music and leftover coffee cups from his weathered, plaid couch. He offered a quick apology for the apartment's disarray. "Sorry, the dudes I live with are kind of pigs." We met shortly after he answered my call for participants that circulated through his college diversity coalition's e-mail list. John W.'s tattoos and facial piercings combined with the safety pins holding his jeans together fit the moniker of "progressive punk rocker" he proudly claimed. He had recently declared himself "gay," but he wasn't sure if that identity resonated as deeply with him.

A 19-year-old white middle-class college student, John W. grew up in a factory town of 10,000 and prided himself on being one of the "edgy kids." He continues to commute on weekends from the college he attends to his hometown. Of his high school, he says, "There really weren't too many different kinds of kids. There were the jocks, which I tried to be. There were the smart kids and a few African-American kids." John W. grew up in a strict Catholic household where sexual desires were not discussed. He recalls memories from as early as five years old when he realized that tying himself to his backyard swing set and hanging from its bars sexually excited him. "I really didn't know what bondage was at that point. Sometimes I even say that maybe my sexual attraction is more toward bondage than male or female." He found friends early on with whom he could share and act out some of these desires: "I don't know if the other cliques got into a little bit more of the alternative lifestyle of having sex or doing sexual things than my group of friends. I would probably think that my group of people was more apt to doing things a little bit different because we were different in the first place." In describing his forays into sexual play, John W. continued:

> I had this friend; I think he's straight. But he would come over, and we would get drunk. We just started tying each other up. I was between 15 and 16. One time we were at his house and we were looking at a Playboy and then there was like a couple pictures in the back of some guys lifting weights, and he was, like, "Do you like that?" "Yeah." He asked me if he could do me up the butt, so I was, like, "Okay, sure." As soon as he came and pulled out, he was, like, "What have I done? I can't do this again." I haven't talked to him in a while. We didn't leave on bad terms. That's just when I started wondering if maybe I was gay.

John W. singles out his move to a mid-sized college town and subsequent access to the Internet as the means through which he acquired what he described as the language for his innate desires:

> In high school, I didn't really have too much access to the Internet because it was newer at the time and slower and, of course, all the school computers had software trackers and filters on them. We didn't have a computer at home either. When I came to college, my sophomore year I got a computer, so I had instant access to the Internet. Before I had a computer, I didn't have any sense of what I'd find online. I just typed in so many things on the computer and just learned about what to type in, what to find. I think with Gay.com I probably just typed in www.gay.com, like randomly, and found that this was the access to all the perverts like me. That's when I started learning about bondage and the terms, what

BDSM was and S&M, and I just, I can't remember how I started looking for groups.

Websites were critical to John W's process of naming his desires, but they also played an important part in his search for local belonging in communities of practice organized around his new identity:

> Three or four years ago you'd have a hard time finding something to do with leather or bondage or whatever around here, but now about every weekend there's a party. So the Internet has allowed all that to come forth.... Before I met my boyfriend [at the campus LGBT group], I was actively involved with a BDSM bondage group that met in the South Central Kentucky area. I would travel and play around with male and females—mostly safe sex. I was actively involved with that group.

For John W., claiming a gay identity was a means toward a more salient identity. As he notes, "I have to emphasize that my sexual interests are a big part of who I am, and my attraction for men . . . I don't know. I'm not all that sure that I feel gay like the other guys I meet who are gay. Like my current boyfriend, he's really gay, wants to settle down with one other guy and isn't into bondage at all." When asked how he was different from other gay men his age, John W. responded that from reading websites and negotiating his current relationship he had the sense that being gay came packaged with a set of expectations, such as monogamy and normality, "like working at a regular job and settling down."

As John W. saw it, "bondage just comes with a desire to play with other people. I'm not just out to have sex. I'm fulfilling this internal need." Identifying as "gay" made it easier for him to find other men with whom to have the intimacy and sexual connection he desired even if a gay identity did not squarely fit his sense of self and his range of desires:

> Gay.com really isn't that great for me because a lot of people aren't into bondage. But I go to the "Kentucky" chat room because you know that you're probably going to find somebody near you. A lot of people will travel two or three hours to meet somebody. You can't just, like, hit on a guy on campus, 'cause you don't know. I can find people on campus that I would have maybe one-night stands, but I really didn't have fun because there was no bondage. If I didn't have access to computers, I don't know what I would do.

The websites and online communities John W. finds don't confirm an identity for him. Rather, he picks up definitions to pragmatically serve his sexual desires. This process of sorting through the available terms led to his identity as a young gay man. But his gay identity is an approximation. He has ambivalence with the category "gay," but he finds utility in it. Digital representations of what it means to be "gay" have been undeniably vital to Brandon's sexuality. But they also underscore the frustration of what philosopher Kenneth Burke long ago noted, "To define or determine a thing is to mark its boundaries" (Burke 1969, 24).

Conclusion

Until recently, Brandon felt his bisexuality was incommensurate with his racial identity. John W. questions whether his identification with bondage fits with his understanding of "gay." Presuming that rural youth in the United States are isolated from LGBT identity formation, from the processes that can queer one's normative sense of self, ignores how identities settle on our skin. The politics of LGBT visibility compel Brandon and John W. to put sexual identity ahead of their familial, racial, and queer desires. But Brandon and John W. teach us that we need to change our perception of the closet as an open or shut door. Closets are, in part, shaped by the "compulsory heterosexuality" that structures our everyday interactions.[10] Culturally, we all work under the assumption that individuals are heterosexual (and "male" or "female") until "proven" otherwise. Rural communities' material dependencies on structures of familiarity and the value placed on conformity as a sign of solidarity intensify the visibility of compulsory heterosexuality's hegemonic sexual and gender norms. Brandon's experience of what is commonly referred to as "the closet" challenges Seidman's assertions of or hopes for an America beyond the closet as long as we hitch a generic and universalizing logic of visibility to queer difference.

Like most teens, Brandon and John W. grew up with gay visibility readily available in the media. They knew what "gay" meant, but it was an identity category otherwise conspicuously unfamiliar to and popularly depicted as out of place in their rural surroundings. Both Brandon and John W. searched for identities that would lend authenticity to their own desires but that they could also experience locally. But identities, as rhetorician and AIDS activist Cindy Patton has argued, "suture those who take them up to specific moral duties" (Patton 1993, 147). The ascribed moral duties of visibility and normative sexual mores that Brandon and John W. associated with the genre of "gay" realness they found online conflicted with the moral duties that already deeply engrossed them locally. The genre of "gay" available to them as a commodity through online coming-out narratives and personal ads provided partial relief to their search for realness. However, the packaging of gay identity's "auxiliary characteristics," those hegemonic behaviors and affective dispositions represented as integral to the status role of "gay," read as incommensurate with other pieces of their sense of self.[11] Their rural locales did not present them with options to tune out this dissonance. This is not a case of the Internet opening netherworlds of desire and identification unavailable in the everyday lives of rural queer youth. Instead, Brandon's and John W.'s engagements with genres of queer realness demonstrate the dialectical production of modern LGBT identities that, by definition, draw on narratives driven by a politics of visibility.

Narratives of isolation reflect the ascendancy and dominance of a self-discovery/disclosure paradigm that structures not only LGBT lives but also modern notions of how identities work (Seidman 2002; Giddens 1992, 200). What we call "the closet" springs from the idea that identities are waiting to be discovered and unfold from the inside out. Authenticity hinges on erasing the traces of others from our work to become who we "really" are. To leave the traces of social interaction visible is to compromise our claims to authenticity and self-determination (Giddens 1992, 185). Genres of queer realness simultaneously expand and consolidate the possibilities of identity. They prompt youth to rework the unmarked categories of heterosexual, male, and female and embrace burgeoning non-normative desires. At the same time, they restabilize and genericize LGBT identities as real, natural, unmediated, and authentic. In this sense, identity, even the most intimate, personal senses of self, can be explored as deeply social and highly mediated. With this in mind, how might we shift from imagining that rural young people's sexualities and genders are unfolding states of essential being stunted by what we presume they lack? How might we come to see identities (theirs and ours) as a cultural process akin to what philosopher Gil Deleuze characterizes as the folding in from the outside?

The transformative power of self-identification to organize politics, culture, and intimacy depends on countless others. Social identities as agents of change are not isolatable to individual bodies or locations. Highly dynamic dialogues between local, material conditions and modern, commercial renderings of LGBT identities produce particular ways to dress, speak, and look for rural youth. For the youth with whom I worked, representations of the real—online coming-out stories and electronic personal ads in particular—were crucial. These genres of queer realness expand their sense of place, home, and belonging within queer social worlds.

Beyond a moment of visibility provided by mainstream television and film, genres of queer realness circulate compelling images of peers on a similar quest for verity and viability. This validation is particularly pressing in rural areas where one relies on being known and knowable—familiar—to people around you. Internet-based genres of queer realness offer rural youth possibilities for both recognition and acknowledgment of seeking that recognition in places one is presumed to already be familiar. This genre of realness has the power to authenticate queerness through the textual and visual rhetoric of LGBT visibility that is (seemingly) real and tangible somewhere if not easily found in a small town. But how is the increased visibility of queer realness through media discourses taken up in people's lives? What are the practical applications of these media texts and discourses? What do these youth do with the expectations of visibility that are so central to the identity politics of the LGBT social movement? Instead of trying to gauge how media effects impact individuals, we should look at everyday uses and practices of media engagement.

6

To Be Real
Transidentification on the Discovery Channel

What you find-ah
What you feel now
What you know-a
To be real.

—Cheryl Lynn, "Got To Be Real," 1978

I argue in the previous chapter that online coming-out stories and personal ads are pivotal to rural young people's negotiations of a queer sense of self. These stories and ads convey generic expectations of what lesbian, gay, bisexual, and transgender (LGBT) identities look like and beckon young people to authenticate their own identity claims through a logic of visibility. I suggest that these narratives of queer realness are compelling not as a particular grouping of cinematic, televisual, or digital texts but as situated, discursive practices that mark the local boundaries of LGBT identities. These practices offer rural queer and questioning youth routes to LGBT community recognition and inclusion. At the same time, rural youth transform queer storylines through their online engagements. They address the "spatial practices" of places that demand familiarity as they respond to the call to make their queer differences visible.[1]

Without question, then, new media operate as a critical node of queer realness in the lives of rural young people. But if online coming-out stories and personal ads are key sites of queer-identity work for today's rural youth, can or should we assume that they signal a radical rupture or epistemological break from other sites and sources for queer identity's mediation? In other words, do new media technologies introduce something that had been missing wholesale from rural communities before the Internet?

The problem with this line of questioning is that it tends to narrowly focus our attention on the imagined capacity of new media technologies to parse out social experiences. It also implicitly reinforces a clear boundary between online and offline mediations of identity. As discussed in the last two chapters and argued by researchers of youth media culture, "on-line spaces are used, encountered and interpreted within the context of young people's off-line everyday lives."[2] In effect, "online" and "offline" experiences of media constitute one another.[3] Moreover, presuming new media do something "new" in isolation of other forms of mediation ignores the rich "media environment" of computers, video games, chat rooms, radios, televisions, phones, and music players that saturate young people's lives and more broadly shape global youth culture.[4] Whether a young person in the United States possesses each technology listed above or not, the target marketing that categorically defines them as "users" of it all shapes all young people's expectations and experiences of new media.

Arguably, new media's qualities (if it could be argued that they have any) cannot be separated from the rhetoric that surrounds their "newness."[5] Attributing the importance of queer realness to its online circulation ignores the politics that elevate one technology's importance as a site of discursive practice over other "cultural circuits" that produce meaning in our daily lives.[6] It also ignores rural young people's complicated and, often, compromised access to computers and Internet connections that hamper their opportunities to participate in these discursive practices online. Lastly, and perhaps most pressing, focusing on the medium ignores the politics that prioritize a rhetoric of realness and visibility over other expressions or configurations of queer experience.

This is not to say media don't matter. The questions I pose in this chapter are in what ways does it matter, and how does it come to matter or to occupy a place of importance in a rural young person's negotiation of queerness? As Martin Meeker persuasively argues in his history of the formation of gay and lesbian community from the 1940s to the 1970s in the United States, innovations in communication—the circulation of early national publications of the homophile movement, mass-media attention to the "problem of the homosexual," and, later, do-it-yourself alternative gay and lesbian travel guidebooks—literally defined and transformed the meaning of gay and lesbian life. While I find Meeker's argument compelling, I am more circumspect about claiming that significant communicative transformations are altering the trajectory of compulsory visibility that dominates LGBT life and representation today. While Meeker describes a moment of definition and consolidation in gay and lesbian political history, the centripetal force of neoliberal gay and lesbian politics makes communicative transformation difficult to imagine. We seem "stuck" on visibility politics. However, historically significant or not, new media are but one social terrain for or manifestation of communicative transformation, and they are by no means rural young people's only venue for sampling (and therefore transforming) the meaning of queer realness.

I take to heart feminist theorist Donna Haraway's contention that media technologies, new and old, are simultaneously "formalizations, i.e., as frozen moments, of the fluid social interactions constituting them" and "instruments for enforcing meanings" (Haraway 1991, 163–64). The value rural young people ascribe to online coming-out stories attests to a qualitative shift in the politics of visibility—the movement of the mass cultural circulation of gay identity to an online context—but this shift and its layered consequences cannot be understood as the product of new media technology in and of itself. And, as Sonia Livingstone contends, "attributing social change to technological innovation is naïve. Moreover, change is not necessarily the same as progress, especially for those who are left out" (Livingstone 2002, 17).

Context Matters: Taking Queer Realness Cross-Platform

With this penultimate chapter, I want to draw attention further away from the aesthetic codes associated with particular media or texts associated with them and, instead, attend to what media scholar Susan Murray refers to as the "context of reception" to try to make sense of how rural young people experience and make use of a range of engagements with queer realness (Murray 2004, 44). I do this because I believe it is in these moments of engagements with queer realness and rural young people's passion to take part in their persuasive power that we can sort out the productivity as well as the constraints of a politics of visibility and media's role in it. Murray argues that media texts can be "manipulated" by marketing and branding "so as to encourage a viewer to understand the meaning of the text through a specific generic lens" (Murray 2004, 44). So, for example, whether an audience member interprets a television show as reality-based programming or as documentary may hinge as much on the register of a genre's aesthetic codes as whether the person watched the show on Fox, the Public Broadcasting Service, or Cable News Network. In arguing for the viewer's "context of reception" to matter in discussions about genre, Murray underscores the limits of studying media as texts divorced from the conditions that shape audiences' reception and interpretations of them. If scholars want to make claims about what media mean and how they matter to people, we cannot solely depend on the particularities gleaned from close textual readings or tallies of media's form and content. We must also attempt to work across media platforms to make sense of the context in which viewers experience, engage, and mobilize an assortment of media.

Redirecting media studies' (inter)disciplinary energies toward the context of reception, engagement, and mobilization also suggests that, if we are to work toward understanding what meaning and impact media have in people's lives, we must move aesthetics and texts out of their leading roles in media studies and give up searching for definitive effects of media that stem from the textual content itself. Analyzing aesthetics and texts compels us to presume static, generic audiences who are either bludgeoned or snubbed by media. While challenging the presumption of a monolithic audience responding to formalistic elements of a media text is certainly not new, many film and media scholars continue to operate from a text-centric position. We may challenge presumptions of who is in the audience and how they experience media texts, but it is more difficult to de-center media itself from the spotlight of analysis. More importantly, as public support for media monitoring systems from film ratings to website filtering software suggest, we culturally construe media as objects with the power to do good or evil rather than cultural resonances incessantly and contextually engaged daily toward different ends.

As a radical rethinking of what media studies has to offer public debates on media's effects (particularly to studies of youth) and how to account for the power of media in everyday life, this chapter examines how AJ and Ashley, two trans-identifying rural young people, experience very different engagements with the same Discovery Channel documentary. What could this made-for-television documentary first aired more than twenty years ago possibly have to do with rural young people defining their identities at the turn of the 21st century? AJ and Ashley serendipitously cited the rebroadcast (literally, the recycling) of the 1985 documentary *What Sex Am I?* aired on the Discovery Channel's Discovery Communications Incorporated (DCI) franchise channel, Discovery Health, as a pivotal moment in the queering of their gender identity. I trace how this film relates to earlier documentary modes of representing LGBT lives and how it came into AJ's and Ashley's lives. I also review the discourses of "real trans identity" circulated by and through *What Sex Am I?* I look at how the documentary puts into words and images who counts as a "real" trans person. To highlight how the interplay between media-generated and -circulated discourses of realness and the materiality of class, location, and society's gender norms shape their queer-identity work, I compare how AJ and Ashley talk about and use this documentary. I argue that the meaning and impact of *What Sex Am I?* to AJ's and Ashley's gender identity cannot be found simply in the content, form, or location of viewing. All these things shape and are shaped by the interplay of AJ's and Ashley's agency as audience members or viewers and the structures that discipline and govern their capacity to discursively practice or rework the narratives available to them. The analysis attempts to push past a moment of reception. Instead, I contextualize how these young people make sense and use of *What Sex Am I?* in their daily lives. How these two young people take up and rework what we might consider a generic, outdated account of transsexuality raises the question of what rural queer and questioning youth do with the resources on hand to transform media consumption into identity production.

Arguably, *What Sex Am I?* and its generic kin, as examples and complications of the genre of queer realness discussed in the previous chapter, set particular expectations of normative transgender embodiment. At the same time, the conditions of young rural people's lives—in this example, most notably class status and its links to physical location and access to health care and societal expectations of what a "real" man or woman looks and sounds like—reconstitute and interpellate popular discourses of authentic trans identity. This chapter explores how rural youth make meaning from mainstream media and the everyday as source materials for queer-identity work.

Continuities of Realness: Technologies of Genre

Scholars Jay Bolter and Richard Grusin maintain that each technological innovation "remediates" or remixes rather than displaces its predecessor. This is a robust theory to help explain how elements of technologies and the social stories we tell about them manage to reincarnate generation after generation. This give and take between old and new to maintain or dazzle producers and consumers creates a sense of consistency and change across media.[7]

Remediation might also be a useful metaphor to apply to the persistence of visibility in gay politics itself. While the appearance and lineup of different queer identities continue to change in the media and are taken to index progress, elements of past representations are regularly repurposed to quickly convey the conventions of a stereotypically queer character (Gross 2001).[8] What has arguably remained constant since the medicalizing of homosexuality at the turn of the 19th century is the press for visibility of some kind—the need to locate and mark queer subjects to distinguish and contain them from normal people. Discursive practices of queer realness also show signs of continuity and crosscurrents of remediation.

Online coming-out stories and personal ads might be characterized by their private consumption and peer-to-peer recognitions, exchanges, and acknowledgments.[9] Online coming-out stories hail rural young people to become visible, and therefore authentic, through the convention of not only claiming an identity but also retelling it as a personal story. Documentaries broadcast on television carry a voice of authority critical to public validation, but they channel their authority through an intimacy produced between viewers and viewed in the domestic sphere.[10] Those watching are meant to feel close to the subjects presented through the use of first-person narratives and direct address. Queer realness, engaged online or through television documentaries, extends affirmation while modeling and streamlining a public narrative of what shape that subjectivity should take. The aesthetic codes of documentary incorporate a public discourse of how it is in real life for the subjects on display and are remediated across media platforms.

Long before its circulation online, then, queer realness flowed piecemeal through other mass media such as news reports and investigative exposés and, later, through first-person narrative documentaries. As scholar Lisa Duggan contends, identities as narratives are "[n]ever created out of whole cloth, never uniquely individual," but rather "each narrative is a retelling, an act of social interaction, a positioned intervention in the shared, contested narratives of a given culture" (Duggan 1993, 793). As will be discussed below, discursive practices of queer realness incorporate the aesthetics of realist narrative forms, such as documentary, but also the discourses of visibility so central to public discussion of gay and lesbian identities since the 1970s. These discursive practices of crafting narrative involve borrowing, incorporating, and reworking not only storylines but also remediating styles of storytelling. What young audiences are able to do with these genres of queer realness depends not only on the hegemonic media discourses and preferred reading strategies in circulation but also on the resources that mark the boundary publics in which they circulate.

The Power of Documenting Queerness

Unlike fictional accounts that offer vicarious stand-ins for queer love (or bodies) or online personals and coming-out stories that narrate connections to kindred spirits, cable television documentaries, as another iteration of queer realness, offer the weightiness of what Bill Nichols refers to as "a discourse of sobriety" (Nichols 1991, 3). Documentary's mode of observational and interactive representation is positioned to tell an instructive story of realness through personal narrative. Its naturalizing rhetoric of biological knowing subtly informs the audience whom to accept and why. As such, documentaries blend authority with authenticity and social discourse with first-person accounts. There is a long history of a genre of realism making a difference in the visibility of queer people's lives. Documentaries premiered in large cities communicated and distributed images of gay and lesbian people that gave shape to the boundaries of these communities of identities. What difference does it make to have this visibility framed in such specific language and packaged in a particular look and feel flow directly into young people's homes? The result is a gravity and relevance that some LGBT youth found particularly compelling in their efforts to assert the existence—the realness—of queer identities to skeptical (or hostile) family and friends.

Because tropes of objectivity, science, and public service frame our reception of documentaries, they occupy a privileged site of truth and revelation, particularly as compared to other television programming.[11] Documentaries, therefore, can do work that other discursive practices within this genre of queer realness cannot. They can legitimize and humanize LGBT people "out there." They provide stories of personhood, family, and place. An audience member might empathize with or relate to the subject of a documentary even if that viewer does not believe such people live in his or her small town. Because they are rebroadcast on basic cable, documentaries are potentially reusable and portable in rural places in ways that independent or mainstream documentary films about LGBT identity may not be. They can be privately devoured or made available for public consumption.

That said, the meaning or significance of a documentary like *What Sex Am I?* as a genre of queer realness cannot be understood simply in terms of its aesthetic codes. Its potential use or disuse is defined by more than the features of the media text or technology of distribution itself. As film scholar Barbara Klinger persuasively argues, "audiences appropriate the films in their midst," transforming films and genres into "texts and groupings of texts that gain their meaning and significance within processes of exhibition and reception" (Klinger 2006, 246).

Contextualizing What Sex Am I?

There is a moment in the 1985 Home Box Office (HBO) documentary *What Sex Am I?* when director and narrator Lee Grant asks an interviewee: "Why did you want to be a woman?" The woman accelerates the cadence of her rocking chair, almost propelling herself out of the camera's frame. She seems surprised by the question. "I just . . . knew I was a woman. It wasn't about wanting to be a woman. I felt that I was misplaced.... I feel like I was born with a birth defect and I finally got it straightened out." The whiteness of the woman's face and the angularity of her nose contrast sharply with her red, tightly curled bangs. Society's relentless gender assignments cast the feminine casualness of her folksy ruffle-sleeved plaid dress as contrary to her square jaw, baritone voice, and Adam's apple. The woman, later introduced in the film as "Jody—a transsexual," appears agitated by the presumption that she is anyone other than who she has always been, even though much of her role in *What Sex Am I?* is to tell the audience about the journey of becoming a woman. A tension played out during the 58-minute-long documentary is foreshadowed here. Some expressions of transgender identity—indeed some transsexuals—are imagined to be more authentic and deserving of acceptance than others.

What Sex Am I? premiered on April 18, 1985, at 10 P.M. Eastern time on the then young cable network channel HBO. Joseph Feury produced the film for HBO's second season of the *America Undercover* (*AU*) documentary series. Lee Grant, the acclaimed actor and filmmaker (and Feury's wife and creative collaborator), directed and narrated the documentary. The film used one-on-one interviews, observational techniques, and the expository scientific testimony of medical experts to examine the plight of transsexuals, transvestites, and gender outlaws who defied categorization.

What Sex Am I? opens with the brief exchange between Grant and Jody described above and abruptly shifts to a montage of men applying makeup, adjusting their bras, twirling in voluminous skirts, and flitting across the screen. We hear Grant's voice: "Transvestites are men with an obsession to wear women's clothes." Next come quick headshots of the film's main subjects, Jody and Cathy, the two male-to-female transsexuals interviewed in the first half of the program. Then Steven and John, female-to-male transsexuals introduced in the second half of *What Sex Am I?* appear as Grant's voice asserts, "Transsexuals feel they were born in the wrong body and are driven to change their sex permanently through surgery." A few pained, ambiguously gendered faces jump-cut across the screen accompanied by a soundtrack of discordant merry-go-round music. The music's tempo picks up as Grant's disembodied voice tells her audience, "This is a film about people living in a gender crisis, whose mind and body are in conflict and must face every day the question: *What Sex Am I?*" The carnivalesque music stops and the frame settles on the film's title and an off-centered shot of a large, white hand, adorned with long red fake nails, pinching a cigarette between two fingers. The film begins with a brief interview between Grant and starlet Christine Jorgensen, the former World War II private who returned from Denmark in 1953 to face a phalanx of reporters after word broke of the successful sexual reassignment surgery of the "GI turned Blond Bombshell." A key figure in the public recognition of transsexuality, Jorgensen's cameo offers a provocative opening to *What Sex Am I?* But Grant quickly swivels away from Jorgensen's celebrity toward what she clearly believes is "the real story." A story befitting HBO's *America Undercover* series. A story of transsexuals living "in the shadows" and "anonymously" in the United States.

During the next hour, we learn about the discrimination transsexual people face as they struggle to find clarity and wholeness through gender transition. For expert analysis, Grant turns to Paul A. Walker, Ph.D., a "Gender Specialist" with the Janus Information Facility of San Francisco, and Norman Fisk, M.D., psychiatrist and co-founder of the Gender Program at Stanford University. Interviewed in talking-head fashion, these experts begin by defining differences among transsexuality, transvestism (or cross-dressing), and homosexuality, then move on to detail the physical and psychological experiences of transsexuals transitioning from one sex to another. Grant also takes us on several detours to explore the life of Clifford, a 35-year-old man "desperately running away from his homosexuality, who had a sex-change operation" in search of a cure for his same-sex desires; "the fringe underground . . . [of transsexual prostitutes called] . . . she-males—women from the waist up, men from the waist down" using "female hormones, silicone, and plastic surgery" so these "drag queens and hookers can fulfill most of their wildest fantasies thanks to medical technology"; and a support group of transvestites, "men in hiding who have an uncontrollable obsession to cross-dress."

Grant spends the rest of the documentary sharing the personal narratives of four main characters. Jody, a male-to-female transsexual, and her lover (former legal wife), Susan, who relocate to San Francisco so that Jody can continue her career as a computer programmer; Cathy, a male-to-female transsexual from a small town, who strips in a Houston bar to earn money for her sexual-reassignment surgery; Steven, a female-to-male transsexual, who is coping with the loss of his job as a gym teacher and girl's basketball coach; and, finally, John, a female-to-male transsexual, who is planning a family with his now legal wife, Susan (former lesbian lover of fifteen years), and works in the shipyards of San Francisco's East Bay. *What Sex Am I?* ends with updates on each of the main characters: John and Susan decided to adopt a child. Steven gave up on being a teacher and is now a construction supervisor. Cathy's surgery was a success, and she is starting a new life as a secretary in a large company. Jody found work as a computer programmer, although Grant informs us "she is earning $10,000 dollars less than she did as a man." As the credits roll and the silhouette of a solitary fair-skinned, gender-ambiguous person smoking at a table in a crowded restaurant fills the screen, Grant shares some final thoughts: "For these people, the battle between the mind and the body is over. They are now the person they want to be. And for the transvestite there are the beginnings of self-acceptance. But for countless others who have to ask themselves, '*What Sex Am I?*' the struggle continues."

Past Lives: A History of Documenting Gay Identity and Its Links to What Sex Am I?

The 1970s saw the rise of new narratives depicting gay identity in documentary filmmaking. These films challenged earlier nonfictional representations, such as the program "CBS Reports: The Homosexuals" (CBS 1967), by recasting "the homosexual" as a part of society rather than a blight tearing at its fabric. *What Sex Am I?* echoes the rhetorical devices found in these early narratives of personhood that sought to counter hegemonic portrayals of homosexuality as an immoral vice through its use of first-person accounts of dignified "coming out" as a legitimate journey of self-discovery. As media scholar Larry Gross argues, these "coming out narratives connected individual experiences to shared experiences and thus solidified a sense of community and identity" (Gross 2001, 70). In doing so, "confessional documentaries" brought a "gay independent citizen" to cinematic life alongside the nascent gay social movement coalescing in the United States (Pullen 2007, 12).

For example, Alan and Susan Raymond's direction of *An American Family*, the 12-hour serialized PBS program (1973) documenting the everyday suburban lives of the Loud Family, reconfigured gay identity by its portrayal of Lance, the family's young gay son, as a part of rather than isolated from "the typical family" (Pullen 2007, 45). The Mariposa Group's independent production *Word Is Out* (1978) redefined homosexuality by featuring gay men and lesbians disclosing memories of childhood, family, love, and coming out. The film's intimate personal interviews between filmmakers and subjects transformed homosexuality from a social "problem" into a legitimate social identity (Pullen 2007, 20).[12]

To carry out this shift toward legitimacy, confessional documentaries must naturalize gay identity—binding it to the logic of sameness and distancing it from pathologizing medical discourses. These confessional documentaries must align gayness to other social identities, like race or gender, and position the audience to see themselves reflected in the "healthy and normal" individuals on display. This might explain why the representations of transsexuality in *What Sex Am I?* produce both empathetic connection and distanced circumspection. The film appeals to sameness with its argument that the main characters are no different from any other man or woman. Grant subtly suggests patriarchy binds us all through these expectations of gender conformity. But the film goes on to undercut these connections by juxtaposing first-person trans narratives and objectifying, sensationalistic, and exoticized representations of cross-dressers and San Francisco trans sex-workers (disparagingly called "she-males"). In the end, this leaves ambivalent whom the film ultimately deems "healthy and normal" and therefore worthy of normative identification.

Finally, *What Sex Am I?* bestows equal time and authority on first-person accounts and medical expertise, thereby interspersing poignant personal narratives from transpeople with interviews of medical experts who define transsexuality as a condition in need of medical intervention. This figures transsexuals as somewhat dependent medicalized subjects instead of full-fledged independent citizens. Transsexuality retains the mystique and sensationalism often affixed to medical discourses of the body and sexuality.[13] In the end, of course, whether an audience identifies with or dismisses the film's subjects depends, at least in part, on what brought them to the film in the first place.

Reactions to What Sex Am I?

Reviewing the documentary for the *New York Times*, John Corry wrote: "*What Sex Am I?* looks sympathetically at transsexuals and transvestites exploring the meaning of gender. How is it defined? The Home Box Office documentary, neither salacious nor exploitative, finds ambiguities. It suggests that gender is, and probably should be, beyond definition."[14] Corry goes on to critique subtly the documentary and its director for taking a clear point of view. He castigates "Miss Grant" for being "excessively solemn" in what is, arguably (at least in part), a cinematic feminist critique of society's demand for normative gender roles. Corry reads as informative Grant's sympathetic portrayal of transsexuals angrily struggling to counter unjust marginalization, most notably in the workplace. However, he also feels the point of the documentary is left "unclear."

More broadly, the review implicitly questions whether the subjects of *What Sex Am I?* warrant documentary's gravitas. Corry's tone suggests it is the study of transsexuality itself that seems pointless, not Grant's take on it. Indeed, he believes *What Sex Am I?*'s explicit discussions of the subjects' sex lives land it in "[famed tabloid talk-show host] Phil Donahue's territory." However, Corry seems less perturbed by Grant's line of questioning than by what the documentary's subjects imply by their sexual pleasure and satisfaction. He snidely remarks toward the end of his review, "Miss Grant asks about [a] couple's sex life. Has it changed? 'Now it's different,' the wife [of a male-to-female transsexual] answers sensibly. We have the feeling that one thing is as good as the other. It may be, of course, although the experience of generations doesn't seem to uphold the point." The review conveys disdain for *What Sex Am I?* by simultaneously admiring the film's novelty while making light of its attempt to give transsexuality social weight through the conventions of the documentary genre. The review's dismissive tone spoke to Corry's sense that the discussion of transsexuality in a made-for-television movie sullied the mission of documentary. In an interview with the American Film Institute, Grant suggests she was not entirely comfortable with the focus either. As she admitted, "Part of the reason why I do things that tend to be sensational is that the people I work for want that" (American Film 1990, 18). But she also noted that, when it came to making a documentary, "I don't care what it is, [as long as it] says, This is something important and special in life, and there's something I want to say about it" (American Film 1990, 18).

Production Values:
Situating Textual Production in Discursive Practices

Grant's own biography put her in a unique position to make a film that could be read as sensational or earnest (or both). Once a rising star in theater, she spent 12 years, 1952–1964, on Senator Joe McCarthy's House Un-American Activities Committee (HUAC) blacklist. She was black-listed for denouncing HUAC's harassment of actor J. Edward Bromberg and for accusing HUAC of contributing to Bromberg's fatal heart attack. Once removed from the blacklist, Grant rebuilt her career through the mid-1960s, mostly on television series like *Peyton Place*. Then, in 1976, she won an Academy Award for her supporting role in *Shampoo* (1975). The film roles that followed her Oscar win freed her from the grind of television production schedules but also left her with plenty of free time. In 1980 Grant joined the small ranks of Hollywood women who success-fully straddled both acting and directing. Six years later, she won an Acad-emy Award for her direction of the feature documentary *Down and Out in America* (1986). The film explored the economic hardship weathered by small farmers, the homeless, and the unemployed at the height of the 1980s Reaganomics-induced recession. Grant understood, on a personal level, the travails of alienation from the mainstream and what it meant to both conform to and work against society's gendered expectations.

Lee Grant and Joseph Feury Productions created the award-winning *Down and Out in America* for the same HBO America Undercover series that, to that New York Times critic's derision, aired *What Sex Am I?* a year earlier. The range of topics HBO chose to broadcast can, in part, explain the growth, popularity, and critical success of its *AU* series. However, *AU* also benefited from what media scholar Susan Murray calls "a significant shift in the market for television documentaries" driven by "the culture wars over arts funding and increasing competition from cable outlets [that] left PBS (the primary venue for television documentaries up un-til that point) in a state of crisis" (Murray 2004, 49). Documentary's aes-thetics of distance and objectivity gave way to a more "interactive mode" concerned with the intimacies and politics of conversation between film-makers and their subjects just as the venues for television documentaries became increasingly commercialized—and public funding untenable (Nichols 1991, 44–56).

Indeed, Sheila Nevins, one of HBO's key creative forces in programming who is credited with the launch of the critically acclaimed *AU* series, considered documentaries "cheap time-fillers" that "cultivated prestige" by airing the work of well-known, award-winning filmmakers, like Lee Grant (Murray 2004, 50). HBO used the series to build credibility and then parlayed that credibility to show material audiences couldn't see elsewhere, particularly on channels with publicly mandated content limitations, like PBS. In an interview about her programming strategy, Nevins notes, "If an advertiser would sponsor it, then I don't want to put it on HBO because people are paying to see something a little spicier" (Murray 2004, 52).

Susan Murray argues that Nevins' programming strategies furthered HBO's branding of nonfictional programming by "incorporat[ing] popular pleasure into a discourse of quality" generally associated with the documentary genre (Murray 2004, 53). As Murray argues, this approach to documentary "allow[ed] the [HBO] network to escape the cultural vilification and calls for censorship that plague broadcast and some basic cable stations" (Murray 2004, 49). As a result, *What Sex Am I?* originated as a provocative boost to the allure of HBO and further blurred the line between serious documentary and "something a little spicier." One can guess that the creators and subsequent critics of *What Sex Am I?* never imagined the film would one day circulate on the most widely distributed cable network channel in the United States—the Discovery Channel.[15]

In 1991 the Federal Communications Commission loosened restrictions on the financing and syndication of network-generated programming (Raphael 2004, 128). This deregulation allowed cable channels like HBO to negotiate rights with their co-producers to sell original content to other networks. Although there is no public record of any sale, this is most likely how *What Sex Am I?* leapt from HBO's archives to the Discovery Channel's scheduling lineup as early as November 7, 1994. At that time, the Discovery Channel had little original content and relied on "sensationalistic subjects, reality-based formats, and historical reenactments . . . as [a] means of producing quantities of low-cost television product" (Chris 2006, 22). Whether or not it was initially produced as a social message documentary, *What Sex Am I?* easily conforms to the "edutainment" programming found across most of DCI's 29 channel brands. Since *What*

Sex Am I?'s repackaging on the Discovery Channel, the channel's parent company, Discovery Communications Inc., has produced three of its own widely watched testimonial-based documentaries about gender identity: *Is It a Boy or a Girl?* (2000), a documentary about intersex people, as well as two separate 50-minute episodes of a 2002 program documenting sexual reassignment surgery, *Changing Sexes: Male to Female* and *Changing Sexes: Female to Male*.[16]

As DCI built its original programming and updated its stock content, it repackaged *What Sex Am I?* one last time. In 1999 DCI launched Discovery Health and included *What Sex Am I?* in the new channel's regular late-night schedule. That is when Ashley first saw the program. *What Sex Am I?* remained in circulation, airing weekly, as late as February 2001, when AJ caught a rebroadcast of the show just as it was cycling off Discovery Health's regular programming schedule.

What should we glean from *What Sex Am I?*'s rhetorical recycling of earlier LGBT representations in documentary film? And what should we make of Grant's admission that she, at times, took on sensational fare (to perhaps support more "serious" work) or Nevins' acknowledgment that some documentaries served as something "a little spicier" for HBO's viewers? Or the subsequent packaging and repackaging of *What Sex Am I?* as "cheap time-filler" not for HBO but for the far more pedestrian, mundane, and accessible Discovery Channel and, later, Discovery Health? What can be said more broadly about the significance of a film like *What Sex Am I?* Was it a serious documentary meant to educate the general public about transsexuality or a titillating film meant to entertain late-night channel surfers? Does the generic ambivalence produced through *What Sex Am I?*'s branding and repackaging make it an early moment in the blurring of the line between documentary and reality programming? These are the kinds of questions that consume many media scholars, and rightly so. They can provide some sense of how industry practices and norms of sexualities and gender cross-pollinate to produce particular strains of visibility and recognition for trans people. I move from the textual and cursory production analysis of this film to the case of how two rural trans-identifying teenagers engaged with the politics of visibility it proffered. Textual analysis alone cannot envisage what these two teens took away from this exemplar of the genre of queer realness because it is too hard to parse out its specific effects. So, analytically, I am drawn to seeing how they engage it as a medical discourse of authority in communities with limited access to medical care or trans-specific communities of support.

What Sex Am I?'s pivotal importance to AJ and Ashley did not turn on the film's associations with the rhetoric of older gay "confessional documentaries," its links to award-winning filmmakers or documentary film series, its shuffle from one cable brand to the next, or its legibility or status as a serious documentary. Yes, all these elements shape the texture of *What Sex Am I?* and therefore AJ's and Ashley's relationship to it. But for these two trans-identifying youth growing up in rural Appalachia, more pressing conditions mediated the role *What Sex Am I?* would play in their lives.

Journey of Self-Discovery

AJ had just turned 18 when we met through one of his friends in the Highland Pride Alliance. He lives in a Kentucky town of 8,000 people less than two hours away from College Town, home to a state-university-based medical school. While his community is among one of the fastest-growing counties in his state, one of the area's larger employers—an auto parts assembly plant—had recently relocated to Mexico, leaving AJ's mother unemployed. AJ's father worked as a machinist in another factory in a nearby county. AJ's mother took workforce "retooling" courses at night through the community college but spent much of her day with AJ as they both tended to an elderly relative. Living in a modest home with his parents and grandmother, AJ's room is crowded with his computer, a weight bench and dumbbell set, and piles of books, DVDs, and magazines. AJ purchased most of his stock at the local chain and discount stores: "I go to many places to buy my videos—Blockbuster video, Wal-Mart, pawn shops . . . and I buy some of my videos in College Town . . . there's many places in the College Town mall that sell videos. But I get most of my GLBT info from the Internet though, because there's not much out there for people in smaller towns."

AJ initially identified as a female-to-male transman, a definition he said he found online at the website for FTM International, one of the largest and most well-known support networks for female-to-male trans people, based in San Francisco. But he also felt increasingly ambivalent about claiming a trans identity in his small town and noted a recent move away from specifically describing himself as "trans."

> I would describe myself as male, a somewhat feminine male because I'm obviously not very masculine for a guy. There are some, few but some,

things I enjoy doing that girls do . . . such as sewing and crafts. But I know I've always been male in my brain, my mind has always been a boy. It seems that just a few months ago I was still labeling myself as an FTM transsexual. I just don't feel comfortable with that label anymore. I want to be something more normal. I can't spend my life being both, or half of each, or whatever others would consider an FTM. I want to be known as a guy, a man, a boy. Not a guy who used to be a girl. Before hormones, I thought it was cool to be considered transsexual. . . . In my mind, I thought I might as well be open about what I am instead of trying to be something I'm not . . . trying to be normal when I wasn't, or I didn't think I was. After I started on hormones, I began to feel like, "Hey, I need to be one sex or the other because people might treat me differently in a bad way if I don't, well, people will make fun of me, because that's how people are. They tend to make fun of what they don't understand." So I toned it down a bit. I thought of the good and bad sides of being so open and being more secretive.

When asked how he first came to identify as trans, AJ is quick to point out the important role a rerun of the Discovery Channel documentary *What Sex Am I?* played in his process of "recognizing" himself as "a transsexual" just before he turned 17:

Well, I've always enjoyed watching TV shows about things that interest me, which is almost anything medical or on forensic science. The Discovery Channel has the best shows about that stuff. I was watching TV and it said, "Next up, *What Sex Am I?*" At that time, I was questioning that myself. I mean, I had been calling myself a lesbian for about two years, but there were things that just didn't make sense, like how much I remember hating my body and wishing I was like my brother. Anyhow, I started watching it. It seemed like a very old TV show too. The narrator came on and was talking about transsexuals or people who feel they were born in the opposite sex's body. The more I watched it, the more I seen that that was what I was going through. An FTM on the show was talking about how he felt on the inside—hatred for his body and female parts, feeling of belonging to the opposite sex, realizing that it was more than just tomboy-ness. That's how I felt too! I hated my body and female parts. I had always been more like a boy growing up—I preferred boy's toys and boy's games, boy's clothing, and I even once asked my mother to cut my hair like a boy's.

AJ found the program so moving that he taped the next rebroadcast of the show later that afternoon. He planned to share the videocassette recording of the film with family members to help explain his own sense of identity. AJ's ability to watch the video with his mother in particular and use the program's first-person narratives to describe and explain his own feelings about his gender became an important part of his experience.

> My mom was at her night class when the show came on, so when she got home, I told mom that I had seen something on TV that I wanted her to see too and that I had recorded it so we could watch it together. I knew it was important to tell my mom about this as soon as I realized what it was so that she could possibly help me out. As we watched the program, halfway through, she finally leaned over and asked me if that's how I felt and if I was sure that this is what I wanted to do. I said yes, I want to change like they [the individuals profiled in the documentary] did. My mom was shocked at first, but I think she knew something was wrong to begin with because I've never been like a normal girl. We talked about the little things I used to do or say that reflects how I felt and how I feel now that got talked about in the film.

Over the next week, AJ and his mother studied their videotaped copy of the Discovery Channel documentary, wrote down the names of the medical procedures described in the first-person accounts of the documentary's trans subjects, and created a list of terms for AJ to research on the Internet. "My family, they're learning more from me because I do research, especially about transsexuals. I would just get on the Internet and just, I don't know. I'd just look up transsexuals and the stuff I learned from the TV.... I had to figure out what to type in, though, 'cause I was typing in and porn coming up." Within six months, AJ and his parents were driving two hours each way to visit doctors willing to help AJ transition. He spent the year between his first viewing of *What Sex Am I?* building a relationship with a local therapist. At the age of 18, he started testosterone injections.

Both the portability and the "realness" of televisual representations of transsexuality played important roles in AJ's work to explain his gender transition to other family members:

> My aunt's first reaction [to the news of AJ's gender transition] was throwing the Bible at me. She often told me, "God doesn't make mistakes like

you think He does" and "You was born a girl, you have to stay a girl. You will always be a girl to me." Then, my aunt watched the program on TV about transsexuals . . . but, I'm not sure if it was the same one . . . you know, there's several of them that have been playing on TV. She called my mom on the phone and apologized, and asked mom to apologize to me for her, and to tell me she just didn't understand before but now she does. She even cried while watching the program. I think those programs are wonderful things. It's opened so many minds. I just wish I could get my brother to watch them.

In this way, AJ takes up the storylines of the *What Sex Am I?* documentary on trans experience and parleys them into material for what he called his "journey of self-discovery" and to prove to his extended family that there were others like him on similar paths. The more versed he became in recalling the story of his journey, the more AJ's narrative normalized his gender in a way that made it imaginable and describable—if not fully acceptable to all his loved ones.

Ashley's Experience of "That Could Be What I Feel"

Ashley turned 17 the month before we met. She lives in what she describes as a "very small town . . . but not so small.... There are roads to pretty much everywhere and a stoplight in the center of the town square." It had been only about a month since she started using Ashley, her chosen name, almost exclusively and identifying as female in online chat rooms or when instant messaging with friends. She met all the people who know her as Ashley through transgender youth websites and web log entries on the popular commercial website LiveJournal.

The people in Ashley's hometown are friendly to pretty much everyone, she says, except "there are a couple of counties across the state line we have as rivals in sports and stuff.... You wouldn't want to be one of those kids in our town after a home game or something . . . you'd get teased pretty bad—not hurt or nothing, but yelled at for sure." There is a nearby lake in this heavily wooded area of KenTennessee, which gives the town three to four marinas and boat docks with restaurants attached to them generating most of the employment and revenue for the local economy. Ashley lives with her mother, father, and two younger twin sisters in a modular three-bedroom home set back from one of the roads that leads to the lake. Her mother works at a gas station and her father works seasonally at the lake during its busy spring and summer and picks up construction jobs in neighboring counties the rest of the year.

Ashley's school is so small that she really can't think of groups that separate the students: "The only divisions are usually between person to person. There's not really any large groups of anyone, and if there are, they're not usually, they're maybe a couple of groups of two or three people, but there aren't people who don't really hang out with everyone."

Ashley and I chatted at a picnic table in a state park an hour's drive away from her hometown. It took more than 30 minutes of casual conversation before she felt comfortable enough to respond to questions about her gender. I asked her if she could recollect one of the first moments that she questioned being raised a boy and what that meant to her. "I've kind of fought it [questioning gender] on and off there for a long time. I just recently came to terms with it. I've tried to fight it there for a long time." Her face became animated with a broad smile and what I read as relief when I asked if she recalled what she might consider an important moment to her sense of who she was as Ashley. Haltingly, she described a documentary she watched five years ago on the Discovery Channel. Although she could only remember bits and pieces of the program beyond its title, Ashley cited this documentary as one of the first defining moments to her sense of who she was:

> When I was about probably 11 or 12, I saw a thing on Discovery Channel, *What Sex Am I?* or something like that. It was talking about that [transsexuality], and that's when I realized, "Hey, that's what I feel." That [show] meant a lot at the time, but over time, it's what's actually helped me the most. If I see anything like that, it just kind of helps, as long as it's not trying to make fun of or put down anything on that. It just helps me out a whole lot. It makes me feel like I'm not alone. I was just trying to be careful because my parents weren't home or anything, so I was just hoping they wouldn't [come home], 'cause it was a show about stuff that I knew that they wouldn't like. They'd tell me to change the channel. I sat there and I was just watching, you know, just to be doing something. Then that story came across. They'd interviewed and told a little bit about the lives of transsexuals that were older. Some of them had been through transition, some of them hadn't. I don't really remember her that much, but there was this one story she [one of the transgender women] told that was close to what happened to me. She was a little older. She was

just talking about when she was young, she was in the attic of her house. She said she found a large dresser kind of thing full of her mom's clothes, and she tried some of them on, and it [her feelings about her gender] just kept growing for her.

Ashley's accidental engagement with *What Sex Am I?* changed not only the way she imagined her future, but also the way she remembered her past:

When I was younger, somewhere between 5 and, I guess 5 and 9, or somewhere in there, just one day, I was in my house and my parents were away. I found a small dress or something, it was like one of my cousin's or something. I tried that on, you know, it's just like something kind of clicked. I realized then that I'd have to hide it, because I'd been told that that [playing dress up or playing like a girl] was wrong, and everything. After I watched that show [*What Sex Am I?*], I put it all together. After the show and hearing that one [transgender woman's] story of dressing in her mom's clothes, I knew what it was. I knew that what I was doing was like her, that I was like her.

For Ashley, however, there was no clear path for what to do with these feelings about her gender:

I know I need a therapist to start any kind of treatments or anything that I may need. Mostly because the people that I've met online had told me that it would be easier with a therapist. They didn't say I necessarily had to have one, but the safest route was to go to a doctor or a therapist.... I haven't really found many groups that are close to my town. There's one for, it was transsexualism and transgender, but they're out of Nashville. I e-mailed them, but something happened to my e-mail server and I don't think it ever got through. But I can't say I didn't try. I never really knew the possibilities of it [sexual reassignment surgery]. I mean, I'd heard about it back whenever I'd saw that a long time ago, when I saw that show [the Discovery Channel documentary], but that was something, you know, they didn't really go into detail about it, they just said they did it. I don't really know anybody that knows quite a bit about that, but online there's, I'm not really sure on the sites, but there's a couple sites that actually go through the steps and everything.

Ashley uses this documentary to not only define her current gender but to narrate its origins. Like AJ, she draws on this documentary program as a resource. As sociologist Zygmunt Bauman argues, "the media supply the raw stuff" that young people like Ashley and AJ use "to tackle the ambivalence of their social placement" (Bauman 2004, 97).

Context of Media Engagement

AJ's and Ashley's distinctly similar yet different media engagements with the same Discovery Channel documentary highlight the importance of context in how media representations are used—and not used—to rework identity, or, as film scholar Barbara Klinger argues, "considering private acts of consumption in relation to the 'ideas and institutions' that animate the encounters between viewers and films" (Klinger 2006, 243). As much as media serve as a source for and site of queer-identity work, the significance of media is always in conversation with other locations of identity formation. To illustrate this point, let us more closely compare just a few key aspects of material conditions that shape AJ's and Ashley's lives.

AJ lives in a town a little less than 80 miles and a two-hour drive from a major medical school and research center. He can easily go online via a computer in his bedroom to research the optional health protocols that accompany his testosterone treatments. But AJ also relies on information he gathers from a network of transmen who live in or near the town where he gets his medical services. When in town for his monthly checkups, AJ and his mother regularly visit with his new friends.

Ashley, on the other hand, lives two hours from a relatively small town with a technical college and more than four hours from a major research hospital with any services for transhealth needs. There are fewer than a dozen licensed mental health care professionals in the vicinity and their offices are 40 or more miles outside Ashley's hometown. As a result of limited, confidential health services in her area, Ashley relies on "researching" website-based information and tips sent via Instant Messenger by friends, but even this source of information is precarious because she shares the family computer, located in the den within easy sight of her parents' bedroom.

AJ and Ashley also have dramatically different family support. AJ's mother is an incredible source of support in his life. When I asked her about her feelings regarding her child's gender-identity work, she responded, "Well, in my book, God don't make trash . . . my child is my child . . . I can't understand any parent rejecting their child for how they feel." But Ashley describes a far less supportive home environment. She says that her parents' hostility toward her questioning her gender is a major source of anxiety and tension in her life.

In addition to the differences in proximity to medical resources and availability of supportive family, AJ's and Ashley's use of the Discovery Channel for identity work is further mediated by their differing class positions and the economics of their hometowns. Although AJ comes from a working-class family and his mother was recently laid off from her local factory job, both he and his mother have job prospects. Plus, AJ's mother and father continue to support him as he finishes his high school equivalency through a Christian correspondence course at home. Removed from the torment and hostilities he felt in high school, most of AJ's social time is spent in the supportive environment of his parents, a few friends, and other transgender youth he talks with online. Youth contact him through his website, online transgender pen-pal lists, and the websites of other trans-identifying young people.

Ashley, however, has remained in public school and has the same friendship circles she has had since kindergarten. Shortly after we met, Ashley lost her online access because her parents discovered e-mail exchanges on the family's computer that she had had with other trans-identifying young people.

While the documentary *What Sex Am I?* as a genre of queer realness resonated for both AJ and Ashley, the degree to which it could be used as a tool or guide in their identity work as trans youth cannot be understood without attending to the different conditions that give meaning and possibility to their identities. AJ started hormone treatments before he had physically matured. He has steady access to health checkups and testosterone. This made his physical transformation relatively smooth as compared to the physical transitions experienced by older trans-identifying people AJ knew. He is also moving into a less marked gender. Although the emotional toll has not been easy, AJ's physical transition to a male body is arguably more culturally achievable and certainly more geographically accessible than it would be for Ashley to produce and perform the category of female.[17]

For her part, Ashley remains ambivalent about physically altering her body. She cannot imagine being able to take part in such bodywork without leaving her hometown—and she cannot afford to support herself away from home. The conditions sketched above make all the difference in how AJ and Ashley think about and use the representations of trans identity circulated through the documentary *What Sex Am I?* The specifics of location, health-care access, and cultural expectations of how normative gender should look fuse with AJ's and Ashley's media engagements and give rise to different trajectories of identity. But the material realities of AJ's and Ashley's lives can also be generalized into categories warranting further analysis, such as the distribution of and access to medical technologies in rural communities, the pathologizing of gender and the scripts required to access mental health services, the school environments of gender-variant children, and the role of class and race in gender practices.

Conclusion

The examples discussed above offer a project of how to understand the significance of media in the lives of queer and questioning youth. The act of viewing media is not what makes this story interesting. The more interesting question is how do youth and others put media engagements to use in their everyday lives? How might we theorize the dialectic between the significance of some media genres over others and the social realities and inequalities they index?

Young people's experiences and understandings of media engagements indicate that they experience these narratives as possibilities—bringing other ways of being to life. These possibilities are always interlocking with the material conditions of their lives. We can never point to an overriding factor that determines or produces the particularities of identities. AJ's and Ashley's different physical, familial, and class locations are necessary parts of the story if we are to understand how media matter to their queer-identity work.

7

Conclusion
Visibility Out in the Country

I began this book with the story of rural young people and their adult allies employing a stalwart practice of gay-visibility politics. They doggedly lobbied legislators for greater awareness and legal recognition of lesbian, gay, bisexual and transgender (LGBT) people. For this kind of lobbying to succeed, particularly at the state and local level, it must mobilize more than appeals to a lawmaker's sense of decency and justice. The recognition of LGBT rights tacitly relies on the financial clout and a critical mass of upstanding, respectable gay and lesbian (sometimes transgender but rarely bisexual) citizens. To advocate publicly for the right to recognition, LGBT-identifying people and their allies must mobilize the social, political, and literal capital that affords them the privilege to visibly claim and prioritize their sexual and gender identities over other identities or alliances. And, they must be able to amass enough of this privilege to sway the interests of local power brokers. These methods fall short in places where the risks of seeming out of place in communities that materially depend on familiarity outweigh the tangible benefits (i.e., access to LGBT social services and community spaces) of making oneself queerly visible.

As the previous three chapters illustrate, rural youth use media and emerging technologies to manage the delicate calculus of gay visibility's benefits and risks. Rural youth also use media engagements, much as they use lobbying, to produce or take part in social moments of gay visibility. However, the media technology in question need not be "new" for such a moment to take place.

For example, when I first met Shaun and several of his friends from the Highland Pride Alliance introduced in chapter 4, they relayed a story of their use of the mundane "information technology" of a static-cling rainbow flag decal. They prominently displayed the sticker in the rear window of Shaun's car, generating gay visibility while riding around out in the country. When traveling through certain counties that they referred to as "hostile territory" due to some past experience with a local kid or just rumor, they peeled off the decal and stored it in the glove box until they felt it was safe enough to stick it back on the window. When I asked Shaun how he felt about having to temporarily hide his gay identity, he laughed and said, "Well, it's not like I stop liking guys when I take the sticker off! And I sure don't need to prove I'm gay by getting beat up driving through a town I know don't like gay people. You got to pick your battles."

Shaun and his friends practice a form of what queer theorist José Esteban Muñoz calls "disidentification"—they neither reject outright nor fully take on the expectations of a dominant ideology, in this case a politics of gay visibility that judges allegiance and mental adjustment to one's identity by a willingness to pronounce it. Instead, Shaun and his friends strategically fly their rainbow flag sticker, "laboring to enact permanent structural change while at the same time valuing the importance of local and everyday struggles of resistance" by recognizing the pragmatic need to blend in as familiar rather than stand out as queer (Muñoz 1999, 11–12). They simultaneously work on stretching their spatial boundaries as young LGBT-identifying rural people and against the notion that their experiences of identity are any less meaningful or real because these boundaries are fragile and impermanent.

Technologies of Identity

Authenticity and coherency define the modern experience of identity and individualism. These expectations compel us to narrate our identities as developmental progress narratives. Popular understandings of how LGBT identities work are no exception. Our identities are imagined to start deep inside, eventually coalescing to visibly resonate with others "like us." The previous chapters offer an ethnographic account of the identities that transpire and take shape when the politics of gay visibility and the media images of LGBT lives these politics produce circulate in rural America. This book tells a story about the work that goes into forging LGBT identities in communities where LGBT people are popularly represented as out of place and the mediation of identity work among rural youth coming of age in a digital era.

Arguably, we have no way to construct our sense of the present without drafting and redrafting social narratives that orient what John Berger called our "ways of seeing" the world around us.[1] Extending this logic, we have no way to articulate our identities without drafting and redrafting narratives gleaned from others. As ethnographer Charlotte Linde argues, stories acquire speakers through the "movement of narratives within a social world that allows and demands that a person produce a particular version of a personal story" (Linde 2001, 629; Linde 1993). In exchange for articulating their queer desires and embodiments as iterations of explicitly LGBT identities, rural youth receive a measure of cultural recognition and a degree of legitimacy and authenticity through their technologically mediated connections with others. The qualities of these connections—how long they last, who is able to take part in them, where they happen—speak to the possibilities, constraints, and practices of gay visibility in a rural U.S. context rather than the attributes of any media technology in and of itself.

Youth growing up in rural Kentucky and along its more desolate borders use a mixture of the tools and materials on hand—national LGBT political advocacy organizations, the intimacies of family, brick-and-mortar public spaces like county libraries and superstores, the new media landscapes of websites, and cable television reruns—to craft familiar identities out of queer desires. To paraphrase anthropologist Clifford Geertz, rural LGBT youth identity is mediation all the way down (Geertz 1973), whether seen in the aisles of Wal-Mart, the browser windows of websites, or the embrace of family.

Local Belonging

All contemporary processes of identity formation, regardless of where they take place, involve a disorientation from the self. A dialogue ensues, as one's sense of bewilderment sorts through connections with others (or otherness) perceived to possess the kind of difference that resonates with one's own ambivalence. Individuals then incorporate this other into a sense of self (Strauss 1959). And through every moment in the flow of these processes, social meanings of "self," "bewilderment," "other," and "difference" are in the thick of the action. But as several theorists referenced throughout this book note, places, often glossed over or presumed to be passive backdrops, are also central to the understanding and articulation of identities.

From their earliest memories, rural LGBT-identifying young people recalled feeling different and queerly out of place. British sociologist Ken

Plummer was one of the first theorists to note that recollection of differentness is a fairly common theme in the life stories of those who come to identify as gay or lesbian. Rather than signaling the origins of homosexuality, Plummer argues, these stories serve as narrative materials individuals use to retrospectively assemble the coherent naturalness and authenticity that has become so central to the meaning of modern homosexual identities.[2] I argue, however, that rural queer youth rework their disorientation from self, in places that prioritize familiarity through codes of sameness, discourage claims to difference, and have relatively few local "others" to turn to for queer recognition. Yet, in our media-saturated world, they are not isolated from narratives about queer difference. When they scan mass media and the Internet for materials to incorporate into their queer sense of self, a politics of LGBT visibility comes up on the screen. These representations organize recognition of queer difference through a grammar of narrowly defined LGBT identities, a "visible minority," underwritten by capital of urban counterpublics that have no equivalents in rural areas. Perhaps even more challenging to rural youth's queer-identity work is that the politics of LGBT visibility narrate rural communities as the last place LGBT-identifying young people should be.

Urban queer and questioning youth can walk or take transit to gay bookstores, coffeehouses, or support centers or cruise the streets outside queer dance clubs and bars (possibly even slip inside a few of them) to test out a sense of local belonging, to see how queer scenes recognize or dismiss their racial, gendered, classed, or other expressions of social embodiment. The politics of LGBT visibility are literally built into the counterpublic landmarks that demarcate gay and lesbian urban community spaces. In contrast, rural queer kids must address the same cultural and political demands for LGBT visibility while balancing the logistical needs to fit in and conform to the familiarity that structures rural life. They walk this fine line amid cultural representations that heighten their sense of feeling out of place and a politics of visibility that fails to see them or their needs for different strategies of recognition.

Rural youth, such as Seth, Jeremy, Dale, Darrin, Shaun, Amy, Clay, Brandon, John, AJ, Ashley, and others introduced to you in this book, are the ones who plan to or have no choice but to stay in their rural towns. With the help of advocates like Mary Bird, Ed McCurley, Gina Cooper, and other adult allies, these youth work every day, through strategies of familiarity, pushing public boundaries of recognition and renarrativizing the meaning of queer realness to reconcile identifying as queerly different from their local communities while still intimately a part of them. More and more small towns wrestle with integrating LGBT and questioning youth in their midst as youth organize and name "the pleasures and possibilities" of their queer difference using the conventions of gay visibility that circulate across mass and digital media (Warner 1999, 7). At the moment, queer desires and embodiments are popularly and politically tethered to prescriptions of exacting kinds of LGBT visibility. These politics and practices of LGBT visibility, however, fail to recognize the price rural LGBT-identifying youth pay for this "claustrophilia."

Coping with the Politics of Visibility

Family can transform queer strangers into local girls and boys, providing much needed "familiar" status. The Grayson County Homemakers Club's effort to host a gay teen informational panel speaks to the power of family to strategically craft a sense of local belonging for LGBT and questioning youth. Few stories are more important to the imagining of rural spaces than family. And the reliance on family was much more than romantic symbolism among the youth I met. Families were important to finding a job, securing housing, and financially surviving in stark economic conditions. Groups like the Homemakers Club create a place for LGBT identities by tenaciously threading the logic of the family through the few community-based organizational structures available. These strategies necessarily embroil local and extralocal sources and therefore demonstrate how local identities are always an exchange with the extralocal.

A complicated history of economic divide delineates the line between rural and urban communities in Eastern Kentucky. Gay-Straight Alliances (GSAs), like the one formed at Boyd County High School, are one strategy for integrating LGBT youth into small towns. Schools were a battleground for class and racial tensions long before Boyd County students added sexuality to the mix by petitioning for a GSA. Boyd County LGBT students gained support for their GSA through a mixture of tepid local support, pressures exacted by the Education Access Act, and state educational reforms meant to give local communities power to block outside influence on school curriculum. In contrast stands the limited success of national LGBT social movement organizations, like the Gay, Lesbian and Straight Education Network (GLSEN), to establish chapters or offices beyond urban centers. The presumption is that if rural communities had the will, they would have found a way to establish chapters. But this ignores

the broader economic realities that make any organizations, beyond local churches, difficult to sustain and does not consider how entrenched
a politics of visibility is in national political strategies. As Gina Cooper,
GLSEN-KY's founder once told me, "You can't really go to the gay-friendly
neighborhood here and knock on doors!" There is no such neighborhood,
no Dupont Circle, Chelsea, or Castro in which to fundraise.[3]

Fragile Publics and Identity Work

As theorist Bruno Latour argued, there are histories embedded in the objects we lean on (literally) every day.[4] The Wal-Marts, websites, church-
sponsored skate parks, and other symbols of rural space come with their
own histories, lessons, and expectations. Youth in this study use these everyday objects of space as props to fashion their identities. In the process,
they bind their surroundings together and transform them in complicated
ways. Boundary publics offer a framework for analyzing how young people engage late-modern identities and the role of social spaces in their
enactment. In rural areas and small towns visited in this book, boundary publics make some renderings of queerness (white, gay, male, gen-
der-conforming, if not normative) more legible than others. The broader
argument of this chapter is to recognize that social identities, exemplified
by the experiences of rural youth, always have spatial contexts that are
critical to the shape and articulation of those identities. If, as anthropologist Keith Basso masterfully argues, we come to understand the world
through a "sensing of place," then identity "sits in places" too (Basso 1996,
143). But in the case of rural LGBT-identifying youth, it does not sit in
one place; it runs around town and circulates through the countryside.

Studying the boundary publics occupied by rural youth suggests that
divisions between "public" and "private" need to be reframed. New media are certainly productive raw materials for the identity work that
happens among these youth, but not in isolation from other sources. In
fact, new media aptly show the constitutive knitting together of multiple
publics that these youth demanded. Websites, for example, proved to be
resilient and significant boundary publics for rural young people. Rural
youth's uses of them also illustrate how privatized space and a sense of
publicness intermingled to provide de facto public space. Nonprofit websites, like that of the Highland Pride Alliance, and for-profit websites, like
PlanetOut.com, were designed to provide this sense of queer public space.
Youth described websites as tangible places with unlimited possibilities

for connection. Analytically, boundary publics illustrate the expansion of a sense of public presence and the complicated interlocking of privacy and publicity.

Media and the Construction of Rural Queer Realities

The analysis of genres of queer realness found in the last two chapters speaks to another critical site of queer-youth identity work. As discussed in the book's introduction, social anxieties have historically accompanied introductions of media innovations. Young people are often the site on which this collective angst is dumped. Fretting about the fate of youth rapt by the powers of "new" media, whether radios, nickelodeons, or video pinball machines, is a part of the social texture and history of technological innovation. This unease, transferred to children and teenagers, provides an outlet to manage the change and unknowns accompanying the introduction of new technologies to our daily routines. By arguing that media intrinsically have the power to produce certain behaviors, from making kids gay or violent to imbuing them with a love of reading or better eye-hand coordination, we give ourselves the feeling of control over life's technosocial complexities, our "cyborg" realities (Haraway 1991, 127).

Sociologist Howard Becker argues that new media studies amounting to "behavior accounting . . . or the 'impact' approach . . . improperly treats the public as an inert mass which doesn't do anything on its own, but rather just reacts to what is presented to it by powerful (usually commercial) organizations and the representatives of dominant social strata" (Becker 2002, 337–40). For better or worse, as Becker suggests, our social interactions with media are not that simple and cannot be reduced to matters of cause and effect.

The media engagements of rural youth illustrate that new media do not carry an inherently transformative essence. At first glance, rural young people's prioritization of what I call genres of queer realness would seem to validate rather than refute the transformative powers of technologies like the Internet and digital cable programming. After all, for young people like Brandon, online coming-out stories paired words and feelings considered foreign in their hometowns. But on closer examination, media tell only half the story. The Internet was certainly a part of Brandon's identity negotiation as a young bisexual man. But the politics of race in his community and the whiteness of the LGBT communities he found online integrally shaped his identity construction.

Ironically, media engagements with queer realness are rarely acknowledged by youth as mediated. The online personal ads, listservs, and chat rooms are seen as direct reflections rather than layered productions of queer reality. But these websites, documentaries, and online discussion forums are, in important ways, mediated by the social, racial, and economic realities of rural communities.

These mediations are examined in depth through the cases of AJ and Ashley. Their engagements with the meaning of "trans" cycled through the same Discovery Channel documentary, *What Sex Am I?* But the degree to which they recruit these depictions as guides to identity work, or explanations of it, are complicated by the social and material contexts that structure what each youth can make of this new language. The material conditions that contour their lives can also be abstracted into categories for further analysis, such as the wider availability of medical technologies in rural communities; the medical coding and standardization of gender and the scripts incorporated into these norms to explain (or pathologize) deviations from these standards; and the gender-identity work produced by different class, gender, and race positions.

Genres of queer realness in fictionalized narratives found in books, films, or television programs dominated rural young people's discussions of media engagements. Cable-produced digitally broadcast documentaries, and Internet-based personals, coming-out stories, and discussions were cited as key resources for identity work more than any other kind of media engagement. To me, this suggests that these engagements shore up "truth narratives" for young people who seek validation of their identity work. But, importantly, these representations of realness are also portable—they can be passed on to families or forwarded to friends. I would argue that these representations of reality carry cultural weight not just because of the genre of story they tell, but also because rural youth can put these images of queerness to work for them. They can deploy them at critical moments to illustrate to their families and peers that there are queer others like them not just out in the world, but more importantly right next door, in the same classroom, and living under the same roof.

Get Out the Roadmap: Directions for Future Research

In assessing the paths this study portends, I return to the question of methods outlined in the book's introduction (and discussed further in the Appendix). The most significant barrier facing studies of queer-youth sexuality and gender is the severely limited access researchers have to a diverse cross-section of youth populations. There are currently only a handful of states that even anonymously survey young adults about sexual health and behavior. These state surveys are some of the few random-sample data sets of youth respondents available for analysis. Practically speaking, as long as it is politically infeasible for researchers to carry out research on sexuality and gender, in collaboration with young people where they gather in the greatest, most diverse numbers (i.e., schools, churches, neighborhood hangouts, etc.), we will continue to have only the murkiest sense of what sexuality and gender identities mean to youth and how to better support them in their negotiations of these meanings.

For the most part, this research project was limited to the networks of peers already receiving some form of support from outside agencies. These were the youth who not only knew about urban-based support services like the Louisville Youth Group and regional college-based LGBT organizations but also had the means to seek them out and participate in them. While my Institutional Review Board imagined these young people would have access to computers and office space where they could participate confidentially in this research project, their communities often had nothing more to offer than a public park or strip mall parking lot to accommodate ethnographic interviewing. It is certainly an important point to note that there are many not readily available to be interviewed. It is frustrating to know that researchers could reach these populations through, for example, school settings that would (potentially) make it safer for them to participate. Until our cultural belief that talking about sex incites sexual behavior gives way to the social reality that the majority of our young people are sexually active before they turn 18, examining what sexuality and gender identity mean to young people will remain politically out of the question.[5] We cannot expect to see further advancement in the sociological or anthropological studies of these topics unless we actively work to change the climate for studies of youth sexuality and gender and it no longer seems odd to suggest researching youth sexuality and gender in the settings in which youth are most likely to candidly discuss their lives.

My fieldsite and my job as a researcher called on me to critically examine the moment of archetypal self-discovery narrated by many of the youth I met and that I have myself recounted as a queer-identifying woman when asked about "coming out." My task was to affirm these narratives as lived experience while also mapping out how they spoke to the rhetorical force of a politics of visibility. I sought to detail the "social me-diation" of these intensely personal narratives of the self, a process film scholar Barbara Klinger describes as "the manner in which people deploy media to shore up, transform, or otherwise operate on individual and col-lective identities" (Klinger 2006, 242–47). I wanted to contextualize what makes it harder for some or easier for other young people to grab hold of particular versions of a socially mediated, visible self and participate in communities that organize around identities to which they are drawn. In focusing on these mediations and their contexts, I came to see how nec-essary it is to argue for resources that open the widest doors possible to youth explorations of identities.

To date, we primarily focus on queer-youth identity formation as an isolated (and isolating) experience. This focus suggests little need for in-vesting in youth support services for anything other than as resources for when things go wrong. It became increasingly clear to me over the course of this research that politically we have a more expansive mandate: to challenge the assumption that young people, particularly queer young people, need to confine their identities to their elders' political goals or go it alone without our active encouragement.

Why haven't LGBT-identifying activists and researchers allied with them, for example, taken up the challenge of trans youth and argued for universal health care that would medically support the gender-identity work of youth without the means to safely do so otherwise? And, why have we not generally invested in public spaces that afford young peo-ple the ability to transform, challenge, and rework identities as they see fit? I would argue that, whether they fit our politics or not, young people queering their senses of sexuality and gender deserve our political energy and collective support. We should strive to see the revolutionary poten-tial of their queer negotiations and rally behind them instead of keeping our distance because we fear accusations of recruitment. If nothing else, LGBT adults' efforts to garner civil rights must acknowledge both how young people are used in our battles and the social fallout they experience from that use.

The case of rural queer and questioning youth illustrates that if we want to make a difference in the lives of people queering desire and embodi-ment in places beyond the benefits of supportive infrastructures (people disenfranchised by class, location, race, ability), then we must push for something other than their right to visibility and recognition. Collective rights to access information, health care, and spaces to gather safe from harassment and public spaces available to all regardless of age and other social identities are issues arguably more worthy of our political rage. As sociologist Barry Adam has argued, "To have an impact in reorganizing the structures of power requires alliances with other democratic movements, such as movements of women, workers, racial minorities, and environmentalists . . . the larger objective of overcoming anti-gay oppression requires change to the larger system of power" (Adam 1995, 178). In funneling our energies into a fight for the "inclusive" rights to marry or retain domestic-partner benefits, we should at the very least acknowledge how these social practices within late-capitalist society marginalize and exclude a host of others.[6] What are the limitations for the youth whose desires or practices don't fit the trajectories of gay and lesbian identities linked to gay marriage, domestic-partner benefits, or rights of survivorship? A narrow focus on rights to privacy that cannot, in practice, be accessed by all ultimately sells short those unable to fit into the trajectories of modern LGBT identities.

One goal of this project is to inspire political actors to reconsider the individual rights-based model of LGBT organizing by examining its universalizing premise. This premise is at odds with the dynamics of how identity formation happens on the ground. In flattening the picture into a universal individual, we push to the side the significant structural differences that make different political projects both necessary and urgent.

Right now, LGBT political and advocacy organizations are grappling with how to welcome others without excluding those with the purchase power to keep these organizations going. In the growing climate of privatized support services and the corporate logic embedded in them, LGBT nonprofit organizations cannot function without appealing to a funding base. Funding bases are essentially networks of individuals with the accumulated capital to support their sense of the world and how the world should work. This base, in turn, drives the mission of an organization and, in the case of LGBT politics in the United States, the direction of a social movement.

What can rural youth communities doing queer-identity work teach us about broadening the scope and queer possibilities of modern LGBT social movements? In the absence of funding bases, rural communities must navigate national images of LGBT organizing, expectations of what chapters of national nonprofits would like them to be, and the material realities of fragile infrastructures for rural public discourse. Because their communities, with few exceptions, cannot live up to the funding demands needed to support local chapters of national 501(c)3 nonprofit organizations, they instead focus on local needs. They build on their sense of unity as neighbors to effect change in more tangible ways than lobbying at the State Capitol affords them. Rural queer organizers raise grocery money for community members who have lost their jobs due to discrimination in the workplace. They find fellow students at the county high schools willing to sign on in support of the formation of a Gay-Straight Alliance. Rural queer-identity work addresses harassment at a very local, personal level when individuals send letters to the editor or to local pastors to complain that someone was harassed in a fast-food parking lot.

These tight-knit communities can be fraught with interpersonal conflicts, the kind that come with working with individuals you have known most of your life. But as much as familiarity might breed contempt, it can also foster comfort and provide resources for queer-identity work. Young people focus on forming makeshift public spaces that can alleviate the disenfranchisement of their daily lives. For people, like me, who worry about how queer organizing will move forward under the corporate structures of nonprofits, increasingly professionalized lobbying groups, and fewer and fewer activists connected to a local volunteer base, rural queer-identity work offers hope for a queerer future.

Epilogue

You Got to Fight for Your Right . . . to Marry?

As I finished my fieldwork in the summer of 2004, Kentucky became one of several battlegrounds over the issue of gay marriage in a state-by-state face-off between the conservative Christian Right and liberal gay-rights advocates. Like ten other states in the 2004 presidential election cycle, anti–gay marriage advocates worked with Republican (and a few Democratic) lawmakers to land a so-called Defense of Marriage Act (DOMA) initiative on Kentucky's November 2004 ballot. The measure, called Amendment 2, asked the Commonwealth's citizens to amend the state constitution to ban recognition of same-sex marriages.[1] August 6, 2004, a coalition of local, state, and national nonprofit lesbian, gay, bisexual, and transgender (LGBT) advocacy groups that initially included a few of the youth and adult allies I met through my research launched Kentucky's "No on Amendment 2" campaign to counter the measure. Sarah Reese, a Kentucky native and longtime National Gay and Lesbian Task Force political field organizer, moved back to the area to lead the effort. With headquarters in Louisville, Kentucky's largest city, the "No on Amendment 2" campaign worked with Kentucky Fairness Alliance (KFA) chapters in every corner of the state to defeat the amendment.

Opponents of Amendment 2 underscored the proposed measure's unnecessary duplication of Kentucky's Defense of Marriage Act passed in 1998 and the federal DOMA legislation signed into law by President Bill Clinton in 1996. "No on Amendment 2" campaigners talked about the principle of fairness for all Kentuckians, a strategy that had successfully rallied support for inclusion of sexual orientation and gender identity in the nondiscrimination ordinances of several larger cities in the state. They made the case that the amendment could be interpreted in ways that threatened benefits that private companies currently offered their employees in domestic partnerships and might drive more progressively minded businesses away from the state. The "No on Amendment 2" campaign fought valiantly to register voters, identify new donors willing to fundraise for the lobbying efforts, and do precinct walks in the larger towns and cities. They raised more money for the few lawmakers who publicly opposed Amendment 2 and identified more LGBT-friendly voters than any organizing endeavor in the history of the state.[2] In the end, none of these arguments or Herculean efforts succeeded in swaying the majority of voters. The Commonwealth voted an overwhelming 75% in favor of the state constitutional amendment banning same-sex marriage.

Some opposed to Amendment 2 argued that the national Democratic Party and its local members and elected officials should have actively come out against the measure and thrown their weight into the fight to block it. Perhaps if the Democrats had nationally done more than sit on the sidelines of most DOMA skirmishes in states like Kentucky, the 2004 presidential elections might have played out differently. Several of my friends back in the Bluest of states, California, argued that places like Kentucky were "lost causes" when it came to the DOMA wars, seeming to forget that back in 2000, California voters passed their own statewide ballot initiative, Proposition 22, defining marriage as a union between one man and one woman.[3] But these lines of discussion and venting ignore a few of the more important lessons young rural people taught me over the course of the past two years.

If the impact of DOMA laws on the outcome of the 2004 elections demonstrates anything, it is that the fates of Red and Blue states are interwoven, and national LGBT advocacy cannot be easily disentangled from local and statewide conditions for that work. There is no conclusive evidence that the DOMA initiatives brought more voters to the polls; rather, they galvanized a core constituency of voters eager to show their support for banning same-sex marriage.[4] Those opposed to referendums like Amendment 2 failed to build a large enough coalition, beyond LGBT-identifying people and stalwart allies, to counter the momentum of those for the ban. In other words, in places like Kentucky, advocates failed to convince strangers to LGBT communities that they shared common cause with them.[5] Those strangers far outnumbered familiar allies. It takes time, resources, and engagement to build politically viable, locally networked coalitions of common cause. National and state-based LGBT advocacy organizations have yet to make local investment in coalitional work their singular priority. Without such a political shift, rural communities—and their queer inhabitants—will remain marginal to queer political organizing even though many LGBT-identifying people likely share common cause with these communities.

The majority of rural citizens have limited access to reliable health care let alone health insurance. They might be swayed to support state legislation for extension of universal health care that would bring resources to youth like AJ and Ashley or HIV prevention information to young men in the Highland Pride Alliance (HPA). Rural community members are arguably less moved by calls for fairness or the extension of benefits to unmarried couples—gay and straight—assumed to live in cities with access to jobs that provide benefits that so many rural community members lack. Tellingly, Marcia Peterson, a retired widow from rural Shelby County, not far from Louisville's city limits, told reporters that she voted for Amendment 2's ban of same-sex marriage not because she objected to gay people's "lifestyle," but because, she argued, "Why should two women or two men live together and have the same privileges as a married person, and probably pay less taxes than a person by themselves?"[6] Peterson, like many rural voters interviewed in exit polls, voiced little interest in the rights of gay people in the name of fairness when they felt so disadvantaged themselves.

As Arlene Stein's research on responses to anti-gay ballot measures in working-class, economically depressed rural towns suggests, arguments that frame protections of LGBT people or their access to marriage as "special rights" prove persuasive to rural constituents. It is not their hatred of queers that motivates them—although surely that is motivation enough for some whether they live in a rural community or a bustling suburb of Los Angeles. Rural voters who reject recognition of LGBT rights telegraph their own feelings of economic vulnerability, lack of access to social-welfare benefits, and reliance on the material more than symbolic preciousness of marriage to span the gaps in a woefully threadbare social safety net. At the same time, the majority of those who typically turn to LGBT communities for support, Democrats running for office most notably, distanced themselves or remained quiet during the debates over Amendment 2.

Several of the youth and adult allies introduced in this book took part in the "No on Amendment 2" campaign, but none played a particularly active role. Mary Bird talked with neighbors about why she opposed the Amendment and sent donations to support the lobbying efforts. Members of the Highland Pride Alliance talked about doing a fundraiser in their community, but, to my knowledge, it was never organized because members thought it would end up costing more money than it would raise. KFA and the "No on Amendment 2" campaign relied on local organizers to identify strategies, like door-to-door voter identification drives or house parties, to fight the measure. But much as Gay, Lesbian and Straight Education Network (GLSEN) members found in their school advocacy efforts described in chapter 3, these strategies seemed ill-suited to all but a few small to midsize towns that already had progressive politics and histories of visible advocacy.

Several of the young people interviewed, like Amy, introduced in chapter 5, expressed ambivalence about the whole marriage movement and whether there was much they could individually offer the cause. As Amy put it:

> I doubt my town is going to get behind gay marriage—ever. I'll send e-mails to friends about it [Amendment 2] because [a KFA volunteer] asked me to help out. But . . . the thing is, my family will support me, but I don't think marriage is really going to make things change all that much. Even if everyone has a gay cousin, they don't think there are really very many gay people here, so why should they do something for gay people?

Amy and others lent some of their energy to the effort to challenge banning gay marriage, but ultimately they did so because that was the political work going on, not because they felt it was the most pressing work to do.

At the same time, the idea of gay marriage was an exciting one to many of the youth with whom I spoke. As Shaun put it, "Of course I want to get married. I can't imagine not wanting to do the whole big wedding thing with cake and presents and all my family. But even though my family would be there for me if I asked them to, they probably wouldn't talk about it with anyone. I don't know if it [gay marriage] being legal would change anything. So, I guess, I care and don't care about the whole gay marriage thing." For Shaun, the tangible benefits of fighting for the legalization of same-sex marriage are less apparent than the imaginable potential of the event itself, legal or not, to bring him closer to his family. He recognizes that the right to marriage might help further normalize him in his family's eyes, but he is aware of how unlikely it is that that will make his family more visible or vocal advocates for LGBT rights in his hometown.

Feminist media scholar Suzanna Walters has argued that "[a]s a civil-rights issue, same-sex marriage is a no-brainer. To deny individuals access to any social and legal institution simply by virtue of their "gayness" is patently discriminatory and should not be tolerated. That said, we need to reckon with why this issue has such enormous ideological salience for advocates and opponents, why a walk down the aisle has replaced a walk on the wild side, and why marriage and familial rhetoric hold such powerful sway.[7] I would add to Walters' call the need to consider how the meaning of family and marriage and the constraints and privileges they are presumed to confer operate differently for advocates and opponents walking on the wild side or down the aisle in a rural context.

Where Are They Now?
Catching Up with Queer Youth and Their Advocates

There is a certain dread and fair amount of guilt that falls on anthropologists when we leave people we have come to know as important sources of expertise or, in some cases, friends and allies on whom we rely to conduct our research. Youth researchers face the particular dilemma of watching our community experts "age out" of their category of expertise. All the young people with whom I worked are now over the age of 18 and some are only a couple of years away from turning 30 (which makes me feel beyond old).

I left my fieldsite wondering what pragmatically would be the more productive line of political work to advocate to support not only the individual youth I met but also rural young people who would later come of age in the communities in which I worked. As several young people suggest, there is more pressing work to be done in their schools and day-to-day lives that seems less directly served by the right to marry. While a few of the youth featured in this book, like Brandon, John W., Dale, Clay, and Amy, have moved away from their small towns to pursue school and work opportunities, the majority of youth remain with their families in their rural communities.

Mary Bird continues to work on representing LGBT interests in her community and has founded a Parents and Friends of Lesbians and Gays (PFLAG) chapter to serve her town and its adjoining counties, bringing the total number of PFLAG chapters in Kentucky to three. She no longer participates in the Grayson County Homemakers Club but remains close to several of the women with whom she worked to put on the Gay Teen presentation at the county library. She tried to hold monthly meetings of the new PFLAG support group over in Elizabethtown, where there is an LGBT-affirming congregation at the Christian Metropolitan Community Church, but she gave up after a year, frustrated with its sparse attendance, what she saw as "too many people afraid of what people will say about them or their families to go to a meeting." Now Mary manages her PFLAG chapter's voicemail, responding to any calls it receives, and makes sure there is a notice in the local paper once a month with the group's address and e-mail.

Despite its triumphs in the court, Boyd County High's Gay-Straight Alliance (GSA) is now defunct. It was unable to draw new members once its founding student members graduated. The dissolution of the Boyd County GSA perhaps attests to the need for GSA advocates to strategically build connections to allied, progressive student groups, like student chapters of Amnesty International and human rights/diversity groups to draw on the productive "cover" of coalitional work to carry forward challenges to heteronormativity in school environments (Miceli 2005, 128).

After GLSEN-KY transformed into the Kentucky Alliance for Education, it too disbanded. The group was unable to continue after Gina Cooper scaled back her involvement when her husband's Army Reserves unit shipped out to Fort Knox to support the deployment of the base's troops to Iraq.

While he finishes courses at a local esthetician school, AJ is living at home trying to address several health issues that arose after his sexual reassignment surgeries. He has stopped identifying as trans but continues to explore what his sexuality means to him. He and I both lost track of Ashley.

Shaun and his closest friends dropped out of the Highland Pride Alliance. They no longer do drag at the Wal-Mart, and he wasn't sure if any of the younger members still involved in the HPA did either. By the time Shaun left, the HPA had grown into 70 active members. Shaun said he and several other HPA'ers lost interest in the group when two of its core members moved away and relationship drama among members seemed to be cycling back. Shaun's breakup with his boyfriend was one of the messier dramas he was trying to sidestep in leaving the HPA. "I'm just getting too old for the drama, I guess," Shaun told me wistfully but with a hint of sarcasm, knowing I had just celebrated a birthday the week before we spoke. But that was far from the end of Shaun's political life.

As Shaun explained to me in an e-mail exchange in 2007 when I asked him if he were still involved in state LGBT politics, "Well most our friends and activism is Hispanic. After leaving the HPA, I made a Gay Mexican

Friend [name of friend] . . . and he introduced me to the local Hispanic community. I even went to Lexington for the Si Se Puede March." After participating in the April 10, 2006, Immigrant Rights Rally that brought more than 10,000 people to Lexington—one of the largest public protests in Kentucky history—Shaun signed up to volunteer at a regional community college to teach English. As Joe, another former HPA member, said, you "get in where you fit in." For Joe, Shaun, and other Springhaven area residents no longer comfortable with the younger scene and tenor of the HPA's gatherings, the area's growing Latino gay men's and queer scene offered new opportunities to continue reworking their queer identities while staying out in the country. How will this work foment? What place will young women and trans rural youth find in this field of identity? What will the crisscrossing of racial lines and blurring of gendered categories of "gayness" mean for white rural residents and queers of color as they collectively rework the structures of familiarity? How might they work together to respond to these structures that push them to the periphery of rural communities in similar yet disparate ways? These are some of the questions that mark the terrain of research waiting for scholars of queer rurality.

Appendix

Methods, Ad-hoc Ethics, and the Politics of Sexuality Studies

My goal in this Appendix is to address the question most city people asked me when I told them about this research: How and where did you find rural gay kids? I think the question, and the fact that it rarely came from people out in the country, is telling. It reveals how widespread the presumption of rural queer invisibility is. But it also signals what should be a concern to anyone who cares about the sexual health and well-being of rural young people—we do not know much about youth sexuality and gender because, as discussed throughout this book, it is a topic we culturally avoid. In discussing the methods and particularly the approval process to move this research forward, I aim to talk about how messy ethical youth research practice can be and the broader politics that compound, respond to, and feed that messiness. In principle, the processes of review and exchange among invested peers and participants are the critical ingredients of ethical inquiry. In part, Institutional Review Boards are meant to facilitate these processes of research production and circulation. In practice, the politics of youth sexuality and gender research may compromise the ability of researchers and university institutions to circulate and extend this scientific dialogue.

As an "aged-out" queer-youth activist with an established record of political organizing, I began the research for this book with strong ties or connections to leaders working in most lesbian, gay, bisexual, and transgender (LGBT) nonprofit youth agencies across the United States. Accordingly, I made initial contact with most of the project participants through snowball sampling from these connections made through personal networks of regional LGBT youth-service workers. My first encounters with youth seeking support were (not surprisingly) with young people who had already found it through these state- or urban-based agencies. These youth had already formed small, informal support networks. As a group, they were visible to me because of their connections to these extralocal agencies. These young people used the conference rooms in public libraries and chain restaurants to hold bimonthly socials and meetings to discuss upcoming events, from Gay Pride picnics in neighboring counties to recent action to include or ban reference to sexual orientation and gender identity in state legislation. They watched television together when someone managed to swing the cable bill. They went to Wal-Mart on late-night drag extravaganzas. These were the youth already involved in statewide campaigns for gay and lesbian civil rights. They traveled hours once or twice a month to attend youth group meetings at college campuses or in larger cities such as Louisville, Lexington, Nashville, and Indianapolis. In fact, I met several of the youth I would later rely on as key participants through support groups for LGBT and questioning young people under 21 like the Louisville Youth Group (LYG).

What little state and private funding available for HIV/AIDS awareness and training made its way to predominantly male peer networks in these groups and their friends living in rural areas. Statewide lobbying bodies such as the Kentucky Fairness Alliance and research funds administered by public research university projects targeted these youth as leaders best positioned to influence their peers. In some cases, young people working with local adults were actively trying to organize themselves into chapters of existing national nonprofit LGBT advocacy organizations, such as Parents and Friends of Lesbian and Gays (PFLAG) and the Gay, Lesbian and Straight Education Network (GLSEN), or as stand-alone community-based organizations designed to meet local needs around employment nondiscrimination and LGBT-specific harassment in local schools, like the Louisville Youth Group or the Tri-State Alliance based in Evansville, Indiana.

Within a matter of days of calling local contacts and sending out an initial electronic call for participants to the statewide LGBT advocacy organizations, I received e-mails from youth interested in talking about why they've stayed in their hometowns and what it is like for them. This necessarily started my study with a bias toward those already engaged in queering their sexual and gender identities, but it was the most logical place to start. The logic of starting with youth connected to LGBT communities warrants three important observations: the overwhelming majority of studies examining youth sexuality and gender are survey-based and administered through public school systems, clinic-based and directed by psychologists in clinical settings, or ethnography-based and rely on participants found at local LGBT service agencies. I was skeptical that I would be allowed to conduct a school-based survey. My real interest was in a decidedly sociological rather than clinical account of identity negotiation. I followed the other research model available and started with agencies as a source of participants. This agency-driven approach, however, has significant drawbacks that will be discussed in detail below. The most critical shortcoming of relying on agencies: most rural communities do not have formal infrastructures of not-for-profit social services beyond faith-based organizations. Working from this initial set of youth participants with connections to urban social services, I shifted to working within their rural towns. Then, I asked these young people to introduce me to their local groups of friends, and friends of friends, and others peripheral to their queer social worlds.

My first month of research, I fanned out across the state and met with any group organizing meetings or providing support to youth seeking information about queer sexualities and genders. Early on, I met Natalie Reteneller, the Louisville Youth Group director. She became one of my key sources of information and contacts with youth and services throughout the area. Natalie introduced me to many of the activists and advocates heard from in this research. She has been the LYG director for close to ten years. Before that, she formed LYG as a peer support group for lesbian, gay, bisexual, trans, and questioning youth with local members of the PFLAG chapter.

I also talked with the adults associated with these loose gatherings of young people. The national nonprofit organization PFLAG has four existing chapters in the areas I worked. Youth attended the monthly PFLAG meetings as liaisons for their college or high school social-justice or LGBT support organization. While high school–based Gay-Straight Alliances do exist in relatively few of the communities in which I worked, it was far more common to find youth associated with a school-based chapter of Amnesty International or groups called "Human Rights" or "Diversity" clubs. These last two clubs were modeled on the area Human Rights Commissions established to address racial tensions. The majority of high school–aged youth I interviewed, however, came from county schools with few extracurricular clubs beyond the omnipresent Fellowship of Christian Athletes, which did not advocate LGBT rights.

I met the friends of youth participants less directly involved in the service agencies and more interested in the parties and gatherings that followed regular meetings. These young people were sometimes interested in the larger political concerns of their friends or the sponsoring service agencies. But they were just as likely to be interested in meeting other young people, particularly new youth participants who found their way to these support organizations. These were the folks who may or may not readily identify as gay, lesbian, bi or trans but voiced their belief in or desire for spaces supporting people wearing such labels. They could as likely be straight advocates of gay rights young people with friends or family who identified as gay.

Because I worked my way outward from a close circle of gay, lesbian, bi, and trans-identifying young people, I limited who I might meet along the way. It is hard for me to imagine how we might encounter a broader spectrum of youth without taking polling and general survey efforts to schools or mainstream youth agencies and asking them to administer questionnaires on sexuality and gender identity. At this historical moment, that seems like an unlikely methodological option. That is a point to ponder when thinking about the methods of studying queer sexualities and genders among youth and an issue I will take up later in this discussion.

Several (though not all) of the youth participants had weathered brutal harassment at their local high schools, dropped out of school before finishing, or graduated high school with a General Equivalency Diploma. They may have moved on to a college not far from their hometowns. In all but a few cases, the young people I spoke with had had conversations with family members and some friends outside their queer peer network about their sexuality or gender. They were "out" by their own decree, although in most cases their families minimally acknowledged or indirectly addressed claims to sexual or gender identity made by these youth.

Sampling and Representation of Research Participants

Accessing a representative sample of young people for my research proved far more difficult. In some ways, I made it even more challenging by depending on the Internet to generate participants beyond those already involved in regional LGBT youth advocacy. After meeting in person with activists and allies involved in the Kentucky Fairness Alliance's Lobby Day events and affiliated with GLSEN-KY, I made my way into the informal peer networks of different rural populations. Beyond the friendship circles of these young people, I attempted to build on my contacts by passing on my e-mail to youth already participating and asking them to let their friends know about my research. I came to appreciate how many youth did not have home Internet access, could not use the Internet as a tool or source of community at their local schools, and had no public access alternative. In fact, several youth I met later in my fieldwork did not feel comfortable enough with their literacy skills to rely on text-based communication.

There are three notable reasons for the lack of young women in this study. Fairly late into my fieldwork, four key female-identifying participants withdrew from the project. The charismatic leader of this peer group had not discussed her queer explorations (and recent forays into online dating) with her parents. Her father, a fairly high-profile city official, found his daughter's web browser history with a cache of PlanetOut.com personal ad pages and confronted her. While she managed to pass his discovery off as "just messing around on the computer with school friends," it shook her to the core. She, and the three friends she was rarely without, thought it would be safer to discontinue meeting and talking with me. The second reason became obvious to me in my first month of fieldwork—at least in the communities I traveled, young rural women were often too busy between work, family, and school commitments to meet with me. Young men, exempted from tending to younger siblings or older relatives more so than young women, simply had more social freedom and leisure time to hang out with their friends. The third explanation may have to do with the drawbacks of snowball sampling in ethnographic research. Once I developed a rapport and reputation with peer groups in a community, I spent most of my time with them. The membership of these peer groups did not change for much of the time I spent with them. In this case, young men replied first and so we became, in a sense, stuck with one another.

Additionally, the corners of community I found online often reproduced the rather closed circles of peer networks I met offline. Young gay-identifying men, almost exclusively white, dominated these groups. As a white self-identifying queer woman, I had some access to young women's lists and online communities, but as a white woman, my access to communities of color and those in the trans community proved more limited. The commercial structure of chat rooms and resources on Gay.com and PlanetOut.com also narrowed the spectrum of enclaves to be found. So, while I could find young men's and women's regional chat rooms, the equivalent did not exist for youth of color or trans and bisexual youth in these regions. I was able to locate some lists and pockets of groups outside the mainstream commercial portals youth mentioned over and over again as the "places to go," such as Gay.com, PlanetOut.com, or more generally chat rooms on Yahoo.com and MSN.com. Finding such online resources off the beaten path was always a matter of luck and happenstance. This is no different from the conditions of "traditional ethnography" and calls for the same diligent triangulation an offline study requires. Whom we find, whom we miss, and how this shapes one's findings is a critical part of the methodological engagement of any researcher, but the browser-friendly, Google-able existence of groups that advertise the identities we're researching can sometimes be too great a temptation or distraction from digging more deeply for potential research participants. Unless our research calls for staying online—say in the rich analysis of linguists like Susan Herring or the exploration of body imagery gaming worlds in the work of T. L. Taylor—I think there is greater impetus to explore offline experiences of phenomena.[1]

Ethnographies of sexualities—like all ethnographies—are ironically most limited by our logistical, methodological need to name and find what it is we are trying to understand. We can't get around this need, as it is the basis of scientific inquiry. But we also must be diligent in recognizing how this shapes what we eventually seek in and draw from our studies.

Seeking Approval: Approaching Studies of Stigmatized Communities

I began to seek consent for my project a year before I had ironed out the details of the study. Sociologist Stefan Timmermans notes his anxieties in seeking Institutional Review Board (IRB) permissions from the hospital in which he would study the life-saving efforts of emergency room workers (Timmermans 1995). In his case, the medical review team not only wanted him to give them credit for the extension of their facilities for the research, but they also wanted paradoxically to remain confidential. They also wanted one of their own doctors listed as first author regardless of the input by the physician. This speaks to norms in the medical and biological sciences that have no precedent in the social sciences. It is another indication of the yawning divide between those researching medical issues and investigating human behavior aside from its medical consequences.

In my case, I spoke with the few program officers staffing the Office of Human Subjects. At the time of my initial submission, there was a non-scientist at the helm. She was a kind person, happy to talk over the finer points of language that should or should not appear in the project pro-posal. It was clear from the direction these informal conferences took that the main goal was to make sure my language was correct, that is, that my proposal effectively incorporated quotes from the codes and subsections of federal guidelines for human research to make my case. First and fore-most, if I wanted to argue that this project should be conducted at all, I needed to show that the risk was minimal. If I wanted waiver of parental consent, what was my rationale to argue such a position? Unfortunately, to make such an argument, I found myself writing a project description that played out and replayed the stereotypes I hoped to challenge about what rural communities were like.

To justify the project, I suggested the study was an intervention: rural youth needed to be learned from because they certainly experienced dis-proportionately horrific abuse and threat their urban peers did not. There are no grounds for such a claim. This perspective is merely experienced as "common sense." I was not doing a comparative study, but the com-parisons to an imagined more liberal, queer-affirming urban environment were difficult to avoid. Who thinks about the rural without invoking the urban? And for queer culture, there is no known rural mark other than the idealizing that people do of country bed and breakfasts or woodsy cruising spots.

So, when I suggested to my IRB that I would be doing groundbreak-ing work, I was not stretching the truth. But I was relying on their own preconceptions of rural places as "backward" or "hostile to difference" to make the argument that my work warranted exceptions to the common rule requiring parental consent because of its scientific importance. Al-though there was initial hesitation on the part of program officers that I would be able to word my project appropriately to gain approval, I did have clearance to do my work the first year out.

May 2002, a year into my fieldwork, marked the anniversary of IRB approval for my research. Unfortunately, I didn't receive notice of the deadline to renew for another month. The IRB sent the first renewal letter to my department mailbox instead of my field address. A newly installed director of human protections with a physician's credentials returned my late renewal application asking me to prepare it for full IRB review. Much to my shock, even though I had no deviations from or incidents with my original project design, my application to continue my work was stamped with a "Pending Approval" label. I thought I would never land in that cat-egory after the painstaking effort put into securing original clearance for my research. I resubmitted a renewal application attempting to decipher the "methodological concerns" outlined in my "Pending Approval" notice. In the letter detailing why I was being held at the gate, the new director (or at least his letterhead) wanted clarification about who I was studying, the hypotheses steering my research, and why I didn't have methods in place that would ensure parental involvement with as many youth as possible. I was stymied by some of the questions. Was I talking to both LGBT and straight youth? If not, why not, and what was I doing to bring LGBT youth with parental consent into the project? What was my hypothesis anyway? When I responded (1) that I was studying youth either accessing or peripherally connected to LGBT-supportive resources but not specifically, or exclusively, LGBT youth, (2) that I was not particularly looking for youth with parental consent or comparing youth to those without parental consent (in rural environments without LGBT centers, I'm looking for any youth who wants to participate!), and (3) that my hypothesis was, "I bet if we asked youth in rural areas how they deal with issues of sexuality and gender we'd know a lot more about them than we do right now (since we haven't asked them much of anything). Furthermore, I didn't think the IRB handled these kinds of details in research design. Suffice to say even my toned-down and appropriately jargoned-up responses sounded huffy.

After a great many letters back and forth, more huffiness exchanged, and some heartfelt and feigned humility worked into my responses, I was able to assuage or effectively respond to nearly all my IRB's concerns. The IRB imparted one resounding message: "Whatever you do, under no circumstances should contact from a minor be made while they're at home!" I thought this last measure was realistically out of my control. I can't keep people from contacting me from their homes! Am I supposed to screen my calls and hang up on anyone who tells me they're calling from their house? Set up a spam filter for "home addresses"? But to get myself over this last IRB hurdle, I promised I'd inform all youth that I would not communicate with them at home unless they had their parents' consent. They were not to call from home, even if in their own judgment that was the safest place from which to call. I gained final approval from my IRB to proceed with my work. Ironically, the year that this process took meant that my next review for renewal was due only 60 days away at that point.

Embedded in what makes social scientific sexuality research "expendable" is the reality that little of this research results in a tangible product that can be heralded in a press release. But there is also a moral economizing at work. Federal oversight, university public relations, and researchers have bestowed on IRBs the moral capital and gatekeeper status to prevent socially disquieting work from ever taking place (Ribeiro 2006). Ultimately, IRBs work from their own standards of what warrants taking a risk (Katz 2006). They evaluate what work is worthy of risk, drawing on institutional standards and notions of what is valuable to know.

My campus IRB worked without any local knowledge of what was practical in my fieldsite, in part because I was working elsewhere. But they also lacked sympathy for the gains to be made through this research. There were no studies to temper their fears that things were worse in rural America for queer folks. And, they operated with an institutional bias toward imagining the worst-case scenario. It is difficult for a researcher not to take an IRB's concern as prioritizing preventing lawsuits over research or benefits to the study population.

In my case, I wanted to fill a gap in the literature concerning the lives of LGBT youth. Psychologist Ritch Savin-Williams, in a critique of literature on LGBT youth suicides, pointed out that we have largely drawn our conclusions and developed our theoretical frameworks on LGBT as "at risk" from a very self-selecting, limited data pool (Savin-Williams 2001). We know relatively little about youth at the margins or beyond the scope of these social services. There are two reasons researchers have methodologically relied on these youth services as sources for data. It seems obvious to say, but what better place to find out about LGBT youth experience than to go to places these youth gather. It is much easier to recruit an otherwise invisible population at "the source" than to find these youth at their schools, in their churches, or in any other circle of young people. But we must ask the question, why is it so hard to find these youth in other locations? Certainly from their own accounts, they are involved in other school and community groups or can be found in the offices of other social-service programs. The rationale for researchers sticking to established, clearly marked LGBT-supportive youth organizations is grounded in the limited access researchers have to these other venues. With few exceptions, we have not ventured out into Boy's and Girl's Clubs, 4-H organizations, or the schools because we, by experience or presumption, see these places as beyond the reach of sexuality and gender scholars.[2] It is imagined that no school would give a researcher permission to distribute a large survey on specifically non-normative sexualities and genders. The politics of asking questions about LGBT sexualities and genders cannot be separated from the methodological and theoretical implications of these politics.

In coding certain groups of folks as "more vulnerable" vis-à-vis genders and sexualities, institutions and researchers end up ignoring the politics that structure who comes to be seen as vulnerable, in need of certain kinds of protection, and how it is that sexualities and genders are imbued with inherent danger. Not coincidentally, these framings carry into the questions we are permitted or even think to ask. Research coded as "appropriate" is embedded with the universalizing blessing of ethical muster while "suspect" projects such as mine are given greater scrutiny that not surprisingly deters us from asking a range of important questions. A worrisome trend can be read into much of what has been approved in sexuality and gender research and where it is allowed to be carried out. Finding individual pathologies is ethically translatable to the biomedical industrial complex. Discussing the complexities of embodied sexual and gender agency is much harder to navigate or contain. This is a problem that can't be solved by retooling methodological design or advocating for greater participation of qualitative researchers on IRBs. These approaches may help, but, as my experiences suggest, something more is needed if we are to broaden the scope of what is "appropriate" in sexuality and gender research.

My project raised question after question as the research design met the realities of daily fieldwork interactions. I list only a small number of them here: What are the ethical considerations introduced by studies of new media? How do issues of sexuality, age of consent, and the moral responsibility to "do no harm" complicate these considerations? So, for example, when reading web logs or downloading audio files of someone talking about their experiences around sexuality and gender, where does the threshold for informed consent begin and the allowance for naturalistic observation end? Does that threshold move when working with a population of 16-year-olds as opposed to 18-year-olds? Should the ethical obligations toward participants met in online contexts differ from those extended to participants interviewed face-to-face? What concerns must I attend to in examining the personal websites of someone like AJ, a trans-identifying young person graphically chronicling his physical transition, when I know I will need to use descriptions of his personal journey in print accounts like this? With each methodological step a researcher takes, her ethical practice attempts to keep pace. Unfortunately, hindsight is often the best teacher when it comes to balancing between the practice of inquiry and its implications for those studied. For most of the questions above, therefore, I have only tentative, partial answers. I am left wondering if any scientific project involving human subjects can guarantee much more than that its researchers will make an earnest effort to identify as many potential risks as possible and honestly acknowledge who stands to gain or be hurt by those risks. Unfortunately, this honesty is compromised by the politics that shape youth sexuality and gender studies noted above.

Additionally, my academic career has introduced competing interests and loyalties. I am no longer a volunteer working with fellow queer-youth activists. Now that I'm a researcher trained to build a career of investigating questions of youth, identities, and queer experience, I have a growing responsibility to a community of scholars working on similar topics and to research institutions funding these investigations. I share this glimpse of my own divided interests because of the importance in making explicit the stakeholders invested in scientific research.[3]

There are multiple audiences addressed by the imperative to "do no harm." For the most part, however, scientific practice has been uncomfortable acknowledging the competing interests and political strain always present just offstage. Ethical positions, like political stakes, are often only visible after safeguards break down. In the charge I make above to assess risks honestly, it is imperative to the growth of ethical scientific practice that, as part of that assessment, we make explicit the negotiation of politics rather than continue to pretend science is above the fray. In the case of ethnographic studies of sexuality, the demands of participant observation must be negotiated in a charged political field that sees sexuality as an intimate and always private matter that propriety deems beyond observation and unethical for a researcher to participate in. For my own research, I travel the circles of multi-site ethnography, tracking actors across fields and through technological sites, with an ethical approach that actively draws those met along the way into the research design.

Notes

1. Assembly Bill 537 (originally Senate Bill 101 and Assembly Bill 1001), the California Student Safety and Violence Prevention Act, introduced by Santa Monica Representative Sheila Kuehl in 1995, finally passed in 2000. For more information on the history of the bill, see the GSANetwork website and the history of the network's founder, Carolyn Laub, who played an integral part in the eventual passage of the measure.

2. Eve Kosofsky Sedgwick, in *Epistemology of the Closet* (Berkeley: University of California Press, 1990), points us to such dyads as "heterosexuality/homosexuality," "urbane/provincial," or "in/out" as rich locations for cultural critique (9–11). Colin Johnson unpacks the significance of Sedgwick's arguments more centrally than I do here. See Colin R. Johnson, "Homosexuals in Unexpected Places? An Introduction," *American Studies* 48 (Summer 2007).

3. Raymond Williams defined the "structures of feeling" as "social experiences in solution, as distinct from other social semantic formations which have been precipitated and are more evidently and more immediately available." In Raymond Williams, *Marxism and Literature* (Oxford: Oxford University Press, 1977), 133–34. I use Williams' phrase to capture that sense of the lived experience pushing against the organized expectations of what life should be and feel like, particularly against and within the logics of familiarity that shape the myth of rural spaces. I also have Ann Cvetkovich's "affective communities" in the back of my mind and how they produce the "presence and promise of cultural formations that bring traumatic histories into the public sphere and use accounts of affective experience to transform our sense of what constitutes a public sphere." In Ann Cvetkovich, *An Archive of Feelings: Trauma, Sexuality, and Lesbian Public Cultures*, Series Q (Durham, NC: Duke University Press, 2003), 15.

4. For the most comprehensive collection of studies concerning the limits of social services in rural communities (although not specific to LGBT-identifying youth), see James Donald Smith and Ronald J. Mancoske, eds., *Rural Gays and Lesbians: Building on the Strengths of Communities* (London: Haworth Press, 1997). For sense of the treatment of new media in this literature, see Anthony M. Haag and Franklin K. Chang's essay in this collection, "The Impact of Electronic

Networking on the Lesbian and Gay Community." See also Paul J. Cody and Peter L. Welch, "Rural Gay Men in Northern New England: Life Experiences and Coping Styles," *Journal of Homosexuality* 33, no. 1 (1997): 51–67.

5. See John D'Emilio, *Sexual Politics, Sexual Communities: The Making of a Homosexual Minority in the United States, 1940–1970* (Chicago: University of Chicago Press, 1983); John D'Emilio, "Capitalism and Gay Identity," *Powers of Desire: The Politics of Sexuality*, ed. Ann Barr Snitow, Christine Stansell, and Sharon Thompson (New York: Monthly Review Press, 1983), 100–113. For other accounts that draw on D'Emilio's history of rural to urban migration, see Elizabeth A. Armstrong, *Forging Gay Identity: Organizing Sexuality in San Francisco, 1950–1994* (Chicago: University of Chicago Press, 2002); Nan Alamilla Boyd, *Wide Open Town: A History of Queer San Francisco to 1965* (Berkeley: University of California Press, 2003); Martin Meeker, *Contacts Desired: Gay and Lesbian Communications and Community, 1940s–1970s* (Chicago: University of Chicago Press, 2006); Marcia M. Gallo, *Different Daughters: A History of the Daughters of Bilitis and the Rise of the Lesbian Rights Movement* (New York: Carroll & Graf, 2006). For the global flow of this argument, see Jeffrey Weeks, *Coming Out: Homosexual Politics in Britain from the Nineteenth Century to the Present* (London: Quartet Books, 1979); Barry D. Adam, Jan Willem Duyvendak, and André Krouwel, eds., *The Global Emergence of Gay and Lesbian Politics: National Imprints of a Worldwide Movement* (Philadelphia: Temple University Press, 1998); and Dennis Altman, *Homosexual: Oppression and Liberation* (New York: Outerbridge and Dienstfrey, 1971). For an important critique of this migration from the perspective of African-American laborers of the same period, see Marlon B. Ross, "Beyond the Closet as Raceless Paradigm," in *Black Queer Studies: A Critical Anthology*, ed. E. Patrick Johnson and Mae G. Henderson (Durham, NC: Duke University Press, 2005), 161–89.

6. See Susan Stryker on her cogent analysis of this shift centrally involving homonormative "gender-policing practices" that became an "important mechanism for shaping the landscape of sexual identity community formations described in the major historiographical accounts." In Susan Stryker, "Transgender History, Homonormativity, and Disciplinarity," *Radical History Review* 100 (Winter 2008): 150.

7. George Chauncey, *Gay New York: Gender, Urban Culture, and the Making of the Gay Male World, 1890–1940* (New York: Basic Books, 1994).

8. For more on the intersections of civil rights and gay rights movements, see John D'Emilio, *Lost Prophet: The Life and Times of Bayard Rustin* (Chicago: University of Chicago Press, 2004); see also Barry D. Adam, *The Rise of a Gay and Lesbian Movement*, Social Movements Past and Present (New York: Twayne Publishers, 1995).

9. See Larry P. Gross, *Up from Invisibility: Lesbians, Gay Men, and the Media in America*, Between Men—Between Women (New York: Columbia University

Press, 2001), 21–55. See Martin Meeker's *Contacts Desired* on the use of alternative gay magazines to build up community and particularly the legend of San Francisco as a gay mecca, and Katherine Sender's *Business, Not Politics: The Making of the Gay Market*, Between Men—Women (New York: Columbia University Press, 2004) on the early marketing of gay media.

10. On the links between radical lesbian separatism and gay liberation movement, see Arlene Stein, "Sisters and Queers: The Decentering of Lesbian Feminism," *Socialist Review* 22, no. 1 (1992): 33–55.

11. This is a reference to French philosopher Michel Foucault's argument about how political positions moralize their arguments by making claims to truth and goodness rather than seeing how truth is circulated as a powerful weapon in the political sphere. In Michel Foucault and Colin Gordon, *Power/Knowledge: Selected Interviews and Other Writings, 1972–1977* (New York: Pantheon Books, 1980), 133. For an excellent articulation of this argument, see Wendy Brown, *States of Injury: Power and Freedom in Late Modernity* (Princeton, NJ: Princeton University Press, 1995), 45.

12. For a concise analysis of feminist critiques of gender as a naturalized category, see Joan W. Scott, "Gender: A Useful Category of Analysis," *American Historical Review* 91, no. 5 (December 1986): 1053–75; and Monique Wittig, "One Is Not Born a Woman," in *The Lesbian and Gay Studies Reader*, ed. Henry Abelove, Michèle Aina Barale, and David M. Halperin, 103–109 (New York: Routledge, 1993).

13. Esther Newton, *Cherry Grove, Fire Island: Sixty Years in America's First Gay and Lesbian Town* (Boston: Beacon Press, 1993); Ellen Lewin, *Lesbian Mothers: Accounts of Gender in American Culture*, Anthropology of Contemporary Issues (Ithaca, NY: Cornell University Press, 1993); Marc Stein, *City of Sisterly and Brotherly Loves: Lesbian and Gay Philadelphia, 1945–1972*, Chicago Series on Sexuality, History, and Society (Chicago: University of Chicago Press, 2000); Martin F. Manalansan IV, *Global Divas: Filipino Gay Men in the Diaspora*, Perverse Modernities (Durham, NC: Duke University Press, 2003); David Valentine, *Imagining Transgender: An Ethnography of a Category* (Durham, NC: Duke University Press, 2007); Martin B. Duberman, *Stonewall* (New York: Dutton, 1993); Elizabeth Lapovsky Kennedy and Madeline D. Davis, *Boots of Leather, Slippers of Gold: The History of a Lesbian Community* (New York: Routledge, 1993); and Lillian Faderman, *Odd Girls and Twilight Lovers: A History of Lesbian Life in Twentieth-Century America*, Between Men—Between Women (New York: Columbia University Press, 1991).

14. Kath Weston noted in her review of the growth in anthropological studies of same-sex desire and gender variance that precisely the rise of a "gay movement in the United States, combined with the efforts of a hardy few who risked not only censure but their careers, allowed homosexuality to move to the center of scholarly attention.". In Kath Weston, "Lesbian/Gay Studies in the House of

Anthropology," *Annual Review of Anthropology* 22 (1993): 339. For the most recent review of gay and lesbian studies in anthropology, see Tom Boellstorff, "Queer Studies in the House of Anthropology," *Annual Review of Anthropology* 36 (2007): 2.1–2.19.

15. Those familiar with the work of Judith Butler, particularly *Gender Trouble: Feminism and the Subversion of Identity*, Thinking Gender(New York: Routledge, 1990), will recognize the central role Newton's work played in understanding the performative rather than prediscursive nature of subjectivity, experiences of identity and the self. Butler, building on Newton's work and that of J. L. Austin, as well as a Foucauldian understanding of the self, argued that social categories of personhood, such as homosexual or heterosexual and man or woman, are the products of "a set of repeated acts within a highly rigid regulatory frame that congeal over time to produce the appearance of substance" (43). Butler cites Newton's *Mother Camp: Female Impersonators in America* (Englewood Cliffs, NJ: Prentice Hall, 1972) as fundamental to her own example of drag and transgender embodiment as examples of the performativity required to produce a gendered body. For productive critiques and elaborations of Butler's arguments, see Jay Prosser, *Second Skins: The Body Narratives of Transsexuality*, Gender and Culture (New York: Columbia University Press, 1998).

16. For a representative sample of this scholarship, see Richard G. Parker, *Bodies, Pleasures, and Passions: Sexual Culture in Contemporary Brazil* (Boston: Beacon Press, 1991); G. W. Dowsett, *Practicing Desire: Homosexual Sex in the Era of AIDS* (Stanford, CA: Stanford University Press, 1996); Ralph Bolton, "Mapping Terra Incognita: Sex Research for AIDS Prevention—an Urgent Agenda for the 1990s," in *The Time of AIDS: Social Analysis, Theory, and Method*, ed. Gilbert H. Herdt and S. Lindenbaum, 124–58 (Newbury Park, CA: Sage, 1991); John M. Carrier, "Sexual Behavior and the Spread of AIDS in Mexico," in *The AIDS Pandemic*, ed. Ralph Bolton, 37–50 (New York: Gordon and Breach, 1989); Gilbert H. Herdt and S. Lindenbaum, eds., *The Time of AIDS: Social Analysis, Theory, and Method* (Newbury Park, CA: Sage, 1991); and Ralph Bolton, ed., *The AIDS Pandemic* (New York: Gordon and Breach, 1989). For a review of more recent contributions to this body of work, see Richard G. Parker, "Sexuality, Culture, and Power in HIV/AIDS Research," *Annual Review of Anthropology* 30 (2001): 163–79. For exemplary work that followed Parker's review, see Héctor Carrillo, *The Night Is Young: Sexuality in Mexico in the Time of AIDS*, Worlds of Desire (Chicago: University of Chicago Press, 2002); and Mark Padilla, *Caribbean Pleasure Industry: Tourism, Sexuality, and AIDS in the Dominican Republic*, Worlds of Desire (Chicago: University of Chicago Press, 2007).

17. For a thorough review of the more recent literature in anthropology, see Boellstorff, "Queer Studies in the House of Anthropology," 2.1–2.19.

18. See Evelyn Blackwood, "Tombois in West Sumatra: Constructing Masculinity and Erotic Desire," *Cultural Anthropology* 13, no. 4 (1998): 491–521; and

Megan Sinnott, *Toms and Dees: Transgender Identity and Female Same-Sex Relationships in Thailand* (Honolulu: University of Hawai'i Press, 2004).

19. See Tom Boellstorff, "Dubbing Culture: Indonesian Gay and Lesbi Subjectivities and Ethnography in an Already Globalized World," *American Ethnologist* 30, no. 2 (2003): 225–42; and Tom Boellstorff, *The Gay Archipelago: Sexuality and Nation in Indonesia* (Princeton, NJ: Princeton University Press, 2005), 58–88.

20. As Manalansan puts it, interactions of norms and locations produce "alternative sex and gender identities and practices." In Manalansan, *Global Divas*, 8.

21. For more critical takes on the visibility of transgender-identifying people, see Victor Silverman and Susan Stryker's film *Screaming Queens: The Riot at Compton's Cafeteria* (San Francisco: Frameline, 2005), and David Valentine's book *Imagining Transgender*.

22. See Williams Hanks' article "Pierre Bourdieu and the Practices of Language" on the saliency of the concept of habitus, in *Annual Review of Anthropology* 34 (2005): 67–83.

23. James Clifford, "On Ethnographic Allegory," in *Writing Culture: The Poetics and Politics of Ethnography: A School of American Research Advanced Seminar*, ed. James Clifford and George E. Marcus, 98–121 (Berkeley: University of California Press, 1986).

24. See Dennis Altman, "Marginality on the Tropic," in *De-Centring Sexualities: Politics and Representations Beyond the Metropolis*, ed. Richard Phillips, Diane Watt, and David Shuttleton, 37–48 (London: Routledge, 2000); Will Fellows, *Farm Boys: Lives of Gay Men from the Rural Midwest* (Madison: University of Wisconsin Press, 1996); Smith and Mancoske, eds., *Rural Gays and Lesbians*; and Jerry Lee Kramer, "Bachelor Farmers and Spinsters: Gay and Lesbian Identities and Communities in Rural North Dakota," in *Mapping Desire: Geographies of Sexualities*, ed. David Bell and Gill Valentine, 200–213 (London: Routledge, 1995). The anthology *De-Centring Sexualities: Politics and Representations Beyond the Metropolis*, ed. Richard Phillips, Diane Watt, and David Shuttleton (London: Routledge, 2000),offers a more complicated treatment of the ways queer rural sexualities are imagined, but these efforts draw from literary criticism rather than sociological approaches to the topic.

25. Kath Weston, "Get Thee to a Big City: Sexual Imaginary and the Great Gay Migration," *GLQ: Gay and Lesbian Quarterly* 2 (1995): 253–77. See also her revision of this essay in her book *Long Slow Burn: Sexuality and Social Science* (New York: Routledge, 1998), 29–56.

26. Halberstam notes how this binary "can also shed light on the strangely similar constructions of nonmetropolitan sexualities in other parts of the world" and cites the important work of scholars, particularly Gayatri Gopinath, *Impossible Desires: Queer Diasporas and South Asian Public Cultures*, Perverse Modernities (Durham, NC: Duke University Press, 2005); Manalansan, *Global Divas*; and M. Jacqui Alexander, *Pedagogies of Crossing: Meditations on Feminism, Sexual*

Politics, Memory, and the Sacred, Perverse Modernities (Durham, NC: Duke University Press, 2005).

27. See the following scholarship that examines queer sexuality and rurality from historical, literary, and human geographical disciplinary perspectives. David Bell and Gill Valentine, eds., *Mapping Desire: Geographies of Sexualities* (London: Routledge, 1995); David Bell, "Eroticizing the Rural," in *De-Centring Sexualities*, 83–101; Walter T. Boulden, "Gay Men Living in a Rural Environment," *Journal of Gay and Lesbian Social Services* 12 (2001): 63–75; C. L. Barney Dews and Carolyn Leste Law, *Out in the South* (Philadelphia: Temple University Press, 2001); Cody and Welch, "Rural Gay Men in Northern New England," 51–67; Robert J. Corber, "Queer Regionalism," *American Literary History* 11, no. 2 (Summer 1999): 391–402; Vicki Lea Eldridge, Lisa Mack, and Eric Swank, "Explaining Comfort with Homosexuality in Rural America," *Journal of Homosexuality* 51, no. 2 (2006): 39–56; Fellows, *Farm Boys*; Ann Forsyth, "Out in the Valley," *International Journal of Urban and Regional Research* 21, no. 1 (1997): 36–60; Haag and Chang, "The Impact of Electronic Networking," 83–94; Scott Herring, "Caravaggio's Rednecks," *GLQ: A Journal of Gay and Lesbian Studies* 12, no. 2 (2006): 217–36; John Howard, "Place and Movement in Gay American History: A Case from the Post–World War II South," in *Creating a Place for Ourselves: Lesbian, Gay, and Bisexual Community Histories*, ed. Brett Beemyn, 211–26 (New York: Routledge, 1997); John Howard, *Men Like That: A Southern Queer History* (Chicago: Chicago University Press, 1999); Kenneth Kirkey and Ann Forsyth, "Men in the Valley: Gay Male Life on the Suburban-Rural Fringe," *Journal of Rural Studies* 17 (2001); Linda McCarthy, "Poppies in a Wheat Field," *Journal of Homosexuality* 39 (2000); Ramona Oswald, "Who Am I in Relation to Them? Gay, Lesbian, and Queer People Leave the City to Attend Rural Family Weddings," *Journal of Family Issues* 23, no. 3 (2002); T. Piontek, "Kinging in the Heartland; or, the Power of Marginality," *Journal of Homosexuality* 43, no. 3–4 (2002): 125–43; James T. Sears, *Rebels, Rubyfruit, and Rhinestones: Queering Space in the Stonewall South* (New Brunswick, NJ: Rutgers University Press, 2001); Darren Smith and Louise Holt, "Lesbian Migrants in the Gentrified Valley and Other Geographies of Rural Gentrification," *Journal of Rural Studies* 21, no. 3 (2005): 313–22; Kathleen Tiemann, Sally Kennedy, and Myrna Haga, "Rural Lesbians' Strategies for Coming Out to Healthcare Professionals," *Journal of Lesbian Studies* 2, no. 1 (1998): 61–75; Kathleen Tiemann, "Why Is Their Picture on the Wedding Page? A Rural Community Responds to a Union Announcement," *Journal of Homosexuality* 51, no. 4 (2006): 119–35; David Knapp Whittier, "Social Conflict Among 'Gay' Men in a Small(er) Southern Town," in *Rural Gays and Lesbians: Building on the Strengths of Communities*, 53–71 (New York: Haworth Press, 1997); Diane Wysocki, "'Growing Up Gay in Rural Nebraska,' or a Feminist Relocates to the Midwest," *Sexuality and Culture* 4, no. 3 (2000): 57–64; David Bell and Gill Valentine, "Queer Country: Rural Lesbian and Gay

Lives," *Journal of Rural Studies* 11, no. 2 (1995): 113–22; David Bell, "Farm Boys and Wild Men: Rurality, Masculinity, and Homosexuality," *Rural Sociology* 65, no. 4 (2000): 547–61; Jean Brashear, "The Friday Night Bunch: A Lesbian Community in West Texas," *Journal of Lesbian Studies* 9, no. 1 (2005): 73–80; Judith Halberstam, *In a Queer Time and Place: Transgender Bodies, Subcultural Lives, Sexual Cultures* (New York: New York University Press, 2005); and Gill Valentine, *From Nowhere to Everywhere: Lesbian Geographies* (New York: Harrington Park Press, 2000).

28. Manuel Castells, *The City and the Grassroots: A Cross-Cultural Theory of Urban Social Movements* (Berkeley: University of California Press, 1983); Larry Knopp, "Some Theoretical Implications of Gay Involvement in an Urban Land Market," *Political Geography Quarterly* 9 (1990): 337–52; Larry Knopp, "Exploiting the Rent-Gap: The Theoretical Significance of Using Illegal Appraisal Schemes to Encourage Gentrification in New Orleans," *Urban Geography* 11 (1990): 48–64; Larry Knopp, "Sexuality and Urban Space: A Framework for Analysis," in *Mapping Desire*, 149–64; and Martin P. Levine, "Gay Ghetto," in *Gay Men: The Sociology of Male Homosexuality*, ed. Martin P. Levine, 182–204 (New York: Harper & Row, 1979).

29. Phillips, Watt, and Shuttleton, eds., *De-Centring Sexualities*.

30. See Martin Meeker, *Contacts Desired*. This is, to date, the only book-length analysis of communication on the formation of gay and lesbian communities. But it focuses primarily on flow of information to and from the urban space of the San Francisco Bay Area.

31. Larry P. Gross, "Foreword," in *Queer Online: Media, Technology, and Sexuality*, ed. Kate O'Riordan and David J. Phillips, ix (New York: Peter Lang, 2007).

32. As media scholar Steve Jones recently argued, that the Internet "comes to us at a screen's remove should not remove from our consideration the realities (socially, politically, economically, or otherwise constructed) within which those who use it live and within which the hardware and software, markets and marketing operate" (Steve Jones, "Foreword: Dreams of Fields: Possible Trajectories of Internet Studies," in *Critical Cyberculture Studies*, ed. David Silver and Adrienne Massanari, xv (New York: New York University Press, 2006).

33. For historical and cultural work on the relationship between moral panics and technologies, see Kirsten Drotner, "Modernity and Media Panics," in *Media Cultures: Reappraising Transnational Media*, ed. Michael Skovmand and Kim Christian Schrøder, 42–62 (London: Routledge, 1992); David E. Nye, *Electrifying America: Social Meanings of a New Technology, 1880–1940* (Cambridge: MIT Press, 1990); Carolyn Marvin, *When Old Technologies Were New: Thinking About Electric Communication in the Late Nineteenth Century* (New York: Oxford University Press, 1988); and Nicholas Sammond, *Babes in Tomorrowland: Walt Disney and the Making of the American Child, 1930–1960* (Durham, NC: Duke University Press, 2005).

34. See Fred Turner's *From Counterculture to Cyberculture: Stewart Brand, the Whole Earth Network, and the Rise of Digital Utopianism* (Chicago: University of Chicago Press, 2006); and James W. Carey's seminal work on the aura of the sublime introduced by the telegraph, in "Technology and Ideology: The Case of the Telegraph," in *Communication as Culture: Essays on Media and Society*, ed. James W. Carey (Boston: Unwin Hyman, 1989), 201–31.

35. Gregory A. Waller, "Situating Motion Pictures in the Prenickelodeon Period: Lexington, Kentucky, 1897–1906," *Velvet Light Trap* 29 (Spring 1990): 12–28. For discussions of the contemporary connection between protection of minors and anxieties over media consumption, see, for example, Ellen Seiter, *Sold Separately: Children and Parents in Consumer Culture*, Rutgers Series in Communications, Media, and Culture (New Brunswick, NJ: Rutgers University Press, 1993); Judith Levine, *Harmful to Minors: The Perils of Protecting Children from Sex* (Minneapolis: University of Minnesota Press, 2002); and Henry Jenkins' seminal collection on the culture of childhood, *The Children's Culture Reader* (New York: New York University Press, 1998).

36. For an overview of ethnographic approaches to media, see the comprehensive edited volumes of Faye D. Ginsburg, Lila Abu-Lughod, and Brian Larkin, *Media Worlds: Anthropology on New Terrain* (Berkeley: University of California Press, 2002); and Kelly Michelle Askew and Richard R. Wilk, *The Anthropology of Media: A Reader*, Blackwell Readers in Anthropology, vol. 1, no 2 (Malden, MA: Blackwell, 2002). For a comprehensive and prescient summary of reception or audience studies in media research, see Janet Staiger, *Media Reception Studies* (New York: New York University Press, 2005). Each of these volumes includes examples of the approaches taken by each discipline with surprisingly sparse interdisciplinary collaboration of conversation.

37. Arguably this is less an issue among critically trained anthropologists and more an anxiety anthropologists of the media express as they see non-anthropologists use the tools of ethnography. For a critique speaking to this concern, see Daniel Miller and Don Slater, *The Internet: An Ethnographic Approach* (Oxford: Berg, 2000).

38. For exemplary scholarship taking ethnographic approaches to young people's media engagements, see Ellen Seiter, *Television and New Media Audiences*, Oxford Television Studies (Oxford: Clarendon Press, 1999); Ellen Seiter, *The Internet Playground: Children's Access, Entertainment, and Mis-Education*, Popular Culture & Everyday Life (New York: Peter Lang, 2005); Sonia M. Livingstone, *Young People and New Media: Childhood and the Changing Media Environment* (London: Sage, 2002); and Sonia M. Livingstone, "Taking Risky Opportunities in Youthful Content Creation: Teenagers' Use of Social Networking Sites for Intimacy, Privacy and Self-Expression," *New Media and Society* 10, no. 3 (2008): 392–411.

39. Lisa Duggan suggests just such an approach in her influential essay "Making It Perfectly Queer," *Socialist Review* 22, no. 1 (1992): 11–31. Duggan cites (on

22) Donna Haraway's 1985 reference to feminist Chela Sandoval's use of the notion of "oppositional consciousness" to construct identities that resisted naturalization but sought, instead, a foundation of coalitional politics built through common cause, in Haraway's "A Manifesto for Cyborgs: Science, Technology, and Socialist Feminism in the 1980s," *Socialist Review* 15, no. 2 (March–April 1985): 65–108.

40. For a comprehensive, exhaustive review of reception studies and the limits of media-effects scholarship, see Staiger, *Media Reception Studies*; and David Gauntlett, *Moving Experiences: Media Effects and Beyond* (Eastleigh, UK: John Libbey, 2005).

41. This is less a critique of Sherry Turkle's work than a critique of how it was taken up—mistakenly, I believe—to support a clear divide between online and offline experiences. See Sherry Turkle, *Life on the Screen: Identity in the Age of the Internet* (London: Weidenfeld and Nicolson, 1995). For additional critiques and work that pushes against this early trend, see Nancy K. Baym, *Tune In, Log On: Soaps, Fandom, and Online Community*, New Media Cultures (Thousand Oaks, CA: Sage, 2000); Lori Kendall, *Hanging Out in the Virtual Pub: Masculinities and Relationships Online* (Berkeley: University of California Press, 2002); and Nina Wakeford, "Cyberqueer," in *The Cybercultures Reader*, ed. David Bell and Barbara M. Kennedy, 403–15 (London: Routledge, 2000). More recent work that illustrates this critical approach to cyberculture studies includes T. L. Taylor, *Play between Worlds: Exploring Online Game Culture* (Cambridge: MIT Press, 2006); Mia Consalvo, *Cheating: Gaining Advantage in Videogames* (Cambridge: MIT Press, 2007); and Kate O'Riordan and David J. Phillips, eds., *Queer Online: Media Technology & Sexuality*, Digital Formations (New York: Peter Lang, 2007).

42. On this point, see Susan Leigh Star, "The Ethnography of Infrastructure," *American Behavioral Scientist* 43, no. 3 (1999): 377–91; and George E. Marcus, "Ethnography in/of the World System: The Emergence of Multi-Sited Ethnography," *Annual Review of Anthropology* 24 (1995): 95–117.

43. J. David Bolter and Richard Grusin, *Remediation: Understanding New Media* (Cambridge: MIT Press, 2000).

44. See Sonia M. Livingstone, "Taking Risky Opportunities," 392–411. For more on this point and a critique of the literature in media studies that attempts to maintain this divide, see Maria Bakardjieva, *Internet Society: The Internet in Everyday Life* (London: Sage, 2005); and Roger Silverstone, "Domesticating Domestication: Reflections on the Life of a Concept," in *Domestication of Media and Technology*, ed. Thomas Berker, Maren Hartmann, Yves Punie, and Katie Ward, 229–48 (Maidenhead, UK: Open University Press, 2006).

45. My use of the word "community" is meant to signal agreement with what sociologist Stephen O. Murray theorized as the "quasi-ethnic" quality of gay and lesbian urban communities that reproduce cultural and social institutions through the scaffolding friendship networks, political will, and other features he

characterizes as aspects of gay and lesbian community. In Stephen O. Murray, "The Institutional Elaboration of a Quasi-Ethnic Community," *International Review of Modern Sociology* 9 (1979): 165–78. See David Woolwine's elaboration of Murray's argument for a more thorough discussion of why the use of community vs. "ghetto" or enclave is particularly important. In David Woolwine, "Community in Gay Male Experience and Moral Discourse," *Journal of Homosexuality* 38, no. 4 (2000): 5–37. On the strategic use of identity by gay and lesbian politics, see Steven Epstein, "Gay Politics, Ethnic Identity: The Limits of Social Constructionism," *Socialist Review* 93/94 (1987): 9–54.

46. On the significance and controversy concerning the removal of homosexuality from the Diagnostic and Statistical Manual (DSM) of the American Psychiatric Association and the replacement of the designation Gender Identity Disorder within a short number of years, see Geoffrey C. Bowker and Susan Leigh Star, *Sorting Things Out: Classification and Its Consequences*, Inside Technology (Cambridge: MIT Press, 1999); Ira B. Pauly, "Terminology and Classification of Gender Identity Disorders," in *Gender Dysphoria: Interdisciplinary Approaches in Clinical Management*, ed. Walter O. Bockting and Eli Coleman, 1–14 (New York: Haworth Press, 1992); John P. De Cecco, *Gay Personality and Sexual Labeling* (New York: Harrington Park Press, 1984); Dan Karasic and Jack Drescher, *Sexual and Gender Diagnoses of the Diagnostic and Statistical Manual (DSM): A Reevaluation* (New York: Haworth Press, 2005); and Frederick Suppe, "Classifying Sexual Disorders: The Diagnostic and Statistical Manual of the American Psychiatric Association," *Journal of Homosexuality* 9, no. 4 (1984): 9–28. It seems critical to note that the history of these two shifts in the medicalizing of sexuality and gender interlock.

47. Ritch C. Savin-Williams, *The New Gay Teenager*, Adolescent Lives, no. 3 (Cambridge: Harvard University Press, 2005).

48. Erik H. Erikson, *Childhood and Society* (New York: W.W. Norton, 1950); and Erik H. Erikson, *Identity: Youth and Crisis* (New York: W.W. Norton, 1968).

49. See Savin-Williams' review of this literature in *The New Gay Teenager* (49–92). See also his earlier essay, Ritch C. Savin-Williams, "A Critique of Research on Sexual-Minority Youths," *Journal of Adolescence* 24 (2001): 5–13.

50. See Janice M. Irvine's observation regarding the statistical "making up [of] children," in *Talk About Sex: The Battles over Sex Education in the United States* (Berkeley: University of California Press, 2002), 108–11.

51. See Audrey Olsen Faulkner and Ann Lindsey, "Grassroots Meet Homophobia: A Rocky Mountain Success Story," *Journal of Gay & Lesbian Social Services* 16, no. 3/4 (2004): 113–28; Colin Flint, *Spaces of Hate: Geographies of Discrimination and Intolerance in the U.S.A.* (New York: Routledge, 2004); and Carol A. Snively, "Building Community-Based Alliances between GLBTQQA Youth and Adults in Rural Settings," *Journal of Gay & Lesbian Social Services* 16, no. 3/4 (2004): 99–112.

52. For a representative sample of studies that approach identity as a sociological construction, see Anselm L. Strauss, *Mirrors and Masks: The Search for Identity* (Glencoe, IL: Free Press, 1959); Anthony Giddens, *Modernity and Self-Identity: Self and Society in the Late Modern Age* (Stanford, CA: Stanford University Press, 1991); George Herbert Mead and Charles W. Morris, *Mind, Self & Society from the Standpoint of a Social Behaviorist* (Chicago: University of Chicago Press, 1934); and Erving Goffman, *The Presentation of Self in Everyday Life* (Garden City, NY: Doubleday, 1959). Specific studies of youth identity include early studies by Margaret Mead, *Coming of Age in Samoa; a Psychological Study of Primitive Youth for Western Civilization* (New York: Blue Ribbon Books, 1932); and William Foote Whyte, *Street Corner Society; the Social Structure of an Italian Slum* (Chicago: University of Chicago Press, 1943). For studies specifically dealing with the career of homosexuals, see Laud Humphreys, *Tearoom Trade: Impersonal Sex in Public Places*, Observations (Chicago: Aldine, 1970); and later on lesbian identities, Barbara Ponse, *Identities in the Lesbian World: The Social Construction of Self*, Contributions in Sociology, no. 28 (Westport, CT: Greenwood Press, 1978). I also draw heavily on the more recent work of Wayne Brekhus' *Peacocks, Chameleons, Centaurs: Gay Suburbia and the Grammar of Social Identity* (Chicago: University of Chicago Press, 2003) and his concept of suburban gay male identities as transmutable categories that can serve as actions, objects, or characteristics depending on the social situation. I hope this project builds a serviceable bridge between interactionist/constructionist perspectives on identity and poststructuralist perspectives on subjectivity. For the latter, the self is much less coherent and more of a "consequence" of discourse and power. Arguably, an interactionist approach and conceptualization of identity makes a bit more room for agency and resistance. On this point, see Jane Flax, *Thinking Fragments: Psychoanalysis, Feminism, and Postmodernism in the Contemporary West* (Berkeley: University of California Press, 1990), 192–221.

53. For a representative sample of this literature, see Patricia A. Adler and Peter Adler, *Peer Power: Preadolescent Culture and Identity* (New Brunswick, NJ: Rutgers University Press, 1998); William A. Corsaro, *The Sociology of Childhood*, Sociology for a New Century (Thousand Oaks, CA: Pine Forge Press, 2005); Gary Alan Fine and Kent L. Sandstrom, *Knowing Children: Participant Observation with Minors*, Qualitative Research Methods 15 (Newbury Park, CA: Sage, 1988); Allison James, Chris Jenks, and Alan Prout, *Theorizing Childhood* (New York: Teachers College Press, 1998); Nancy Lesko, *Act Your Age! The Cultural Construction of Adolescence*, Critical Social Thought (New York: RoutledgeFalmer, 2001); and Jens Qvortrup, *Childhood Matters: Social Theory, Practice, and Politics*, Public Policy and Social Welfare (Aldershot, UK: Avebury, 1994).

54. Qvortrup, *Childhood Matters*.

55. For a recent and thorough review of this literature and its implications for youth research, see Amy L. Best's introduction to *Representing Youth: Methodological Issues in Critical Youth Studies* (New York: New York University Press, 2007), 1–38.

56. Many readers will recognize that this approach to identity is indebted to the work of Judith Butler and her use of Esther Newton's notion of performance as iterative acts that produce the chimera of a stable identity, in *Gender Trouble*. See also Barbara H. Smith's work on the social construction of personal narrative, in "Narrative Versions, Narrative Theories," in *On Narrative*, ed. W. J. Thomas Mitchell, 209–32 (Chicago: University of Chicago Press, 1981).

57. For an overview of the seminal work of Roland Barthes on mythology and cultural representations, see Roland Barthes, "Myth Today," in *Media and Cultural Studies: Keywords*, ed. Meenakshi Gigi Durham and Douglas Kellner, 122–28 (Malden, MA: Blackwell, 1999). For Barthes' extended argument, see *Mythologies*, trans. Annette Lavers (New York: Hill and Wang, 1972).

58. For a rich and poignant description of the freedom and mobility cars represent in youth culture, see Amy L. Best, *Fast Cars, Cool Rides: The Accelerating World of Youth and Their Cars* (New York: New York University Press, 2006). Best, quoting James Kunstler, notes that "the car promises 'liberation from the daily bondage of place' but goes on to suggest that it is the 'freedom of movement between places that perhaps matters even more'" (138). In the case of rural LGBT-identifying and questioning youth, I think it is a matter of moving between but actually expanding a sense of what counts as one's daily place that takes precedence. I will return to this issue in subsequent chapters.

59. For a summary of what constitutes the ARC and a demographic overview of this area that encompassed my fieldsites, see Kelvin Pollard, "Appalachia at the Millennium: An Overview of Results from Census 2000," Washington D.C.: Appalachian Regional Commission/Population Reference Bureau, 2003.

60. There is a small but rich literature on sociocultural aspects of this region sometimes referred to as Appalachia. See Paul J. Cloke's review of the cultural turn in rural studies away from an area studies or strictly political economic treatment of this area, in "Country Backwater to Virtual Village? Rural Studies and 'the Cultural Turn,'" *Journal of Rural Studies* 13, no. 4 (1997): 367–75. For analysis of the most recent Census report of the Appalachian Regional Commission, see Phillip J. Obermiller, "Introduction to Appalachia Counts: The Region in the 2000 Census, a Special Issue of the Journal of Appalachian Studies," *Journal of Appalachian Studies* 10, no. 3 (2004): 245–54. See also Richard Couto's important work challenging the easy distinctions and homogenization of this area, in Richard A. Couto, "Appalachia," in *Appalachia: Social Context Past and Present*, ed. Phillip J. Obermiller and Michael E. Maloney (Dubuque, IA: Kendall/Hunt, 2002). In the field of rural sociology, see the work of Dwight B. Billings and Kathleen M. Blee, *The Road to Poverty: The Making of Wealth and Hardship in Appalachia* (Cambridge: Cambridge University Press, 2000); Dwight B. Billings and Ann Tickamyer, "Uneven Development in Appalachia," in *Forgotten Places: Uneven Development in Rural America*, ed. Thomas A. Lyson and William W. Falk, Rural America (Lawrence: University Press of Kansas, 1993), 7–29;

Dwight B. Billings, Gurney Norman, and Katherine Ledford, eds., *Confronting Appalachian Stereotypes: Back Talk from an American Region* (Lexington: University Press of Kentucky, 1999); Mary K. Anglin, "Engendering the Struggle: Women's Labor and Traditions of Resistance in Rural Southern Appalachia," in *Fighting Back in Appalachia: Traditions of Resistance and Change*, ed. Stephen L. Fisher (Philadelphia: Temple University Press, 1993), 263–82; Kenneth L. Deavers and Robert A. Hoppe, "Overview of the Rural Poor in the 1980s," in *Rural Poverty in America*, ed. Cynthia Duncan, 3–20 (New York: Auburn House, 1992); Emery N. Castle and Clifton Wharton Jr., eds., *The Changing American Countryside: Rural People and Places* (Lawrence: University Press of Kansas, 1995); J. W. Williamson, *Hillbillyland: What the Movies Did to the Mountains and What the Mountains Did to the Movies* (Chapel Hill: University of North Carolina Press, 1995); Paul J. Cloke and Jo Little, eds., *Contested Countryside Cultures: Otherness, Marginalisation and Rurality* (London: Routledge, 1997). In my case, I am working with one of the more racially and socioeconomically consolidated areas, and still there is much diversity in how individuals and families cope with the poverty and whiteness that shapes their worlds. I resist using "Appalachia" as a specific place marker to describe the areas where I conducted my research in an effort to avoid suggesting any clear divisions between "Appalachia" and the other communities youth traveled to in and beyond its imagined borders. Tethering this project to a specific area works against illustrating the interdependencies and boundary-crossings that constitute both rural and metropolitan communities. At the same time, there are political and economic reasons for rural sociologists and economists to study the ARC as a unified area. I do not intend to dismiss its productiveness as an analytical concept to those scholars but to recognize its limits for this project.

61. Marcus, "Ethnography on/of the World System," 95–117.

62. See Kathleen Stewart, *A Space on the Side of the Road: Cultural Poetics in an "Other" America* (Princeton, NJ: Princeton University Press, 1996); Allen W. Batteau, *The Invention of Appalachia*, Anthropology of Form and Meaning (Tucson: University of Arizona Press, 1990); and Henry D. Shapiro's landmark study, *Appalachia on Our Mind: The Southern Mountains and Mountaineers in the American Consciousness, 1870–1920* (Chapel Hill: University of North Carolina Press, 1978). Most of these accounts carry forward James Agee's efforts in his 1941 book *Let Us Now Praise Famous Men* to present the sheer weight of detail to, as Kathleen Stewart says, "be read not for its truth value and congruence with fact but for its tense, halting evocation of difference and desire at the very heart of a doubly constructed 'real' or the very impossibility of representing the harsh realities of poverty and destitution Agee found" (Stewart, *A Space on the Side of the Road*, 23).

63. The Oxford English Dictionary (2008) defines queer as "strange, odd, peculiar, eccentric. Also: of questionable character; suspicious, dubious." I am using

the term "queer" throughout this discussion in this sense but also as a moniker for lesbian, gay, bisexual, trans, and questioning identities, as these were the non-normative identities in which I was most interested and able to access. While "queer" certainly retains its own identity currency among some youth, the majority of young people in this study did not identify as "queer."

64. See Wilburn Hayden, "Appalachian Diversity: African-America, Hispanic/Latino, and Other Populations," *Journal of Appalachian Studies* 10, no. 3 (2004): 293–306.

65. I did not assume face-to-face interviews were "more" real than e-mail or chat-based interviews. On the complexities of multi-sited ethnographies that involve media, see Star, "The Ethnography of Infrastructure," 377–91, and Nicole Green, "Disrupting the Field: Virtual Technologies and 'Multisited' Ethnographic Methods," *American Behavioral Scientist* 43, no. 3 (1999): 409–21. In my case, my interest was seeing the context in which new media—including e-mail—were used, so I focused on engaging with youth who I thought I would be able to meet in person and particularly meet in their hometowns. This touches on the broader issue of the role of new media as a tool for ethnographic fieldwork, but that is outside the scope of this discussion. See the Appendix for additional methodological notes.

66. For a discussion of identities as verbs, nouns, and adjectives that, through variations of "duration, durability, and dominance," mark and perform identities differently, see Wayne Brekhus' ethnography of suburban gay men, *Peacocks, Chameleons, and Centaurs.*

67. For prescient critiques of homonormativity in gay and lesbian political and social organizing, see Lisa Duggan, *The Twilight of Equality? Neoliberalism, Cultural Politics, and the Attack on Democracy* (Boston: Beacon Press, 2003); Judith Halberstam's discussion of "homo-normative" gender codes that specifically call out the dismissal of masculine women by gays, lesbians, and straight people alike, in *Female Masculinity* (9); and Susan Stryker's more recent genealogy of homonormativity and the use of it to dismiss different embodiments and modes of knowing in gay and lesbian scholarship, in "Transgender History, Homonormativity, and Disciplinarity," 145–57.

68. My own understanding of community draws heavily on the notion as developed by anthropologist Cheleen Mahar in her study of rural New Zealanders, in "On the Moral Economy of Country Life," *Journal of Rural Studies* 7, no. 4 (1991): 363–72. Mahar's concept of community draws on British sociological and anthropological studies of rural communities that configure community as a "notion of belonging [to] a social space in which various households are linked by kin, social and economic ties, a sense of a shared history and expectations of certain behavior, and a cycle of religious and social activities" (363–64). But Mahar's insights from the villagers with whom she worked more specifically defined rural communities in terms of individuals' "self-conception in relation to each other

and to the various social and economic associations which tied them to this locality, as well as by their sense of difference from other people and communities
which in their view clearly lay 'outside'" (363).

69. I am referencing the critical work of theorist Benedict Anderson in my
citation of "imagined communities." Anderson used his study of the rise of nationalism in Indonesia and its links to print culture, particularly nationally circulated newspapers at the turn of the 19th century, to argue the centrality of what
he called "print capitalism"—the commercial mass mediation and distribution of
information where face-to-face interaction is not possible—to the construction
of a shared sense of identity as a citizen of a nation-state. In Benedict Anderson,
Imagined Communities: Reflections on the Origin and Spread of Nationalism (London: Verso, 1991).

NOTES TO CHAPTER 2

1. Berea College, founded in 1855, was the first coeducational, integrated college opened in the South. Kentuckian Cassius M. Clay donated the land for the
founding of the ecumenical Christian private college, and Berea's first president,
Reverend John G. Fee, recruited faculty from nearby Oberlin College to bring
an ethic of emancipation and equality to the state despite (or in response to) the
college's proximity to supporters of slavery in Madison County. Berea College's
mission continues a tradition of extending free education to admitted students
with the goal of educating working poor, academically promising Appalachians.

2. For a discussion of the effort to pass Kentucky's Fairness Bill and its links
to local organizing in Louisville, Kentucky, see Melanie D. Otis, "One Community's Path to Greater Social Justice: Building on Earlier Successes," *Journal of
Gay & Lesbian Social Services* 16, no. 3/4 (2004): 17–33; and Erlene Grise-Owens,
Jeff Vessels, and Larry W. Owens, "Organizing for Change: One City's Journey
toward Justice," *Journal of Gay & Lesbian Social Services* 16, no. 3/4 (2004): 1–15.

3. On the politics and rhetoric of family values that anchor the analysis in
this chapter, see the work of Judith Stacey, *In the Name of the Family: Rethinking
Family Values in the Postmodern Age* (Boston: Beacon Press, 1996).

4. Feminist media scholar Suzanna Walters argues any "acceptance" garnered
by gay visibility in the media is "predicated on a comparative model: the straight
person (or character in a film or TV show) can only 'accept' the gay person once
he or she has interpreted that person as 'just like me.'" In Suzanna Danuta Walters, *All the Rage: The Story of Gay Visibility in America* (Chicago: University of
Chicago Press, 2001), 16.

5. The notion of disidentifications will be addressed later in the book, draw-
ing on the arguments of queer theorist José Esteban Muñoz in *Disidentifications:
Queers of Color and the Performance of Politics*, Cultural Studies of the Americas
(Minneapolis: University of Minnesota Press, 1999).

6. This is the crux of Walters' argument in *All the Rage*. See also Larry P. Gross, *Up from Invisibility: Lesbians, Gay Men, and the Media in America*, Between Men—Between Women (New York: Columbia University Press, 2001), and his earlier work chronicling the rise in gay visibility in popular media, in Larry P. Gross and James D. Woods, *The Columbia Reader on Lesbians and Gay Men in Media, Society, and Politics*, Between Men—Between Women (New York: Columbia University Press, 1999).

7. Raymond Williams, *The Country and the City* (New York: Oxford University Press, 1973), 96.

8. For a discussion of the "rural idyll" and the nostalgia of rural communities as static serene spaces, see G. E. Mingay, *The Rural Idyll* (London: Routledge, 1989); Raymond Williams, *The Country and the City* (New York: Oxford University Press, 1973); Paul J. Cloke, Terry Marsden, and Patrick H. Mooney, *Handbook of Rural Studies* (London: Sage, 2006); Mark Lawrence, "Heartlands or Neglected Geographies? Liminality, Power and the Hyperreal Rural," *Journal of Rural Studies* 13 (1997): 1–17; Michael Keith and Steve Pile, *Place and the Politics of Identity* (New York: Routledge, 1993); Marilyn Strathern, *Kinship at the Core: An Anthropology of Elmdon, a Village in North-West Essex in the Nineteen-Sixties* (Cambridge: Cambridge University Press, 1981); Keith Halfacree, "Locality and Social Representation: Space, Discourse and Alternative Definitions of the Rural," *Journal of Rural Studies* 9, no. 1 (1993): 23–37; and Jo Little, *Gender and Rural Geography: Identity, Sexuality and Power in the Countryside* (Harlow, UK: Prentice Hall, 2002).

9. Alfred Shuetz specifically exempted "children" from his definition of a stranger as "an adult individual of our times and civilization who tries to be permanently accepted or at least tolerated by the group which he approaches." In Alfred Shuetz, "The Stranger: An Essay in Social Psychology," *American Journal of Sociology* 49, no. 6 (1944): 499. For other sociological discussions of the stranger, see Paul C. P. Siu, "The Sojourner," *American Journal of Sociology* 58, no. 1 (1952): 34–44; Georg Simmel, "The Stranger," in *The Sociology of Georg Simmel*, trans. Kurt H. Wolff, 402–408 (Glencoe, IL: Free Press, 1950); and Zygmunt Bauman, "Making and Unmaking of Strangers," *Thesis Eleven* 43, no.1 (1995): 1–16.

10. For a thorough analyses and persuasive arguments of this point, see Deborah Thorne, Ann Tickamyer, and Mark Thorne. "Poverty and Income in Appalachia," *Journal of Appalachian Studies* 10, no. 3 (2004): 341–58; and Richard A. Couto, *An American Challenge: A Report on Economic Trends and Social Issues in Appalachia* (Dubuque, IA: Kendall/Hunt, 1994).

11. Thorne, Tickamyer, and Thorne, "Poverty and Income in Appalachia," 350.

12. Richard A. Couto, "Appalachia and Market Economics: The Invisible Hand and Its Powerful Arm," *Journal of Appalachian Studies* 10, no. 3 (2004): 407–20. See also Paul J. Cloke, Sarah Johnson, and Jon May, "The Periphery of Care: Emergency Services for Homeless People in Rural Areas," *Journal of Rural Studies* 23 (2007): 387–401.

13. I'm sure Napier would not recognize the Marxist critique of homosexuality as one of the litany of vices produced by the fetishism of capital.

14. All voting data are drawn from the United States Election Project available online at www.elections.gmu.edu and managed by Dr. Michael McDonald, Department of Public and International Affairs, George Mason University.

15. Annual salaries for state Assembly members are bound to $12,000 by a 1949 amendment to the Kentucky state constitution. Legal cases have interpreted this amendment to refer to the 1949 value of the dollar (allowing Assembly members to receive pay raises without having to publicly change the salary cap amendment). The current pay range for senators and representatives is nearly $30,000 to just more than $55,000 per year. Assembly sessions run annually, but they only meet for a maximum of 60 days unless the governor calls for a special session, which Governor Ernie Fletcher did most recently in 2007 to challenge the University of Kentucky's decision to extend health benefits to any adult living with a university employee. This measure effectively provided domestic-partner benefits to same and differently gendered couples. The governor and state Republicans threatened to block university funding if the campus did not reverse the measure, but the proposed legislation failed to make it out of the House Health and Welfare Committee in a 2007 special session.

16. Ann E. Kingsolver, *NAFTA Stories: Fears and Hopes in Mexico and the United States* (Boulder, CO: Lynne Rienner Publishers, 2001); Couto, "Appalachia and Market Economics." For a historical approach to the class structure of these areas, see Pem Davidson Buck, *Worked to the Bone: Race, Class, Power, and Privilege in Kentucky* (New York: Monthly Review Press, 2001).

17. The national average is $43,084. Compared to a national average of 24.4%, the Central Appalachia region where I conducted my research has the lowest college attainment rates, with only 10.5 percent of males and 10.8 percent of females holding a college degree. See Melissa Latimer and Ann M. Oberhauser, "Exploring Gender and Economic Development in Appalachia, *Journal of Appalachian Studies* 10, no. 3 (2004).

18. Jessica Fields, "Normal Queers: Straight Parents Respond to Their Children's 'Coming Out,'" *Symbolic Interaction* 24, no. 2 (2001): 165–87.

19. Fields, drawing on Erving Goffman, defines this as "courtesy stigma" (Fields, "Normal Queers").

NOTES TO CHAPTER 3

1. A fifth GSA existed at Louisville's Atherton High School and had been running for two years at that point, but it was not registered with GLSEN at the time. John Hudson, Atherton's principal, said that despite a few complaints when the group first formed, all criticism had died off.

2. Mark Pitsch, "Gay-Straight Group Wants to Meet at Boyd School; Council Denied Request, Will Reconsider Tonight," *Courier-Journal*, October 28, 2002.

3. See the early work of John Dewey on the relationship between public education and democracy, in *Democracy and Education; an Introduction to the Philosophy of Education* (New York: Macmillan, 1916). For more contemporary debates, see Eamonn Callan, *Creating Citizens: Political Education and Liberal Democracy*, Oxford Political Theory (Oxford: Oxford University Press, 2004); and Kevin McDonough and Walter Feinberg, *Education and Citizenship in Liberal-Democratic Societies: Teaching for Cosmopolitan Values and Collective Identities* (Oxford: Oxford University Press, 2003). For readings on the role of schools in the battles for civil rights, see Danielle S. Allen, *Talking to Strangers: Anxieties of Citizenship since Brown v. Board of Education* (Chicago: University of Chicago Press, 2004); Richard Kluger, *Simple Justice: The History of Brown v. Board of Education and Black America's Struggle for Equality* (New York: Knopf, 2004); and Juan Williams, *Eyes on the Prize: America's Civil Rights Years, 1954–1965* (New York: Penguin Books, 1988). For research on schools as sites of anti-war protest, see Kenneth J. Heineman, *Campus Wars: The Peace Movement at American State Universities in the Vietnam Era* (New York: New York University Press, 1993).

4. For the importance of considering theories of intersectionality—the ways "sexuality is intertwined with the cultural creation of other categories of inequality (race, class, and gender)"—see Joshua Gamson and Dawne Moon, "The Sociology of Sexualities," *Annual Review of Sociology* 30 (2004): 49, and see 52–56 specifically for a review of this literature. See also the work of Kimberle Crenshaw, "Mapping the Margins: Intersectionality, Identity Politics, and Violence against Women of Color," *Stanford Law Review* 43 (1991): 1241–99; Patricia Hill Collins, *Black Feminist Thought: Knowledge, Consciousness, and the Politics of Empowerment* (New York: Routledge, 2000); Gloria T. Hull, Patricia Bell-Scott, and Barbara Smith, *All the Women Are White, All the Blacks Are Men, But Some of Us Are Brave: Black Women's Studies* (Old Westbury, NY: Feminist Press, 1982); Cherríe Moraga and Gloria Anzaldúa, *This Bridge Called My Back: Writings by Radical Women of Color* (New York: Kitchen Table, Women of Color Press, 1983); Joane Nagel, *Race, Ethnicity, and Sexuality: Intimate Intersections, Forbidden Frontiers* (New York: Oxford University Press, 2003); Jyoti Puri, *Woman, Body, Desire in Post-Colonial India: Narratives of Gender and Sexuality* (New York: Routledge, 1999); Kevin J. Mumford, *Interzones: Black/White Sex Districts in Chicago and New York in the Early Twentieth Century*, Popular Cultures, Everyday Lives (New York: Columbia University Press, 1997); Cathy J. Cohen, "Punks, Bulldaggers, and Welfare Queens: The Radical Potential of Queer Politics," *GLQ: A Journal of Gay and Lesbian Studies* 3 (1997): 437–65; and Cathy J. Cohen, *The Boundaries of Blackness: AIDS and the Breakdown of Black Politics* (Chicago: University of Chicago Press, 1999).

5. For a discussion of the role people of color play even where we assume their absence, see the incomparably moving work by Toni Morrison, *Playing in the Dark: Whiteness and the Literary Imagination* (Cambridge: Harvard University Press, 1992).

6. Richard A. Couto, "Appalachia and Market Economics: The Invisible Hand and Its Powerful Arm," *Journal of Appalachian Studies* 10, no. 3 (2004): 407–20.

7. For more discussion of "Sundown Towns," see James W. Loewen, *Sundown Towns: A Hidden Dimension of American Racism* (New York: Touchstone, 2006); and Elliot Jaspin, *Buried in the Bitter Waters: The Hidden History of Racial Cleansing in America* (New York: Basic Books, 2007). For the broader history and legacy of racial violence in the United States, see Christopher Waldrep, *Lynching in America: A History in Documents* (New York: New York University Press, 2006); and Charles P. Henry, *Long Overdue: The Politics of Racial Reparations* (New York: New York University Press, 2007).

8. The year before, the Kentucky Legislature passed the School Improvement Act of 1984. This gave the Kentucky Department of Education the right to take over management of any school district unable to meet a set of minimum performance standards based on matriculation, attendance, and test scores. This state intervention without an exchange of resources to bring failing schools up to speed registered as a betrayal of local stewardship of education and was the last straw for several of the districts that took part in the 1985 suit.

9. Rose v. Council for Better Education, 790 S.W.2d 186, 60 Ed. Law Rep. 1289 (1989).

10. Ibid.

11. This was the first agreement made by a school without a court order. David Buckel, senior attorney for Lambda Legal, a gay- and lesbian-rights advocacy organization, obtained the first agreement made through court petition for a young man in Arkansas.

12. Instead of putting Brad through another year at Somerset High, Gina moved her family just outside the city limits and transferred her son to Pulaski County High School. Drawing more than 900 students from the surrounding towns too small to have their own high schools, Pulaski County High's boundaries of familiarity and difference run along lines of race, class, and county more than any other marker of difference.

13. Brad's case settled out of court in November 2000. The school paid Brad $135,000 toward counseling and a fund for his college education and agreed to adopt a tougher anti-harassment policy that included sexual harassment based on "actual or perceived sexual orientation." See Putman v. Board of Education of Somerset Independent Schools et al., C.A. No. 00-145 for the case's details.

14. According to correspondence dated February 12, 2007, with Shawn Gaylord, director of GLSEN's chapter organizing, GLSEN does not have on record more than the Letter of Intent to form a GLSEN Kentucky Chapter,

submitted to GLSEN National's offices in New York City August 29, 2000. No accreditation applications are on file. The only other document in the file is a "thank you" written to GLSEN-KY for sending in its first quarterly report in 2000. They are fairly positive the Kentucky chapter was never accredited, but GLSEN-KY used GLSEN's official banners in all its functions and was regularly in contact with Brenda Barron, GLSEN's then Southern Field Organizer.

15. From Melinda Miceli, *Standing Out, Standing Together: The Social and Political Impact of Gay-Straight Alliances* (New York: Routledge, 2005), 97, based on interviews with Project 10's founder Virginia Uribe.

16. This 1989 USHHSD Report is still widely cited today as reason for increases in funding and attention to LGBT youth as an "at risk" population. Scholar Janice Irvine has noted that these early studies of gay and lesbian youth suicide rates in fact helped to stabilize the notion that these youth were a distinct minority population. See Janice M. Irvine, *Talk About Sex: The Battles over Sex Education in the United States* (Berkeley: University of California Press, 2002), 108–11). More recently, psychologist Ritch Savin-Williams has identified this study as one of the key moments in the construction of gay youth as an at-risk population. For a complication of this report's findings and use of suicide rates to define LGBT youth as "at risk," see Ritch C. Savin-Williams, "A Critique of Research on Sexual-Minority Youths," *Journal of Adolescence* 24 (2001): 5–13.

17. Mark Pitsch, "Gay-Straight Group Wants to Meet at Boyd School; Council Denied Request, Will Reconsider Tonight," *Courier-Journal*, October 28, 2002.

18. Ibid.

19. Ibid.

20. Ibid.

21. Mark Pitsch, "Gay-Rights Decision Protested at E. Kentucky School: Allowing Group to Meet Sparks Student Boycott," *Courier-Journal*, November 5, 2002.

22. Ibid.

23. Ibid.

24. Ibid.

25. Ibid.

26. Mark Pitsch, "'We Have to Protect Our Children' Rally Targets Gay-Rights Group: Boyd High Urged to Change Curriculum," *Courier-Journal*, November 11, 2002.

27. Ibid.

28. Ibid.

29. Ibid.

30. David Ryan Alexander, "Kentucky Gay Student Group Protested Again," Gay.com/PlanetOut.com Network, November 11, 2002.

31. Ibid.

32. Gay.com/PlanetOut.com Network, "Kentucky School's Gay Club Wins Appeal," November 27, 2002.

33. Kentucky Department of Education Office of Communication, *Results Matter: A Decade of Difference in Kentucky's Public Schools 1990–2000* (2000).

34. William H. Hoyt, "An Evaluation of the Kentucky Education Reform Act," in *Kentucky Annual Economic Report*, 21–36, 1999. See also Beverly M. Klecker, Jerry Austin, and Leonard Burns, "An In-Depth Analysis of Decisions Made by Kentucky's School-Based Decision Making Councils," in *Annual Meeting of the American Educational Research Association*, 1–29, Quebec, Canada, 1999; Eddy J. Van Meter, "Implementing School-Based Decision Making in Kentucky," *National Association of Secondary School Principals (NASSP) Bulletin* 78 (1994): 61–70; and Jane C. Lindle, "Developing School-Based Decision Making Capacities in Kentucky: Communication Satisfaction after the Pilot Year," Education Resources Information Center, 1992, 1–28.

35. Alan Maimon, "Attempt to Block Gay-Rights Club at Boyd High School Is Stymied," *Courier-Journal*, December 18, 2002.

36. Alan Maimon, "Boyd Bans Club Meetings at Schools: Gay-Rights Group Sparked Controversy," *Courier-Journal*, December 21, 2002.

37. For more on the Phelps' organization and its history of protesting gay rights, most notably the funeral of Matthew Shepard, see Beth Loffreda, *Losing Matt Shepard: Life and Politics in the Aftermath of Anti-Gay Murder* (New York: Columbia University Press, 2000).

38. *Gay People's Chronicle* (January 17, 2003, edition by Anthony Glassman) reported 300 attendees, while the *Lexington Herald-Leader* (January 17, 2003, by Steve Lannen) reported 200 participants.

39. Anthony Glassman, "Hundreds Counter Phelps Clan's Pickets of School Gay-Straight Alliance," *Gay People's Chronicle*, January 17, 2003.

40. "Rally for Unity in Ashland Responds to Anti-Gay Group; Kansas Protesters Condemn America, Kentucky Churches," *Lexington Herald-Leader*, January 13, 2003.

41. Glassman, "Hundreds Counter Phelps Clan's Pickets."

42. "Rally for Unity in Ashland."

43. Steve Lannen, "Kansas Church Returns to Protest Boyd Club: Demonstrators Again Outnumbered by Police, 200 Unity Ralliers," *Lexington Herald-Leader*, January 13, 2003.

44. Ibid.

45. Mark Pitsch, "ACLU Files Gay-Rights Suit against Boyd School Leaders," *Courier-Journal*, January 23, 2003.

46. Ibid.

47. Ibid.

48. Ibid.

49. Bunning referenced one incident in an English class in which students stated "that they needed to take all the (expletive) faggots out in the back woods and kill them" and another instance at a school basketball game when students chanted anti-gay epithets through megaphones at one of the GSA members suing the school. Reported by Kenneth Hart, "GSA Allowed to Meet," *Ashland Daily Independent*, April 19, 2003.

50. Mark Pitsch, "Boyd Gay-Rights Club to Meet Again; School District Ponders Appeal of Ruling against Ban," *Courier-Journal*, April 23, 2003.

51. Hart, "GSA Allowed to Meet.

52. On the racial tension in rural communities around immigration, see Ann E. Kingsolver, *NAFTA Stories: Fears and Hopes in Mexico and the United States* (Boulder, CO: Lynne Rienner Publishers, 2001); Emery N. Castle and Clifton Wharton Jr., eds., *The Changing American Countryside: Rural People and Places* (Lawrence: University Press of Kansas, 1995); Stephen L. Fisher, ed., *Fighting Back in Appalachia: Traditions of Resistance and Change* (Philadelphia: Temple University Press, 1993); Colin Flint, *Spaces of Hate: Geographies of Discrimination and Intolerance in the U.S.A.* (New York: Routledge, 2004); and Wilburn Hayden, "Appalachian Diversity: African-America, Hispanic/Latino, and Other Populations," *Journal of Appalachian Studies* 10, no. 3 (2004): 293–306.

53. Melissa Latimer and Ann M. Oberhauser, "Exploring Gender and Economic Development in Appalachia," *Journal of Appalachian Studies* 10, no. 3 (2004): 269–92; Robert L. Seufert and Mark A. Carrozza, "Economic Advances and Disadvantages in Appalachia: Occupation, Labor Force Participation, and Unemployment," *Journal of Appalachian Studies* 10, no. 3 (2004): 331–40; and Deborah Thorne, Ann Tickamyer, and Mark Thorne, "Poverty and Income in Appalachia," *Journal of Appalachian Studies* 10, no. 3 (2004): 341–58.

NOTES TO CHAPTER 4

1. For a more detailed analysis of popular representations that perpetuate these ideologies, see Ronald L. Lewis, "Beyond Isolation and Homogeneity: Diversity and the History of Appalachia," in *Appalachia: Social Context Past and Present*, ed. Michael E. Maloney and Phillip J. Obermiller, chapter 13 (Dubuque, IA: Kendall/Hunt, 2007); and Ronald L. Lewis and Dwight B. Billings, "Appalachian Culture and Economic Development: A Retrospective View on the Theory and Literature," *Journal of Appalachian Studies* 3, no 1 (1997): 3–41.

2. John Howard, "Of Closets and Other Rural Voids," *GLQ: A Journal of Gay and Lesbian Studies* 13, no. 1 (2006): 100–102; see also the GLQ issue on *Brokeback Mountain* edited by Scott Herring, "*Brokeback Mountain* Dossier," *GLQ: A Journal of Gay and Lesbian Studies* 13, no. 1 (2006): 93–109. For a complication of the way race configures Jack and Ennis' love as particularly white, see Martin F. Manalansan IV, "Colonizing Time and Space: Race and Romance in *Brokeback*

Mountain," GLQ: A Journal of Gay and Lesbian Studies 13, no. 1 (2006): 97–100; and Dwight A. McBride, "Why I Hate That I Loved *Brokeback Mountain," GLQ: A Journal of Gay and Lesbian Studies* 13, no. 1 (2006): 95–97.

3. James T. Sears, *Rebels, Rubyfruit, and Rhinestones: Queering Space in the Stonewall South* (New Brunswick, NJ: Rutgers University Press, 2001); Will Fellows, *Farm Boys: Lives of Gay Men from the Rural Midwest* (Madison: University of Wisconsin Press, 1996); and for an important exception and complication, see John Howard, *Men Like That: A Southern Queer History* (Chicago: University of Chicago Press, 1999).

4. On rural crime rates that report that "intimate violence"—between relatives and longtime acquaintances—is more consistent with rates of random violence in urban centers whereas rural communities report far less crime around property, see the work of Cynthia Barnett and F. Carson Mencken, "Social Disorganization Theory and the Contextual Nature of Crime in Nonmetropolitan Counties," *Rural Sociology* 67, no. 3 (2002): 372–93; and Matthew R. Lee, Michael O. Maume, and Graham C. Ousey, "Social Isolation and Lethal Violence across the Metro/Nonmetro Divide: The Effects of Socioeconomic Disadvantage and Poverty Concentration on Homicide," *Rural Sociology* 68, no. 1 (2003): 107–31.

5. See Larry P. Gross, *Up from Invisibility: Lesbians, Gay Men, and the Media in America*, Between Men—Between Women (New York: Columbia University Press, 2001), 233; Suzanna Danuta Walters, *All the Rage: The Story of Gay Visibility in America* (Chicago: University of Chicago Press, 2001); Katherine Sender, "Sex Sells: Sex, Class, and Taste in Commercial Gay and Lesbian Media," *GLQ: A Journal of Gay and Lesbian Studies* 9, no. 3 (2003): 331–65; and Katherine Sender, *Business, Not Politics: The Making of the Gay Market*, Between Men—Between Women (New York: Columbia University Press, 2004). See also Martin Meeker, *Contacts Desired: Gay and Lesbian Communications and Community, 1940s–1970s* (Chicago: University of Chicago Press, 2006).

6. James R. Kincaid, *Erotic Innocence: The Culture of Child Molesting* (Durham, NC: Duke University Press, 1998). See also Anne Higonnet, *Pictures of Innocence: The History and Crisis of Ideal Childhood* (New York: Thames and Hudson, 1998).

7. See Wayne Brekhus' overview of the "tradition of researchers who have located identity as an interactional accomplishment rather than a fixed identity," in *Peacocks, Chameleons, Centaurs: Gay Suburbia and the Grammar of Social Identity* (Chicago: Chicago University Press, 2003), 21. Brekhus cites theorists from Garfinkel and Goffman to Anderson, West and Zimmerman, and Butler. To this list I would add Anselm L. Strauss, *Mirrors and Masks: The Search for Identity* (Glencoe, IL: Free Press, 1959); Barbara Ponse, *Identities in the Lesbian World: The Social Construction of Self*, Contributions in Sociology, no. 28 (Westport, CT: Greenwood Press, 1978); and Geoffrey C. Bowker and Susan Leigh Star, *Sorting Things Out: Classification and Its Consequences*, Inside Technology (Cambridge: MIT Press, 1999).

8. Jürgen Habermas, *The Structural Transformation of the Public Sphere: An Inquiry into a Category of Bourgeois Society*, Studies in Contemporary German Social Thought (Cambridge: MIT Press, 1989).

9. This rubric is drawn from the work of media scholar L. J. Kensicki, "Speaking of New Media: Oral Explorations into Social Change through the Internet," paper presented at the Minnesota-Amsterdam Symposium, Minneapolis, September 2002.

10. The genealogy of the term "counterpublics," often attributed to Fraser, actually begins elsewhere. Fraser references and attributes the notion to Rita Felski's use of it in *Beyond Feminist Aesthetics: Feminist Literature and Social Change* (Cambridge: Harvard University Press, 1989). Fraser did add Spivak's "altern" as a prefix. Felski cites the term from Oskar Negt and Alexander Kluge, who used the German "Gegenoffentlichkeit." Felski, however, doesn't claim to be the first person to use the word in English. She notes, "It was very much 'in the air' at the time" (personal correspondence, 2003).

11. Susan Leigh Star, "The Structure of Ill-Structured Solutions: Heterogeneous Problem-Solving, Boundary Objects and Distributed Artificial Intelligence," paper presented at the 8th AAAI Workshop on Distributed Artificial Intelligence, Department of Computer Science, University of Southern California, 1988; and Susan Leigh Star and James Griesemer, "Institutional Ecology, 'Translations,' and Boundary Objects: Amateurs and Professionals in Berkeley's Museum of Vertebrate Zoology, 1907–1939," *Social Studies of Science* 19 (1989): 387–420.

12. Ponse, *Identities in the Lesbian World*, 59–74.

13. There is a rich scholarly literature in anthropology and sociology that examines peer networks and their role in the social construction and expansion of gay and lesbian "communities." For example, see Murray on the meaning of "community" and his convincing argument that if "community" is a sociologically viable category, gays and lesbians typify it through their collective action, shared sense of territoriality, and reliance on friends as a primary group. In Stephen O. Murray, *American Gay*, Worlds of Desire (Chicago: University of Chicago Press, 1996), 182–214. On friendship networks and their role as fundamental units of support, see David Woolwine, "Community in Gay Male Experience and Moral Discourse." *Journal of Homosexuality* 38, no. 4 (2000): 5–37.

14. FTM International is an educational organization for female-to-male transgender people and transsexual-identifying men.

15. On this point, see Sara Diamond's two influential books, *Roads to Dominion: Right-Wing Movements and Political Power in the United States* (New York: Guilford Press, 1995), and *Not by Politics Alone: The Enduring Influence of the Christian Right* (New York: Guilford Press, 1998), as well as Heather Hendershot, *Shaking the World for Jesus: Media and Conservative Evangelical Culture* (Chicago: University of Chicago Press, 2004).

16. See Susan Stryker on the history of this effort by early and contemporary gay- and lesbian-rights organizing in San Francisco, in particular in

· "Transgender History, Homonormativity, and Disciplinarity," *Radical History Review* 100 (Winter 2008): 150. See also David Valentine's recent critique of gay and lesbian social-service organizations that maintain a policing among categories of gay, lesbian, bi, and trans, often denying clients' sense of the interconnectedness of their gender and sexual modalities. In David Valentine, *Imagining Transgender: An Ethnography of a Category* (Durham, NC: Duke University Press, 2007).

17. In fact, the U.S. House of Representatives voted to pass legislation called the Matthew Shepard Act to expand existing federal hate-crime laws authorizing the Department of Justice to investigate and prosecute bias-motivated crimes based on the victim's actual or perceived sexual orientation, gender, gender identity, or disability. Current law only includes race, color, religion or national origin; eliminates the restrictions currently in place that limit federal involvement to cases in which a victim of a bias-motivated crime was attacked because he/she was engaged in a specified federally protected activity such as voting, serving on a jury or attending school; and adds "gender" and "gender identity" to the Hate Crimes Statistics Act to keep national statistics on LGBT-related hate crimes. For more on the discussion of hate crimes, see Judith Butler, *Excitable Speech: Contemporary Scenes of Politics* (New York: Routledge, 1997); for reading on hate crimes and their relationship to the Shepard murder, see Beth Loffreda, *Losing Matt Shepard: Life and Politics in the Aftermath of Anti-Gay Murder* (New York: Columbia University Press, 2000).

18. See Lisa Henderson, "The Class Character of *Boys Don't Cry*," *Screen* 42, no. 3 (2001): 299–303; and Judith Halberstam, *In a Queer Time and Place: Transgender Bodies, Subcultural Lives*, Sexual Cultures (New York: New York University Press, 2005): 22–46.

19. Delany characterizes the structural difference between urban and small-town violence this way: urban violence is more random and small-town violence is more personal and predictable based on memories of his own experiences living for a single winter in a small Pennsylvania town in 1967. Samuel R. Delany, *Times Square Red, Times Square Blue*, Sexual Cultures (New York: New York University Press, 1999), 154–56. Arguably, urban violence is random—certainly the greater numbers of poor queer youth of color killed in Manhattan suggest that rural queer kids have statistically better odds of not being killed.

20. Again, see the work of Barnett and Mencken, "Social Disorganization," 372–93; and Lee, Maume, and Ousey, "Social Isolation and Lethal Violence," 107–31.

NOTES TO CHAPTER 5

1. David Grazian, *Blue Chicago: The Search for Authenticity in Urban Blues Clubs* (Chicago: University of Chicago Press, 2003), 10–11.

2. Mittell doesn't specifically have ethnographic studies of media in mind, but his culturally situated notion of genre resonates with work in anthropology

that examines how audiences and listeners interact with generic conventions. For exemplars of this approach to genres as discursive practices, see the work of William Hanks, "Discourse Genres in a Theory of Practice," *American Ethnologist* 14, no. 4 (1987): 668–92; Richard Bauman, *Story, Performance, and Event: Contextual Studies of Oral Narrative* (Cambridge: Cambridge University Press, 1986); and more recently, Sara L. Friedman, "Watching Twin Bracelets in China: The Role of Spectatorship and Identification in an Ethnographic Analysis of Film Reception," *Cultural Anthropology* 21, no. 4 (2006): 603–32.

3. I draw from the work of scholars on drag and the importance of "realness" in performing gender as a category, such as Judith Butler, *Gender Trouble: Feminism and the Subversion of Identity*, Thinking Gender(New York: Routledge, 1990); Judith Butler, *Bodies That Matter: On the Discursive Limits of "Sex"* (New York: Routledge, 1993); Judith Halberstam, *Female Masculinity* (Durham, NC: Duke University Press, 1998); and the earlier work of Esther Newton, *Mother Camp: Female Impersonators in America* (Englewood Cliffs, NJ: Prentice Hall, 1972). Unlike hyperbolic performances of gender popularly associated with drag, "realness" seeks to embody rather than parody gender norms.

4. There is an ongoing, vibrant discussion of the critical role of information and communication technologies (ICTs) in the construction of spaces. For example, David Morley and Kevin Robins, in *Spaces of Identity: Global Media, Electronic Landscapes and Cultural Boundaries* (London: Routledge, 1995), offer a theoretical analysis of how ICTs—particularly globally circulated mass-media consumption—disrupt the traditional boundaries of the nation-state. These authors argue that ICTs afford a different kind of geography and assert corresponding global/local dialectics. Anthropologist Debra Spitulnik takes a more linguistic approach to the ways in which communicative practices and their everyday discursive engagements with media technologies, such as portable radios in Zambia, produce spaces of cultural mobility. In Debra Spitulnik, "Mobile Machines and Fluid Audiences: Rethinking Reception through Zambian Radio Culture," *Media Worlds: Anthropology on New Terrain*, ed. Faye D. Ginsburg, Lila Abu-Lughod, and Brian Larkin, 337–54 (Berkeley: University of California Press, 2002). Zizi Papacharissi more recently argued that the virtual spaces of new media offer potential for a revival of the public sphere. In Zizi Papacharissi, "The Virtual Sphere: The Internet as Public Sphere," *New Media and Society* 4, no. 1 (2002): 9–27. For a more provocative discussion of the distinction between "space" and "place" that bears heavily on whether new media can be considered locations of any sort, see Michael Curry, *The Work in the World: Geographical Practice and the Written Word* (Minneapolis: University of Minnesota Press, 1996).

5. PlanetOut and Gay.com merged in 2001. For a discussion of their business model, see John Edward Campbell, "Outing PlanetOut: Surveillance, Gay Marketing and Internet Affinity Portals," *New Media and Society* 7, no. 5 (2005): 663–83.

6. See Campbell, "Outing PlanetOut"; Joshua Gamson, "Gay Media, Inc.: Media Structures, the New Gay Conglomerates, and Collective Sexual Identities," in *Cyberactivism: Online Activism in Theory and Practice,* ed. Martha McCaughey and Michael D. Ayers, 255–78 (New York: Routledge, 2003); and Jonathan Alexander, "Homo-Pages and Queer Sites: Studying the Construction and Representation of Queer Identities on the World Wide Web," *International Journal of Sexuality and Gender Studies* 7, no. 2–3 (2002): 85–106.

7. Studies from the late 1980s to present have consistently shown that U.S. rural communities have few, and more often no, shelters, outreach programs, or minimal services. Homelessness is often invisible because individuals with insecure housing use car campers, parks, and private homes as temporary shelters and there are no centralized support services where these individuals could be counted. See Housing Assistance Council, "Taking Stock: Rural People, Poverty, and Housing at the Turn of the 21st Century," available at www.ruralhome.org, 2002; G. A. Hoover and M. V. Carter. "The Invisible Homeless: Non-Urban Homeless in Appalachian East Tennessee," *Rural Sociologist* 11, no. 4 (1991): 3–12; Janet Fitchen, "On the Edge of Homelessness: Rural Poverty and Housing Insecurity," *Rural Sociology* 57 (1992): 173–93; and Paul J. Cloke, Sarah Johnson, and Jon May, "The Periphery of Care: Emergency Services for Homeless People in Rural Areas," *Journal of Rural Studies* 23 (2007): 387–401.

8. For examples of interesting analyses of Kentuckiana's complicated race and labor rights history, see Catherine Fosl's biography of a civil rights organizer, *Subversive Southerner: Anne Braden and the Struggle for Racial Justice in the Cold War South* (New York: Palgrave Macmillan, 2002); and Pem Davidson Buck's historical ethnography of Kentucky's rural working poor, *Worked to the Bone: Race, Class, Power, and Privilege in Kentucky* (New York: Monthly Review Press, 2001).

9. On this point, see Martin F. Manalansan IV, *Global Divas: Filipino Gay Men in the Diaspora*, Perverse Modernities (Durham, NC: Duke University Press, 2003), 23.

10. Adrienne Rich described this notion in her now classic essay, "Compulsory Heterosexuality and Lesbian Existence," *Signs: Journal of Women in Culture and Society* 5 (Summer 1980): 631–60.

11. Wayne Brekhus, *Peacocks, Chameleons, Centaurs: Gay Suburbia and the Grammar of Social Identity* (Chicago: University of Chicago Press, 2003), 1–2; see also Everett Hughes, "Dilemmas and Contradictions of Status," *American Journal of Sociology* 50 (1945): 353–59.

NOTES TO CHAPTER 6

1. Some readers may recognize my reference to the notion of place-identities and the importance of place in shaping action as discussed by literary theorist Michel de Certeau in *The Practice of Everyday Life* (Berkeley: University

of California Press, 1984). Building on Foucault's analyses of the structures of power, de Certeau asserted that *"spatial practices . . .* structure the determining conditions of social life" and, drawing on this premise, he argued for considering how individual strategies and tactics engage representations of self and society to rework relations of power on the ground (96).

2. Sarah Holloway and Gill Valentine, *Cyberkids: Children in the Information Age* (London: Routledge, 2003), 12.

3. See Tom Boellstorff's recent argument for maintaining a distinction between "offline" and "online" or "actual" and "virtual" worlds, particularly in ethnographic studies of virtual worlds. While Boellstorff claims that "[i]n virtual worlds, *techne* [human innovation and creative action] *can take place inside* [virtual worlds], rather than solely in the actual world," creating a *"gap between actual and virtual in the realm of the virtual"* (italics in the original), I think that, as Boellstorff suggests in his discussion of ethnographic approaches to the study of the virtual, the degree of permeability or gap between "offline" and "online" depends entirely on the questions the researcher asks and the experiences of the participants. See Tom Boellstorff, *Coming of Age in Second Life: An Anthropologist Explores the Virtually Human* (Princeton, NJ: Princeton University Press, 2008), 58 and 62. In other words, if I am interested in the "actual-world cultures" that engage new media practices, I am more concerned with how people talk about these experiences as deeply separate worlds and whether those claims of deep separation between offline and online hold constant under ethnographic scrutiny.

4. See Sonia M. Livingstone, *Young People and New Media* (London: Routledge, 2002), 15. See also Ellen Seiter, *Television and New Media Audiences*, Oxford Television Studies (Oxford: Clarendon Press, 1999).

5. On the "electronic sublime" and rhetorical aura of media innovations, see Carolyn Marvin, *When Old Technologies Were New: Thinking about Electric Communication in the Late Nineteenth Century* (New York: Oxford University Press, 1988); and James W. Carey, *Communication as Culture: Essays on Media and Society* (Boston: Unwin Hyman, 1989).

6. For more on the notion of cultural circuits and the production of social meaning through and across producers, texts, and consumers, see Stuart Hall, *Representation: Cultural Representations and Signifying Practices* (London: Sage, 1997). For a critical elaboration of these flows as nonlinear and historically layered, see Leah A. Lievrouw and Sonia M. Livingstone, "Introduction," in *Major Works in New Media*, ed. L. Lievrouw and S. Livingstone (London: Sage, in press).

7. J. David Bolter and Richard Grusin, *Remediation: Understanding New Media* (Cambridge: MIT Press, 2000), 55.

8. This is less a criticism of the limits of media representation and more an acknowledgment of how representation works through archetypal characters. For

critical essays on the power of representation and gay iconography, see Richard Dyer, *The Matter of Images: Essays on Representation* (London: Routledge, 1993), 11–51.

9. On the consumption and production of individual web pages by queer and questioning youth, see Jonathan Alexander, "Homo-Pages and Queer Sites: Studying the Construction and Representation of Queer Identities on the World Wide Web," *International Journal of Sexuality and Gender Studies* 7, no. 2–3 (2002): 85–106.

10. For more on the domestication of television, see Lynn Spigel, *Make Room for Television: Television and the Family Ideal in Postwar America* (Chicago: University of Chicago Press), 1992; Roger Silverstone, *Television and Everyday Life* (London: Routledge, 1994); and Roger Silverstone and Eric Hirsch, eds., *Consuming Technologies: Media and Information in Domestic Spaces* (London: Routledge, 1992).

11. For more on the cultural place of television in popular culture, see Michael Curtin, *Redeeming the Wasteland: Television Documentary and Cold War Politics*, Communications, Media, and Culture (New Brunswick, NJ: Rutgers University Press, 1995); and Spigel, *Make Room for TV*.

12. The Mariposa Film Group consisted of Peter Adair, Nancy Adair, Veronica Selvor, Andrew Brown, Robert Epstein, and Lucy Massie Phenix. *Word Is Out* was produced by Peter Adair. See also Nancy Adair and Casey Adair, *Word Is Out: Stories of Some of Our Lives* (San Francisco: New Glide Publications, 1978).

13. On the configuring of the queer body through medical scientific discourses, see Jennifer Terry, *An American Obsession: Science, Medicine, and Homosexuality in Modern Society* (Chicago: University of Chicago Press, 1999).

14. John Corry, "HBO's *What Sex Am I?*" *New York Times*, April 18, 1985.

15. The Discovery Channel and its brands reach 92.5 million U.S. households, according to the National Cable and Telecommunications Association, and a global audience of 431 million homes in 170 countries and territories, according to DCI's marketing information available online at www.dsc.discovery.com.

16. *What Sex Am I?* is not for sale through DCI. At one point, DCI did sell DVD versions of these three films listed above, but now only *Changing Sexes: Female to Male* (2002) is available through the DCI website.

17. Community United Against Violence, a San Francisco–based LGBT hate-crimes watchdog organization, reports that 98% of reported cases of anti-transgender hate violence were directed against trans women, suggesting that trans men more readily "pass" avoiding the scrutiny that might endanger them. Suzanne J. Kessler and Wendy McKenna argue that people "see" male as the default and affix maleness to a body even in the presence of "feminine" markers more easily than they attribute femaleness to a body with "masculine" markers. In Suzanne J. Kessler and Wendy McKenna, "Gender Construction in Everyday Life: Transsexualism (Abridged)," *Feminism and Psychology* 10, no. 1 (2000):

11–29. Marjorie Garber, *Vice Versa: Bisexuality and the Eroticism of Everyday Life* (New York: Simon & Schuster, 1995), also discusses the asymmetry of sex change in *Vested Interests: Cross-dressing and Cultural Anxiety* (New York: Routledge, 1997), arguing that a male body is culturally less scrutinized and, therefore, easier to achieve. See also David Valentine, *Imagining Transgender: An Ethnography of a Category* (Durham, NC: Duke University Press, 2007), for a discussion of the construction of the category "transgender."

NOTES TO CHAPTER 7

1. John Berger, *Ways of Seeing* (London: Penguin Books, 1972).

2. Kenneth Plummer, *Sexual Stigma: An Interactionist Account* (London: Routledge & Kegan Paul, 1975).

3. There is a slight irony here in that the Castro's efforts to "clean up" its streets have involved campaigns to push the homeless youth, many queer-identifying ones who presume the gay neighborhood to be a safe space for them, off the streets without an equal effort to provide shelters for these youth.

4. Bruno Latour, "On Interobjectivity," *Mind, Culture, and Activity* 3, no. 4 (1996): 228–45.

5. Janice M. Irvine, *Talk About Sex: The Battles over Sex Education in the United States* (Berkeley: University of California Press, 2002): 131–32.

6. See Vincent Doyle's persuasive argument on this point in "'But Joan! You're My Daughter!' Gay and Lesbian Alliance Against Defamation and the Politics of Amnesia," *Radical History Review* 100 (Winter 2008).

NOTES TO THE EPILOGUE

1. According to a 2006 study of DOMA initiatives, their voter support, and their impact on the 2004 elections, "State legislatures in Georgia (76 percent yes), Kentucky (75 percent yes), Mississippi (86 percent yes), Oklahoma (76 percent yes), and Utah (66 percent yes) placed referendums on the ballot. Initiatives were on the ballot in Arkansas (75 percent yes), Michigan (56 percent yes), Montana (67 percent yes), North Dakota (73 percent yes), Ohio (62 percent yes), and Oregon (57 percent yes)." See Daniel A. Smith, Matthew DeSantis, and Jason Kassel, "Same-Sex Marriage Ballot Measures and the 2004 Presidential Election," *State and Local Government Review* 38, no. 2 (2006): 78–91. The text of Kentucky's amendment read: "Only a marriage between one man and one woman shall be valid or recognized as a marriage in Kentucky. A legal status identical or substantially similar to that of marriage for unmarried individuals shall not be valid or recognized." Passage of Amendment 2 made Kentucky the seventh of the 37 DOMA states to define marriage strictly as a legal union between a man and woman, to deny recognition of same-sex marriages performed in other states,

and to make same-sex marriage a violation of public policy. The other six states are Alabama, Arkansas, Georgia, Michigan, Pennsylvania, and Missouri.

2. The Kentucky Senate approved a state constitutional marriage amendment for the state ballot by a vote of 33–5. The Kentucky House passed the amendment 85–11.

3. Proposition 22 was ruled unconstitutional by the California Supreme Court in May 2008. A ballot measure amending the state constitution to override the Supreme Court's ruling is headed to voters in November 2008.

4. For a comprehensive literature review and prescient analysis of the impact of DOMA initiatives on the 2004 elections comparing the red state of Ohio and the blue state of Michigan in particular, see Smith, DeSantis, and Kassel, "Same-Sex Marriage Ballot Measures," 78–91.

5. Arguably, statewide LGBT advocacy efforts are at a particular disadvantage in places with deeply grooved divides between urban and rural communities because LGBT advocacy organizations rarely have the resources to build a local presence and ethos of coalition in rural areas that might offer entrée when the debate turns to an anti-LGBT measure.

6. Associated Press article in the online edition of *USA Today*, "Kentucky Voters Approve Same-Sex Marriage Ban Amendment," November 2, 2004, http://www.usatoday.com/news/politicselections/vote2004/2004-11-02-ky-initiative-gay-marriage_x.htm.

7. Suzana Danuta Walters, "Threat Level Lavender: The Truthiness of Gay Marriage," *Chronicle of Higher Education*, January 19, 2007, B12.

NOTES TO THE APPENDIX

1. For discussions of the qualifications and limits of containing studies to "online" engagements, see Susan Herring, "Content Analysis for New Media: Rethinking the Paradigm," paper presented at the New Research for New Media: Innovative Research Methodologies Symposium Working Papers and Readings, 2004; Susan Herring, "Slouching toward the Ordinary: Current Trends in Computer-Mediated Communication," *New Media and Society* 6, no. 1 (2004): 26–36; and T. L. Taylor, *Play between Worlds: Exploring Online Game Culture* (Cambridge: MIT Press, 2006). More recently, anthropologist Tom Boellstorff has compellingly argued for maintaining the distinction between offline and online, or actual and virtual, particularly for ethnographies of immersive virtual worlds. I think, as Boellstorff suggests, this speaks less to the importance of maintaining a distinction between "actual" and "virtual" and more to the need for researchers to assume they won't know whether the distinction matters until they have the questions and context to determine the importance of the boundary to participants. See Tom Boellstorff, *Coming of Age in Second Life: An Anthropologist Explores the Virtually Human* (Princeton, NJ: Princeton University Press, 2008), 18–19).

2. The work of health sociologist Rick Zimmerman and his research team at the University of Kentucky stands out as an exemplary exception to the rule. See their work in Rostosky et al., "Associations among Sexual Attraction Status, School Belonging, and Alcohol and Marijuana Use," *Journal of Adolescence* 26, no. 6 (December 2003): 741–51. See also Herdt et al., "Sexual Inequality, Youth Empowerment, and the GSA: A Community Study in California," in *Sexual Inequalities and Social Justice*, ed. Niels Teunis and Gilbert Herdt (Berkeley: University of California Press, 2006).

3. For rich examples of references discussing the politics of science and technology research, see the work of Bruno Latour and Steve Woolgar, *Laboratory Life: The Construction of Scientific Facts* (Princeton, NJ: Princeton University Press, 1986); Steve Woolgar, *Virtual Society? Technology, Cyberbole, Reality* (Oxford: Oxford University Press, 2002); and Steven Shapin, Simon Schaffer, and Thomas Hobbes, *Leviathan and the Air-Pump: Hobbes, Boyle, and the Experimental Life: Including a Translation of Thomas Hobbes, Dialogus Physicus De Natura Aeris by Simon Schaffer* (Princeton, NJ: Princeton University Press, 1985).

Bibliography

Abelove, Henry, Michèle Aina Barale, and David M. Halperin, eds. *The Lesbian and Gay Studies Reader*. New York: Routledge, 1993.

Adair, Nancy, and Casey Adair. *Word Is Out: Stories of Some of Our Lives*. San Francisco: New Glide Publications, 1978.

Adam, Barry D. *The Rise of a Gay and Lesbian Movement*. 1987. Rev. ed, *Social Movements Past and Present*. New York: Twayne Publishers, 1995.

Adam, Barry D., Jan Willem Duyvendak, and André Krouwel, eds. *The Global Emergence of Gay and Lesbian Politics: National Imprints of a Worldwide Movement*. Philadelphia: Temple University Press, 1998.

Addison, Joanne, and Michelle Comstock. "Virtually Out: The Emergence of Lesbian, Bisexual, and Gay Youth Cyberculture." In *Generations of Youth: Youth Cultures and History in the Twentieth Century*, edited by Joe Austin and Michael Willard. New York: New York University Press, 1998.

Adler, Patricia A., and Peter Adler. *Peer Power: Preadolescent Culture and Identity*. New Brunswick, NJ: Rutgers University Press, 1998.

Agee, James, and Walker Evans. *Let Us Now Praise Famous Men*. Boston: Houghton Mifflin, 1941.

Alexander, David Ryan. "Kentucky Gay Student Group Protested Again," *Gay.com/PlanetOut.com Network*, November 11, 2002.

Alexander, Jonathan. "Homo-Pages and Queer Sites: Studying the Construction and Representation of Queer Identities on the World Wide Web." *International Journal of Sexuality and Gender Studies* 7, no. 2–3 (2002): 85–106.

Alexander, M. Jacqui. *Pedagogies of Crossing: Meditations on Feminism, Sexual Politics, Memory, and the Sacred*. Perverse Modernities. Durham, NC: Duke University Press, 2005.

Allen, C. "What's Wrong with the 'Golden Rule'? Conundrums of Conducting Ethical Research in Cyberspace." *Information Society* 12, no. 2 (1996): 175–87.

Allen, Danielle S. *Talking to Strangers: Anxieties of Citizenship since Brown v. Board of Education*. Chicago: University of Chicago Press, 2004.

Altman, Dennis. *Homosexual: Oppression and Liberation*. New York: Outerbridge & Dienstfrey, 1971.

———. "Marginality on the Tropic." In *De-Centring Sexualities: Politics and Representations Beyond the Metropolis*, edited by Richard Phillips, Diane Watt, and David Shuttleton, 37–48. London: Routledge, 2000.

American Film Institute. Center for Advanced Film and Television Studies. "Lee Grant: The Actress-Director Charts Her Climb from the Blacklist to the A-List." *American Film* 15, no. 5 (1990): 16–22.

Anderson, Benedict. *Imagined Communities: Reflections on the Origin and Spread of Nationalism*. Rev. and extended ed. London: Verso, 1991.

Anglin, Mary K. "Engendering the Struggle: Women's Labor and Traditions of Resistance in Rural Southern Appalachia." In *Fighting Back in Appalachia: Traditions of Resistance and Change*, edited by Stephen L. Fisher, 263–82. Philadelphia: Temple University Press, 1993.

Argyle, K., and R. Shields. "Is There a Body in the Net?" In *Cultures of the Internet: Virtual Spaces, Real Histories, Living Bodies*, edited by R. Shields, 58–69. London: Sage, 1996.

Armstrong, Elizabeth A. *Forging Gay Identities: Organizing Sexuality in San Francisco, 1950–1994*. Chicago: University of Chicago Press, 2002.

Asencio, Marysol. *Sex and Sexuality among New York's Puerto Rican Youth*. Boulder, CO: Lynne Rienner Publishers, 2002.

Askew, Kelly Michelle, and Richard R. Wilk. *The Anthropology of Media: A Reader*. Blackwell Readers in Anthropology, vol. 1, no. 2. Malden, MA: Blackwell, 2002.

Associated Press. "Kentucky Voters Approve Same-Sex Marriage Ban Amendment." *USA Today*, November 2, 2004.

Bakardjieva, Maria. *Internet Society: The Internet in Everyday Life*. London: Sage, 2005.

Barnett, Cynthia, and F. Carson Mencken. "Social Disorganization Theory and the Contextual Nature of Crime in Nonmetropolitan Counties." *Rural Sociology* 67, no. 3 (2002): 372–93.

Barthes, Roland. *Mythologies*. Translated by Annette Lavers. New York: Hill and Wang, 1972.

———. "Myth Today." In *Media and Cultural Studies: Keyworks*, edited by Meenakshi Gigi Durham and Douglas Kellner, 122–28. Malden, MA: Blackwell, 1999.

Basso, Keith H. *Wisdom Sits in Places: Landscape and Language among the Western Apache*. Albuquerque: University of New Mexico Press, 1996.

Batteau, Allen W. *The Invention of Appalachia*. Anthropology of Form and Meaning. Tucson: University of Arizona Press, 1990.

Bauman, Richard. *Story, Performance, and Event: Contextual Studies of Oral Narrative*. Cambridge: Cambridge University Press, 1986.

———. "Genre." *Journal of Linguistic Anthropology* 9, no. 1–2 (2000): 84–87.

———. *Voices of Modernity: Language Ideologies and the Politics of Inequality*.

Studies in the Social and Cultural Foundations of Language. Cambridge: Cambridge University Press, 2003.

Bauman, Richard, and Joel Sherzer. *Explorations in the Ethnography of Speaking.* 2d ed. Cambridge: Cambridge University Press, 1989.

Bauman, Zygmunt. "Making and Unmaking of Strangers." *Thesis Eleven* 43, no. 1 (1995): 1–16.

Bauman, Zygmunt, and Benedetto Vecchi. *Identity: Conversations with Benedetto Vecchi.* Themes for the 21st Century. Cambridge: Polity Press, 2004.

Baym, Nancy K. *Tune In, Log On: Soaps, Fandom, and Online Community.* New Media Cultures. Thousand Oaks, CA: Sage, 2000.

———. "Finding the Quality in Qualitative Research." In *Critical Cyberculture Studies*, edited by David Silver and Adrienne Massanari, 79–87. New York: New York University Press, 2006.

Becker, Howard Saul. *Outsiders: Studies in the Sociology of Deviance.* New York: Free Press, 1973.

———. *Art Worlds.* 1st ed. Berkeley: University of California Press, 1984.

———. "Studying New Media." *Qualitative Sociology* 25, no. 3 (Fall 2002): 337–43.

Beemyn, Brett, ed. *Creating a Place for Ourselves: Lesbian, Gay, and Bisexual Community Histories.* New York: Routledge, 1997.

Bell, David. "Farm Boys and Wild Men: Rurality, Masculinity, and Homosexuality." *Rural Sociology* 65, no. 4 (2000): 547–61.

———. "Eroticizing the Rural." In *De-Centring Sexualities: Politics and Representations Beyond the Metropolis*, edited by Richard Phillips, Diane Watt, and David Shuttleton, 83–101. London: Routledge, 2000.

Bell, David, and Barbara M. Kennedy. *The Cybercultures Reader.* London: Routledge, 2000.

Bell, David, and Gill Valentine. "Queer Country: Rural Lesbian and Gay Lives." *Journal of Rural Studies* 11, no. 2 (1995): 113–22.

Bell, David, and Gill Valentine, eds. *Mapping Desire: Geographies of Sexualities.* London: Routledge, 1995.

Benjamin, Walter, and Hannah Arendt. *Illuminations.* New York: Schocken Books, 1986.

Berger, John. *Ways of Seeing.* London: Penguin Books, 1972.

Bergman, R. "The World at Their Fingertips—Rural Providers Turn to Internet." *Hospitals & Health Networks* 68, no. 14 (1994): 52.

Berker, Thomas, Maren Hartmann, Yves Punie, and Katie Ward. *Domestication of Media and Technology.* Maidenhead, UK: Open University Press, 2006.

Berlant, L., and M. Warner. "Sex in Public." *Critical Inquiry* 24, no. 2 (1998): 547–66.

Berry, Chris, Fran Martin, and Audrey Yue. *Mobile Cultures: New Media in Queer Asia.* Console-Ing Passions. Durham, NC: Duke University Press, 2003.

Best, Amy L. *Prom Night: Youth, Schools, and Popular Culture.* New York: Routledge, 2000.

―――. *Fast Cars, Cool Rides: The Accelerating World of Youth and Their Cars.*
New York: New York University Press, 2006.

―――. *Representing Youth: Methodological Issues in Critical Youth Studies.* New
York: New York University Press, 2007.

Billings, Dwight B., and Ann Tickamyer. "Uneven Development in Appalachia."
In *Forgotten Places: Uneven Development in Rural America*, edited by Thomas
A. Lyson and William W. Falk, 7–29. Rural America. Lawrence: University
Press of Kansas, 1993).

Billings, Dwight B., and Kathleen M. Blee. *The Road to Poverty: The Making of Wealth
and Hardship in Appalachia.* Cambridge: Cambridge University Press, 2000.

Billings, Dwight B., Gurney Norman, and Katherine Ledford, eds. *Confronting
Appalachian Stereotypes: Back Talk from an American Region.* Lexington: University Press of Kentucky, 1999.

Binnie, Jon, and Gill Valentine. "Geographies of Sexuality—a Review of Progress." *Progress in Human Geography* 23, no. 2 (1999): 175–87.

Blackwood, Evelyn. "Tombois in West Sumatra: Constructing Masculinity and
Erotic Desire." *Cultural Anthropology* 13, no. 4 (1998): 491–521.

Blumer, Herbert, David R. Maines, and Thomas J. Morrione. *Industrialization
as an Agent of Social Change: A Critical Analysis.* Communication and Social
Order. New York: Aldine de Gruyter, 1990.

Blumer, Herbert, and Tamotsu Shibutani. *Human Nature and Collective Behavior;
Papers in Honor of Herbert Blumer.* Englewood Cliffs, NJ: Prentice Hall, 1970.

Bockting, Walter O., and Eli Coleman, eds. *Gender Dysphoria: Interdisciplinary
Approaches in Clinical Management.* New York: Haworth Press, 1992.

Boehlefeld, Sharon P. "Doing the Right Thing: Ethical Cyberspace Research." *Information Society* 12, no. 2 (1996): 141–52.

Boellstorff, Tom. "Dubbing Culture: Indonesian Gay and Lesbi Subjectivities and
Ethnography in an Already Globalized World." *American Ethnologist* 30, no. 2
(2003): 225–42.

―――. *The Gay Archipelago: Sexuality and Nation in Indonesia.* Princeton, NJ:
Princeton University Press, 2005.

―――. "Queer Studies in the House of Anthropology." *Annual Review of Anthropology* 36 (2007): 2.1–2.19.

―――. *Coming of Age in Second Life: An Anthropologist Explores the Virtually Human.* Princeton, NJ: Princeton University Press, 2008.

Bolter, J. David, and Richard Grusin. *Remediation: Understanding New Media.* 1st
ed. Cambridge: MIT Press, 2000.

Bolton, Ralph, ed. *The AIDS Pandemic.* New York: Gordon and Breach, 1989.

Bolton, Ralph. "Mapping Terra Incognita: Sex Research for AIDS Prevention—an
Urgent Agenda for the 1990s." In *The Time of AIDS: Social Analysis, Theory,
and Method*, edited by Gilbert H. Herdt and S. Lindenbaum, 124–58. Newbury
Park, CA: Sage, 1991.

Boulden, Walter T. "Gay Men Living in a Rural Environment." *Journal of Gay and Lesbian Social Services* 12 (2001): 63–75.

Bowker, Geoffrey C., and Susan Leigh Star. *Sorting Things Out: Classification and Its Consequences*. Inside Technology. Cambridge: MIT Press, 1999.

Boyd, Nan Alamilla. *Wide Open Town: A History of Queer San Francisco to 1965*. Berkeley: University of California Press, 2003.

Brashear, Jean. "The Friday Night Bunch: A Lesbian Community in West Texas." *Journal of Lesbian Studies* 9, no. 1 (2005): 73–80.

Brekhus, Wayne. *Peacocks, Chameleons, Centaurs: Gay Suburbia and the Grammar of Social Identity*. Chicago: University of Chicago Press, 2003.

Broad, K. L., Sara Crawley, and Lara Foley. "Doing 'Real Family Values': The Interpretive Practice of Families in the GLBT Movement." *Sociological Quarterly* 45, no. 3 (2004): 509–27.

Brown, Jane D., Jeanne R. Steele, and Kim Walsh-Childers. *Sexual Teens, Sexual Media: Investigating Media's Influence on Adolescent Sexuality*. LEA's Communication Series. Mahwah, NJ: Lawrence Erlbaum Associates, 2002.

Brown, Wendy. *States of Injury: Power and Freedom in Late Modernity*. Princeton, NJ: Princeton University Press, 1995.

Bruckman, Amy. "Gender Swapping on the Internet." In *High Noon on the Electronic Frontier*, edited by Peter Ludlow, 9–34. Cambridge: MIT Press, 1996.

Bryant, Jennings, and Dolf Zillmann. *Media Effects: Advances in Theory and Research*. 2d ed. LEA's Communication Series. Mahwah, NJ: Lawrence Elbaum Associates, 2002.

Bucholtz, Mary, A. C. Liang, and Laurel A. Sutton. *Reinventing Identities: The Gendered Self in Discourse*. New York: Oxford University Press, 1999.

Buck, Pem Davidson. *Worked to the Bone: Race, Class, Power, and Privilege in Kentucky*. New York: Monthly Review Press, 2001.

Burke, Kenneth. *A Grammar of Motives*. Berkeley: University of California Press, 1969.

Burke, Susan. "In Search of Lesbian Community in an Electronic World." *CyberPsychology and Behavior* 3, no. 4 (2000): 591–604.

Butler, Judith. *Gender Trouble: Feminism and the Subversion of Identity*. Thinking Gender. New York: Routledge, 1990.

———. *Bodies That Matter: On the Discursive Limits of "Sex."* New York: Routledge, 1993.

———. *Excitable Speech: Contemporary Scenes of Politics*. New York: Routledge, 1997.

Calhoun, Craig J., ed. *Habermas and the Public Sphere*. Studies in Contemporary German Social Thought. Cambridge: MIT Press, 1992.

Callan, Eamonn. *Creating Citizens: Political Education and Liberal Democracy*. Oxford Political Theory. Oxford: Oxford University Press, 2004.

Campbell, John Edward. *Getting It on Online: Cyberspace, Gay Male Sexuality, and Embodied Identity*. New York: Harrington Park Press, 2004.

————. "Outing PlanetOut: Surveillance, Gay Marketing and Internet Affinity Portals." *New Media and Society* 7, no. 5 (2005): 663–83.

Capsuto, Steven. *Alternate Channels: The Uncensored Story of Gay and Lesbian Images on Radio and Television.* 1st ed. New York: Ballantine Books, 2000.

Carey, James W, ed "Technology and Ideology: The Case of the Telegraph." In *Communication as Culture: Essays on Media and Society* Boston: Unwin Hyman, 1989.

Carrier, John M. "Sexual Behavior and the Spread of AIDS in Mexico." In *The AIDS Pandemic*, edited by Ralph Bolton, 37–50. New York: Gordon and Breach, 1989.

Carrillo, Héctor. *The Night Is Young: Sexuality in Mexico in the Time of AIDS.* Worlds of Desire. Chicago: University of Chicago Press, 2002.

Cassell, Justine, and Henry Jenkins. *From Barbie to Mortal Kombat: Gender and Computer Games.* Cambridge: MIT Press, 1998.

Castells, Manuel. *The City and the Grassroots: A Cross-Cultural Theory of Urban Social Movements.* Berkeley: University of California Press, 1983.

————. *The Power of Identity.* Malden, MA: Blackwell, 1997.

————. *The Rise of the Network Society.* 2d ed. Oxford: Blackwell, 2000.

Castle, Emery N., and Clifton Wharton Jr., eds. *The Changing American Countryside: Rural People and Places.* Lawrence: University Press of Kansas, 1995.

Castoriadis, Cornelius. *The Imaginary Institution of Society.* 1st ed. Cambridge: MIT Press, 1987.

Cavanagh, Allison. "Behavior in Public? Ethics in Online Ethnography." *Cybersociology*, no. 6 (1999): unpaginated.

Certeau, Michel de. *The Practice of Everyday Life.* Berkeley: University of California Press, 1984.

Chauncey, George. *Gay New York: Gender, Urban Culture, and the Making of the Gay Male World, 1890–1940.* New York: Basic Books, 1994.

Chris, Cynthia. *Watching Wildlife.* Minneapolis: University of Minnesota Press, 2006.

Clarke, Adele. "Social Worlds Theory as Organization Theory." In *Social Organization and Social Process: Essays in Honor of Anselm Strauss*, edited by Anselm L. Strauss and David R. Maines, 119–58. New York: Aldine de Gruyter, 1991.

Clifford, James. "On Ethnographic Allegory." In *Writing Culture: The Poetics and Politics of Ethnography: A School of American Research Advanced Seminar*, edited by James Clifford and George E. Marcus, 98–121. Berkeley: University of California Press, 1986.

Clifford, James, George E. Marcus, and School of American Research (Santa Fe, NM), eds. *Writing Culture: The Poetics and Politics of Ethnography: A School of American Research Advanced Seminar.* Berkeley: University of California Press, 1986.

Cloke, Paul J. "Country Backwater to Virtual Village? Rural Studies and 'the Cultural Turn.'" *Journal of Rural Studies* 13, no. 4 (1997): 367–75.

Cloke, Paul J., Sarah Johnson, and Jon May. "The Periphery of Care: Emergency Services for Homeless People in Rural Areas." *Journal of Rural Studies* 23 (2007): 387–401.

Cloke, Paul J., and Jo Little, eds. *Contested Countryside Cultures: Otherness, Marginalisation, and Rurality*. London: Routledge, 1997.

Cloke, Paul J., Terry Marsden, and Patrick H. Mooney. *Handbook of Rural Studies*. London: Sage, 2006.

Cody, Paul J., and Peter L. Welch. "Rural Gay Men in Northern New England: Life Experiences and Coping Styles." *Journal of Homosexuality* 33, no. 1 (1997): 51–67.

Cohen, Cathy J. "Punks, Bulldaggers, and Welfare Queens: The Radical Potential of Queer Politics." *GLQ: A Journal of Gay and Lesbian Studies* 3 (1997): 437–65.

———. *The Boundaries of Blackness: AIDS and the Breakdown of Black Politics*. Chicago: University of Chicago Press, 1999.

Cohen-Kettenis, Peggy Tine, and Friedemann Pfäfflin. *Transgenderism and Intersexuality in Childhood and Adolescence: Making Choices*. Thousand Oaks, CA: Sage, 2003.

Consalvo, Mia. *Cheating: Gaining Advantage in Videogames*. Cambridge: MIT Press, 2007.

Cooley, Charles Horton. *Social Organization; a Study of the Larger Mind*. New York: C. Scribner's Sons, 1929.

Corber, Robert J. "Queer Regionalism." *American Literary History* 11, no. 2 (Summer 1999): 391–402.

Correll, S. "The Ethnography of an Electronic Bar: The Lesbian Café." *Journal of Contemporary Ethnography* 24, no. 3 (1995): 270–98.

Corry, John. "HBO's *What Sex Am I?*" *New York Times*, April 18, 1985.

Corsaro, William A. *The Sociology of Childhood*. 2d ed. Sociology for a New Century. Thousand Oaks, CA: Pine Forge Press, 2005.

Couch, Carl J., David R. Maines, and Shing-Ling Chen. *Information Technologies and Social Orders*. Communication and Social Order. New York: Aldine de Gruyter, 1996.

Couldry, Nick, and James Curran. *Contesting Media Power: Alternative Media in a Networked World*. Critical Media Studies. Lanham, MD: Rowman & Littlefield, 2003.

Couto, Richard A. *An American Challenge: A Report on Economic Trends and Social Issues in Appalachia*. Dubuque, IA: Kendall/Hunt, 1994.

———. "Appalachia and Market Economics: The Invisible Hand and Its Powerful Arm." *Journal of Appalachian Studies* 10, no. 3 (2004): 407–20.

————. "Appalachia." In *Appalachia: Social Context Past and Present*, edited by Phillip J. Obermiller and Michael E. Maloney. Dubuque, IA: Kendall/Hunt, 2007.

Crenshaw, Kimberle. "Mapping the Margins: Intersectionality, Identity Politics, and Violence against Women of Color." *Stanford Law Review* 43 (1991): 1241–99.

Cruz, Arnaldo, and Martin F. Manalansan IV. *Queer Globalizations: Citizenship and the Afterlife of Colonialism*. New York: New York University Press, 2002.

Curry, Michael R. *The Work in the World: Geographical Practice and the Written Word*. Minneapolis: University of Minnesota Press, 1996.

Curtin, Michael. *Redeeming the Wasteland: Television Documentary and Cold War Politics*. Communications, Media, and Culture. New Brunswick, NJ: Rutgers University Press, 1995.

Cvetkovich, Ann. *An Archive of Feelings: Trauma, Sexuality, and Lesbian Public Cultures*. Series Q. Durham, NC: Duke University Press, 2003.

D'Augelli, Anthony R., and Charlotte Patterson. *Lesbian, Gay, and Bisexual Identities and Youth: Psychological Perspectives*. Oxford: Oxford University Press, 2001.

D'Emilio, John. *Sexual Politics, Sexual Communities: The Making of a Homosexual Minority in the United States, 1940–1970*. Chicago: University of Chicago Press, 1983.

————. "Capitalism and Gay Identity." *Powers of Desire: The Politics of Sexuality*, ed. Ann Barr Snitow, Christine Stansell, and Sharon Thompson, 100–113. New York: Monthly Review Press, 1983.

————. *Lost Prophet: The Life and Times of Bayard Rustin*. Chicago: University of Chicago Press, 2004.

Dahlgren, Peter. *Television and the Public Sphere: Citizenship, Democracy and the Media*. London: Sage, 1995.

Dahlgren, Peter, and Colin Sparks. *Communication and Citizenship: Journalism and the Public Sphere in the New Media Age*. London: Routledge, 1991.

Day, Ronald E. *The Modern Invention of Information: Discourse, History, and Power*. Carbondale: Southern Illinois University Press, 2001.

Deavers, Kenneth L., and Robert A. Hoppe. "Overview of the Rural Poor in the 1980s." In *Rural Poverty in America*, edited by Cynthia Duncan, 3–20. New York: Auburn House, 1992.

De Cecco, John P. *Gay Personality and Sexual Labeling*. New York: Harrington Park Press, 1984.

De Cecco, John P., and Sonya L. Jones. *A Sea of Stories: The Shaping Power of Narrative in Gay and Lesbian Cultures: A Festschrift for John P. De Cecco*. New York: Harrington Park Press, 2000.

Delany, Samuel R. *Times Square Red, Times Square Blue*. Sexual Cultures. New York: New York University Press, 1999.

Denes, Shary. "Teens Prefer Internet over TV." *Rural Telecommunications* 21, no. 4 (2002): 8.

Denzin, Norman. *Studies in Symbolic Interaction*. Greenwich, CT: JAI Press, 1985.

Dewey, John. *Democracy and Education; an Introduction to the Philosophy of Education*. New York: Macmillan, 1916.

———. *Human Nature and Conduct; an Introduction to Social Psychology*. New York: H. Holt, 1922.

Dews, C. L. Barney, and Carolyn Leste Law. *Out in the South*. Philadelphia: Temple University Press, 2001.

Diamond, Sara. *Roads to Dominion: Right-Wing Movements and Political Power in the United States*. New York: Guilford Press, 1995.

———. *Not by Politics Alone: The Enduring Influence of the Christian Right*. New York: Guilford Press, 1998.

Dicks, B., and B. Mason. "Hypermedia and Ethnography: Reflections on the Construction of a Research Approach." *Sociological Research Online* 3, no. 3 (1998).

Dines, Gail, and Jean McMahon Humez. *Gender, Race, and Class in Media: A Text-Reader*. 2d ed. Thousand Oaks, CA: Sage, 2003.

Doty, Alexander. *Flaming Classics: Queering the Film Canon*. New York: Routledge, 2000.

Dowsett, G. W. *Practicing Desire: Homosexual Sex in the Era of AIDS*. Stanford, CA: Stanford University Press, 1996.

Doyle, Vincent. "'But Joan! You're My Daughter!' Gay and Lesbian Alliance Against Defamation and the Politics of Amnesia." *Radical History Review* 100 (Winter 2008): 209–21.

Driver, Susan. "Beyond 'Straight' Interpretations: Researching Queer Youth Digital Video." In *Representing Youth: Methodological Issues in Critical Youth Studies*, edited by Amy L. Best, 304–24. New York: New York University Press, 2007.

———. *Queer Youth Cultures*. Interruptions—Border Testimony(Ies) and Critical Discourse/S, SUNY. Albany: State University of New York Press, 2008.

Drotner, Kirsten. "Modernity and Media Panics." In *Media Cultures: Reappraising Transnational Media*, edited by Michael Skovmand and Kim Christian Schrøder, 42–62. London: Routledge, 1992.

Duberman, Martin B. *Stonewall*. New York: Dutton, 1993.

Duggan, Lisa. "Making It Perfectly Queer." *Socialist Review* 22, no. 1 (1992): 11–31.

———. "The Trials of Alice Mitchell: Sensationalism, Sexology, and the Lesbian Subject in Turn-of-the-Century America." *Signs* 18, no. 4 (1993): 791–814.

———. *The Twilight of Equality? Neoliberalism, Cultural Politics, and the Attack on Democracy*. 1st ed. Boston: Beacon Press, 2003.

Duncan, Cynthia M., ed. *Rural Poverty in America*. New York: Auburn House, 1992.

Durham, Meenakshi Gigi, and Douglas Kellner, eds. *Media and Cultural Studies: Keyworks*. Rev. ed, Keyworks in Cultural Studies. Malden, MA: Blackwell, 2006.

Dyer, Richard. *The Matter of Images: Essays on Representation*. London: Routledge, 1993.

Ebo, B., ed. *Cyberghetto or Cybertopia? Race, Class, and Gender on the Internet*. Westport, CT: Praeger, 1998.

Eckert, Penelope. *Jocks and Burnouts: Social Categories and Identity in the High School*. New York: Teachers College Press, 1989.

Edelman, Lee. *No Future: Queer Theory and the Death Drive*. Durham, NC: Duke University Press, 2004.

Egan, Jennifer, and Brian Cronin. "Lonely Gay Teen Seeking Same." *New York Times Magazine*, December 10, 2000.

Eisenstein, Elizabeth. *The Printing Press as an Agent of Change: Communications and Cultural Transformations in Early-Modern Europe*. Cambridge: Cambridge University Press, 1979.

———. *The Printing Revolution in Early Modern Europe*. Cambridge: Cambridge University Press, 1983.

Elder, Glen H., and Rand Conger. *Children of the Land: Adversity and Success in Rural America*. John D. and Catherine T. MacArthur Foundation Series on Mental Health and Development, Studies on Successful Adolescent Development. Chicago: University of Chicago Press, 2000.

Eldridge, Vicki Lea, Lisa Mack, and Eric Swank. "Explaining Comfort with Homosexuality in Rural America." *Journal of Homosexuality* 51, no. 2 (2006): 39–56.

Epstein, Steven. "Gay Politics, Ethnic Identity: The Limits of Social Constructionism." *Socialist Review* 93/94 (1987): 9–54.

———. *Impure Science: AIDS, Activism, and the Politics of Knowledge*. Medicine and Society, no. 7. Berkeley: University of California Press, 1996.

Erikson, Erik H. *Childhood and Society*. 1st ed. New York: W.W. Norton, 1950.

———. *Identity: Youth, and Crisis*. 1st ed. New York: W.W. Norton, 1968.

Erzen, Tanya. *Straight to Jesus: Sexual and Christian Conversions in the Ex-Gay Movement*. Berkeley: University of California Press, 2006.

Escobar, A. "Welcome to Cyberia: Notes on the Anthropology of Cyberculture." In *Cyberfutures: Culture and Politics on the Information Superhighway*, edited by Z. Sardar and J. R. Ravetz, 111–37. London: Pluto, 1996.

Escoffier, Jeffrey, and eScholarship (Online service). *American Homo Community and Perversity*. Berkeley: University of California Press, 1998.

Faderman, Lillian. *Odd Girls and Twilight Lovers: A History of Lesbian Life in Twentieth-Century America*. Between Men—Between Women. New York: Columbia University Press, 1991.

Faulkner, Audrey Olsen, and Ann Lindsey. "Grassroots Meet Homophobia: A Rocky Mountain Success Story." *Journal of Gay & Lesbian Social Services* 16, no. 3/4 (2004): 113–28.

Fausto-Sterling, Anne. *Sexing the Body: Gender Politics and the Construction of Sexuality*. 1st ed. New York: Basic Books, 2000.

Feenberg, Andrew, and Alastair Hannay. *Technology and the Politics of Knowledge*. Indiana Series in the Philosophy of Technology. Bloomington: Indiana University Press, 1995.

Fellows, Will. *Farm Boys: Lives of Gay Men from the Rural Midwest*. Madison: University of Wisconsin Press, 1996.

Felski, Rita. *Beyond Feminist Aesthetics: Feminist Literature and Social Change*. Cambridge: Harvard University Press, 1989.

Fields, Jessica. "Normal Queers: Straight Parents Respond to Their Children's 'Coming Out.'" *Symbolic Interaction* 24, no. 2 (2001): 165–87.

Fine, Gary Alan, and Kent L. Sandstrom. *Knowing Children: Participant Observation with Minors*. Qualitative Research Methods 15. Newbury Park, CA: Sage, 1988.

Fisher, Stephen L., ed. *Fighting Back in Appalachia: Traditions of Resistance and Change*. Philadelphia: Temple University Press, 1993.

Fitchen, Janet. "On the Edge of Homelessness: Rural Poverty and Housing Insecurity." *Rural Sociology* 57 (1992): 173–93.

Flax, Jane. *Thinking Fragments: Psychoanalysis, Feminism, and Postmodernism in the Contemporary West*. Berkeley: University of California Press, 1990.

Flint, Colin. *Spaces of Hate: Geographies of Discrimination and Intolerance in the U.S.A.* New York: Routledge, 2004.

Fontaine, J. H. "Queer Kids: The Challenges and Promise for Lesbian, Gay, and Bisexual Youth (1998) (English) by R. E. Owens Jr." *Psychology of Women Quarterly* 24, no. 2 (2000): 204.

Forsyth, Ann. "Out in the Valley." *International Journal of Urban and Regional Research* 21, no. 1 (1997): 36–60.

Fosl, Catherine. *Subversive Southerner: Anne Braden and the Struggle for Racial Justice in the Cold War South*. 1st ed. New York: Palgrave Macmillan, 2002.

Foucault, Michel. *The History of Sexuality: An Introduction*. 1st ed. New York: Vintage Books, 1980.

———. *The Care of the Self: The History of Sexuality, Volume Three*. 1st ed. New York: Vintage Books, 1986.

———. *The Care of the Self*. 1st ed. New York: Vintage Books, 1988.

Foucault, Michel, and Colin Gordon. *Power/Knowledge: Selected Interviews and Other Writings, 1972–1977*. New York: Pantheon Books, 1980.

Fraser, Nancy. "Rethinking the Public Sphere: A Contribution to the Critique of Actually Existing Democracy." In *Habermas and the Public Sphere: Studies in Contemporary German Social Thought*, edited by Craig J. Calhoun, 109–42. Cambridge: MIT Press, 1992.

Friedman, Sara L. "Watching Twin Bracelets in China: The Role of Spectatorship and Identification in an Ethnographic Analysis of Film Reception." *Cultural Anthropology* 21, no. 4 (2006): 603–32.

Galison, Peter Louis, and David J. Stump. *The Disunity of Science: Boundaries, Contexts, and Power*. Writing Science. Stanford, CA: Stanford University Press, 1996.

Gallo, Marcia M. *Different Daughters: A History of the Daughters of Bilitis and the Rise of the Lesbian Rights Movement*. 1st ed. New York: Carroll & Graf, 2006.

Gamson, J. "Reflections on Queer Theory and Communication." *Journal of Homosexuality* 45, no. 2–4 (2003): 385–89.

Gamson, Joshua. *Freaks Talk Back: Tabloid Talk Shows and Sexual Nonconformity*. Chicago: University of Chicago Press, 1998.

———. "Gay Media, Inc.: Media Structures, the New Gay Conglomerates, and Collective Sexual Identities." In *Cyberactivism: Online Activism in Theory and Practice*, edited by Martha McCaughey and Michael D. Ayers, 255–78. New York: Routledge, 2003.

Gamson, Joshua, and Dawne Moon. "The Sociology of Sexualities." *Annual Review of Sociology* 30 (2004): 47–64.

Garber, Marjorie. *Vice Versa: Bisexuality and the Eroticism of Everyday Life*. New York: Simon & Schuster, 1995.

———. *Vested Interests: Cross-dressing and Cultural Anxiety*. 1st ed. New York: Routledge, 1997.

Gauntlett, David. *Web.Studies: Rewiring Media Studies for the Digital Age*. London: Arnold, 2000.

———. *Moving Experiences: Media Effects and Beyond*. 2d ed. Eastleigh, UK: John Libbey, 2005.

Gay.com/PlanetOut.com Network. "Kentucky School's Gay Club Wins Appeal," November 27, 2002.

Geertz, Clifford. *Interpretation of Cultures: Selected Essays*. New York: Basic Books, 1973.

Gibson, William. *Neuromancer*. New York: Ace Science Fiction Books, 1984.

Giddens, Anthony. *Modernity and Self-Identity: Self and Society in the Late Modern Age*. Stanford, CA: Stanford University Press, 1991.

———. *The Transformation of Intimacy: Sexuality, Love, and Eroticism in Modern Societies*. Stanford, CA: Stanford University Press, 1992.

Ginsburg, Faye D., Lila Abu-Lughod, and Brian Larkin. *Media Worlds: Anthropology on New Terrain*. Berkeley: University of California Press, 2002.

Glassman, Anthony. "Hundreds Counter Phelps Clan's Pickets of School Gay-Straight Alliance." *Gay People's Chronicle*, January 17, 2003.

Goffman, Erving. *The Presentation of Self in Everyday Life*. Garden City, NY: Doubleday, 1959.

———. *Stigma: Notes on the Management of Spoiled Identity*. New York: Simon & Schuster, 1986.

Gopinath, Gayatri. *Impossible Desires: Queer Diasporas and South Asian Public Cultures*. Perverse Modernities. Durham, NC: Duke University Press, 2005.

Grazian, David. *Blue Chicago: The Search for Authenticity in Urban Blues Clubs.* Chicago: University of Chicago Press, 2003.

Green, Nicole. "Disrupting the Field: Virtual Technologies and 'Multisited' Ethnographic Methods." *American Behavioral Scientist* 43, no. 3 (1999): 409–21.

Grise-Owens, Erlene, Jeff Vessels, and Larry W. Owens. "Organizing for Change: One City's Journey toward Justice." *Journal of Gay & Lesbian Social Services* 16, no. 3/4 (2004): 1–15.

Gross, Larry P. *Up from Invisibility: Lesbians, Gay Men, and the Media in America.* Between Men—Between Women. New York: Columbia University Press, 2001.

——. "Foreword." In *Queer Online: Media, Technology, and Sexuality,* edited by Kate O'Riordan and David J. Phillips, vii–x. New York: Peter Lang, 2007.

Gross, Larry P., and James D. Woods. *The Columbia Reader on Lesbians and Gay Men in Media, Society, and Politics.* Between Men—Between Women. New York: Columbia University Press, 1999.

Grosswiler, Paul, and Institute of Policy Alternatives (Montreal, Quebec). *The Method Is the Message: Rethinking McLuhan through Critical Theory.* Montreal: Black Rose Books, 1998.

Gunn, Eileen P. "PlanetOut Goes Mainstream." *Advertising Age,* June 19, 2000, 60.

Haag, Anthony M., and Franklin K. Chang. "The Impact of Electronic Networking on the Lesbian and Gay Community." In *Rural Gays and Lesbians: Building on the Strengths of Communities,* 83–94. New York: Harrington Park Press, 1997.

Habermas, Jürgen. *The Structural Transformation of the Public Sphere: An Inquiry into a Category of Bourgeois Society.* Studies in Contemporary German Social Thought. Cambridge: MIT Press, 1989.

Hakken, David. *Cyborgs@Cyberspace: An Ethnographer Looks to the Future.* New York: Routledge, 1999.

Hakken, David, and ebrary Inc. "Cyborgs@Cyberspace? An Ethnographer Looks to the Future." New York: Routledge, 1999.

Halberstam, J. "Reflections on Queer Studies and Queer Pedagogy." *Journal of Homosexuality* 45, no. 2–4 (2003): 361–64.

Halberstam, Judith. *Female Masculinity.* Durham, NC: Duke University Press, 1998.

——. *In a Queer Time and Place: Transgender Bodies, Subcultural Lives.* Sexual Cultures. New York: New York University Press, 2005.

Halfacree, Keith. "Locality and Social Representation: Space, Discourse and Alternative Definitions of the Rural." *Journal of Rural Studies* 9, no. 1 (1993): 23–37.

Hall, Stuart. *Representation: Cultural Representations and Signifying Practices.* London: Sage, 1997.

Hanks, William. "Discourse Genres in a Theory of Practice." *American Ethnologist* 14, no. 4 (1987): 668–92.

———. "Pierre Bourdieu and the Practices of Language." *Annual Review of Anthropology* 34 (2005): 67–83.

Haraway, Donna. "A Manifesto for Cyborgs: Science, Technology, and Socialist Feminism in the 1980s." *Socialist Review* 15, no. 2 (March–April 1985): 65–108.

Haraway, Donna Jeanne. *Simians, Cyborgs, and Women: The Reinvention of Nature.* London: Free Association Books, 1991.

Hart, Kenneth. "GSA Allowed to Meet." *Ashland Daily Independent*, April 19, 2003.

Harvey, David. *The Condition of Postmodernity: An Enquiry into the Origins of Cultural Change.* Oxford: Blackwell, 1989.

Hayden, Wilburn. "Appalachian Diversity: African-American, Hispanic/Latino, and Other Populations." *Journal of Appalachian Studies* 10, no. 3 (2004): 293–306.

Hayles, N. Katherine. *How We Became Posthuman: Virtual Bodies in Cybernetics, Literature, and Informatics.* Chicago: University of Chicago Press, 1999.

Heath, Deborah, Erin Koch, and Barbara Ley. "Nodes and Queries: Linking Locations in Networked Fields of Inquiry." *American Behavioral Scientist* 43, no. 3 (1999): 450–63.

Heineman, Kenneth J. *Campus Wars: The Peace Movement at American State Universities in the Vietnam Era.* New York: New York University Press, 1993.

Heins, Marjorie. *Not in Front of the Children: Indecency, Censorship, and the Innocence of Youth.* New Brunswick, NJ: Rutgers University Press, 2007.

Hemmings, Clare. *Bisexual Spaces: A Geography of Sexuality and Gender.* New York: Routledge, 2002.

Hemphill, Paul. *The Ballad of Little River: A Tale of Race and Restless Youth in the Rural South.* New York: Free Press, 2000.

Hendershot, Heather. *Shaking the World for Jesus: Media and Conservative Evangelical Culture.* Chicago: University of Chicago Press, 2004.

Henderson, Lisa. "The Class Character of *Boys Don't Cry.*" *Screen* 42, no. 3 (2001): 299–303.

Henderson, L. "Queer Theory, New Millennium." *Journal of Homosexuality* 45, no. 2–4 (2003): 375–79.

Henry, Charles P. *Long Overdue: The Politics of Racial Reparations.* New York: New York University Press, 2007.

Herdt, Gilbert H., and Andrew Boxer. *Children of Horizons: How Gay and Lesbian Teens Are Leading a New Way out of the Closet.* Boston: Beacon Press, 1993.

Herdt, Gilbert H., and S. Lindenbaum, eds. *The Time of AIDS: Social Analysis, Theory, and Method.* Newbury Park, CA: Sage, 1991.

Herdt, Gilbert, Stephen T. Russell, Jeffrey Sweat, and Michelle Marzullo. "Sexual Inequality, Youth Empowerment, and the GSA: A Community Study in California." In *Sexual Inequalities and Social Justice*, edited by Niels Teunis and Gilbert Herdt. Berkeley: University of California Press, 2006.

Herring, Scott. "Caravaggio's Rednecks." *GLQ: A Journal of Gay and Lesbian Studies* 12, no. 2 (2006): 217–36.

———. "*Brokeback Mountain* Dossier." *GLQ: A Journal of Gay and Lesbian Studies* 13, no. 1 (2006): 93–109.

Herring, Susan. "Content Analysis for New Media: Rethinking the Paradigm." Paper presented at the New Research for New Media: Innovative Research Methodologies Symposium Working Papers and Readings, 2004.

———. "Slouching toward the Ordinary: Current Trends in Computer-Mediated Communication." *New Media and Society* 6, no. 1 (2004): 26–36.

Higonnet, Anne. *Pictures of Innocence: The History and Crisis of Ideal Childhood.* New York: Thames and Hudson, 1998.

Hill, Annette. *Restyling Factual TV: Audiences and News, Documentary and Reality Genres.* London: Routledge, 2007.

Hill Collins, Patricia. *Black Feminist Thought: Knowledge, Consciousness, and the Politics of Empowerment.* 2d ed. New York: Routledge, 2000.

Hine, Christine. *Virtual Ethnography.* London: Sage, 2000.

———. *Virtual Methods: Issues in Social Research on the Internet.* Oxford: Berg, 2005.

Hirsch, E. "Bound and Unbound Entities: Reflections on the Ethnographic Perspectives of Anthropology vis-à-vis Media and Cultural Studies." In *Ritual, Performance, Media*, edited by F. Hughes-Freeland, 208–28. London: Routledge, 1998.

Holloway, Sarah L., and Gill Valentine. *Cyberkids: Children in the Information Age.* London: Routledge, 2003.

Hoover, G. A., and M. V. Carter. "The Invisible Homeless: Non-Urban Homeless in Appalachian East Tennessee." *Rural Sociologist* 11, no. 4 (1991): 3–12.

Housing Assistance Council. "Taking Stock: Rural People, Poverty, and Housing at the Turn of the 21st Century." Available at www.ruralhome.org, 2002.

Howard, John. *Carryin' on in the Lesbian and Gay South.* New York: New York University Press, 1997.

———. "Place and Movement in Gay American History: A Case from the Post–World War II South." In *Creating a Place for Ourselves: Lesbian, Gay, and Bisexual Community Histories*, edited by Brett Beemyn, 211–26. New York: Routledge, 1997.

———. *Men Like That: A Southern Queer History.* Chicago: University of Chicago Press, 1999.

———. "Of Closets and Other Rural Voids." *GLQ: A Journal of Gay and Lesbian Studies* 13, no. 1 (2006): 100–102.

Hoyt, William H. "An Evaluation of the Kentucky Education Reform Act." In *Kentucky Annual Economic Report*, 1999, 21–36.

Hughes, Everett. "Dilemmas and Contradictions of Status." *American Journal of Sociology* 50 (1945): 353–59.

Hull, Gloria T., Patricia Bell-Scott, and Barbara Smith. *All the Women Are White, All the Blacks Are Men, But Some of Us Are Brave: Black Women's Studies.* 1st ed. Old Westbury, NY: Feminist Press, 1982.

Humphreys, Laud. *Tearoom Trade: Impersonal Sex in Public Places.* Observations. Chicago: Aldine, 1970.

Incite! Women of Color Against Violence. *The Revolution Will Not Be Funded: Beyond the Non-Profit Industrial Complex.* Cambridge, MA: South End Press, 2007.

Ingram, Gordon Brent, Anne-Marie Bouthillette, and Yolanda Retter. *Queers in Space: Communities, Public Places, Sites of Resistance.* Seattle: Bay Press, 1997.

Irvine, Janice M. *Talk About Sex: The Battles over Sex Education in the United States.* Berkeley: University of California Press, 2002.

Jacobson, David. "Doing Research in Cyberspace." *Field Methods* 11, no. 2 (1999): 127–45.

Jakobsen, Janet R., and Ann Pellegrini. *Love the Sin: Sexual Regulation and the Limits of Religious Tolerance.* Sexual Cultures. New York: New York University Press, 2003.

James, Allison, Chris Jenks, and Alan Prout. *Theorizing Childhood.* New York: Teachers College Press, 1998.

Jaspin, Elliot. *Buried in the Bitter Waters: The Hidden History of Racial Cleansing in America.* New York: Basic Books, 2007.

Jenkins, Henry. *The Children's Culture Reader.* New York: New York University Press, 1998.

———. *Convergence Culture: Where Old and New Media Collide.* New York: New York University Press, 2006.

Johns, Adrian. *The Nature of the Book: Print and Knowledge in the Making.* Chicago: University of Chicago Press, 1998.

Johnson, Colin R. "Homosexuals in Unexpected Places? An Introduction." *American Studies* 48 (Summer 2007).

———. "Casual Sex: Towards a 'Prehistory' of Gay Life in Bohemian America." *Interventions* 10, no. 3 (2008): 303–20.

Johnson, E. Patrick, and Mae Henderson, eds. *Black Queer Studies: A Critical Anthology.* Durham, NC: Duke University Press, 2005.

Jones, Steve, ed. *Cybersociety 2.0: Revisiting Computer-Mediated Communication and Community.* Thousand Oaks, CA: Sage, 1998.

———. *Doing Internet Research: Critical Issues and Methods for Examining the Net.* Thousand Oaks, CA: Sage, 1999.

———. "Foreword: Dreams of Fields: Possible Trajectories of Internet Studies." In *Critical Cyberculture Studies*, edited by David Silver and Adrienne Massanari, ix–xvii. New York: New York University Press, 2006.

Karasic, Dan, and Jack Drescher. *Sexual and Gender Diagnoses of the Diagnostic and Statistical Manual (DSM): A Reevaluation*. New York: Haworth Press, 2005.

Katz, Elihu, Paul Felix Lazarsfeld, and Columbia University. Bureau of Applied Social Research. *Personal Influence; the Part Played by People in the Flow of Mass Communications*. Glencoe, IL: Free Press, 1955.

Katz, Jack. "Ethical Escape Routes for Underground Ethnographers." *American Ethnologist* 33, no. 2 (2006): 499–506.

Kaufman, Gershen, and Lev Raphael. *Coming Out of Shame: Transforming Gay and Lesbian Lives*. New York: Main Street Books/Doubleday, 1997.

Keith, Michael, and Steve Pile. *Place and the Politics of Identity*. New York: Routledge, 1993.

Kellner, Douglas. *Media Spectacle*. New York: Routledge, 2003.

Kendall, Lori. *Hanging Out in the Virtual Pub: Masculinities and Relationships Online*. Berkeley: University of California Press, 2002.

Kennedy, Elizabeth Lapovsky. "'But We Would Never Talk About It': The Structures of Lesbian Discretion in South Dakota, 1928–1933." In *Inventing Lesbian Cultures in America*, edited by Ellen Lewin, viii, 232. Boston: Beacon Press, 1996.

Kennedy, Elizabeth Lapovsky, and Madeline D. Davis. *Boots of Leather, Slippers of Gold: The History of a Lesbian Community*. New York: Routledge, 1993.

Kenney, Moira. *Mapping Gay L.A.: The Intersection of Place and Politics*. American Subjects. Philadelphia: Temple University Press, 2001.

Kensicki, L. J. "Speaking of New Media: Oral Explorations into Social Change through the Internet." Paper presented at the Minnesota-Amsterdam Symposium, Minneapolis, September 2002.

Kentucky Department of Education Office of Communication. *Results Matter: A Decade of Difference in Kentucky's Public Schools 1990–2000*, 2000.

Kessler, Suzanne J., and Wendy McKenna. "Gender Construction in Everyday Life: Transsexualism (Abridged)." *Feminism and Psychology* 10, no. 1 (2000): 11–29.

Kincaid, James R. *Erotic Innocence: The Culture of Child Molesting*. Durham, NC: Duke University Press, 1998.

Kingsolver, Ann E. *NAFTA Stories: Fears and Hopes in Mexico and the United States*. Boulder, CO: Lynne Rienner Publishers, 2001.

Kirkey, Kenneth, and Ann Forsyth. "Men in the Valley: Gay Male Life on the Suburban-Rural Fringe." *Journal of Rural Studies* 17 (2001): 421–41.

Klecker, Beverly M., Jerry Austin, and Leonard Burns. "An In-Depth Analysis of Decisions Made by Kentucky's School-Based Decision Making Councils." In *Annual Meeting of the American Educational Research Association*, 1–29. Quebec, Canada, 1999.

Kline, Ronald R. *Consumers in the Country: Technology and Social Change in Rural America*. Revisiting Rural America. Baltimore: Johns Hopkins University Press, 2000.

Klinger, Barbara. *Beyond the Multiplex: Cinema, New Technologies, and the Home*. Berkeley: University of California Press, 2006.

Kluger, Richard. *Simple Justice: The History of Brown v. Board of Education and Black America's Struggle for Equality*. Rev. and expanded ed. New York: Knopf, 2004.

Knopp, Larry. "Some Theoretical Implications of Gay Involvement in an Urban Land Market." *Political Geography Quarterly* 9 (1990): 337–52.

———. "Exploiting the Rent-Gap: The Theoretical Significance of Using Illegal Appraisal Schemes to Encourage Gentrification in New Orleans." *Urban Geography* 11 (1990): 48–64.

———. "Sexuality and Urban Space: A Framework for Analysis." In *Mapping Desire: Geographies of Sexualities*, edited by David Bell and Gill Valentine, 149–64. London: Routledge, 1995.

Kollock, P., and M. A. Smith, eds. *Communities in Cyberspace*. London: Routledge, 1999.

Kraack, Anna, and Jane Kenway. "Place, Time and Stigmatised Youthful Identities: Bad Boys in Paradise." *Journal of Rural Studies* 18, no. 2 (2002): 145–55.

Kramer, Jerry Lee. "Bachelor Farmers and Spinsters: Gay and Lesbian Identities and Communities in Rural North Dakota." In *Mapping Desire: Geographies of Sexualities*, edited by David Bell and Gill Valentine, 200–213. London: Routledge, 1995.

Krieger, Susan. *The Mirror Dance: Identity in a Women's Community*. Philadelphia: Temple University Press, 1983.

Laegran, Anne Sofie. "The Petrol Station and the Internet Cafe: Rural Technospaces for Youth." *Journal of Rural Studies* 18, no. 2 (2002): 157–68.

Lancaster, Roger N. *The Trouble with Nature: Sex in Science and Popular Culture*. Berkeley: University of California Press, 2003.

Lannen, Steve. "Kansas Church Returns to Protest Boyd Club: Demonstrators Again Outnumbered by Police, 200 Unity Ralliers." *Lexington Herald-Leader*, January 13, 2003.

Latimer, Melissa, and Ann M. Oberhauser. "Exploring Gender and Economic Development in Appalachia." *Journal of Appalachian Studies* 10, no. 3 (2004): 269–92.

Latour, Bruno. *We Have Never Been Modern*. Cambridge: Harvard University Press, 1993.

————. "On Interobjectivity." *Mind, Culture, and Activity* 3, no. 4 (1996): 228–45.

Latour, Bruno, and Steve Woolgar. *Laboratory Life: The Construction of Scientific Facts.* Princeton, NJ: Princeton University Press, 1986.

Laumann, Edward O. *The Social Organization of Sexuality: Sexual Practices in the United States.* Chicago: University of Chicago Press, 1994.

Lave, Jean, and Etienne Wenger. *Situated Learning: Legitimate Peripheral Participation.* Cambridge: Cambridge University Press, 1991.

Lawrence, Mark. "Heartlands or Neglected Geographies? Liminality, Power and the Hyperreal Rural." *Journal of Rural Studies* 13 (1997): 1–17.

Lee, Matthew R., Michael O. Maume, and Graham C. Ousey. "Social Isolation and Lethal Violence across the Metro/Nonmetro Divide: The Effects of Socioeconomic Disadvantage and Poverty Concentration on Homicide." *Rural Sociology* 68, no. 1 (2003): 107–31.

Lesko, Nancy. *Act Your Age! A Cultural Construction of Adolescence.* Critical Social Thought. New York: RoutledgeFalmer, 2001.

Levine, Judith. *Harmful to Minors: The Perils of Protecting Children from Sex.* Minneapolis: University of Minnesota Press, 2002.

Levine, Martin P. *Gay Men: The Sociology of Male Homosexuality.* 1st ed. New York: Harper & Row, 1979.

————. "Gay Ghetto." In *Gay Men: The Sociology of Male Homosexuality*, edited by Martin P. Levine, 182–204. New York: Harper & Row, 1979.

Lewin, Ellen. *Lesbian Mothers: Accounts of Gender in American Culture.* Anthropology of Contemporary Issues. Ithaca, NY: Cornell University Press, 1993.

————, ed. *Inventing Lesbian Cultures in America.* Boston: Beacon Press, 1996.

Lewin, Ellen, and William Leap. *Out in Theory: The Emergence of Lesbian and Gay Anthropology.* Urbana: University of Illinois Press, 2002.

Lewis, Ronald L. "Beyond Isolation and Homogeneity: Diversity and the History of Appalachia." In *Appalachia: Social Context Past and Present*, edited by Michael E. Maloney and Phillip J. Obermiller, chapter 13. Dubuque, IA: Kendall/Hunt, 2007.

Lewis, Ronald L., and Dwight B. Billings. "Appalachian Culture and Economic Development: A Retrospective View on the Theory and Literature." *Journal of Appalachian Studies* 3, no. 1 (1997): 3–41.

Leyshon, Michael. "On Being 'in the Field': Practice, Progress and Problems in Research with Young People in Rural Areas." *Journal of Rural Studies* 18, no. 2 (2002): 179–91.

Lievrouw, Leah A., and Sonia M. Livingstone. *Handbook of New Media: Social Shaping and Consequences of ICTs.* London: Sage, 2002.

————. "Introduction." In *Major Works in New Media*, edited by L. Lievrouw and S. Livingstone. London: Sage, in press.

Linde, Charlotte. *Life Stories: The Creation of Coherence.* New York: Oxford University Press, 1993.

———. "The Acquisition of a Speaker by a Story: How History Becomes Memory and Identity." *Ethos* 28, no. 4 (2001): 608–32.

Lindle, Jane C. "Developing School-Based Decision Making Capacities in Kentucky: Communication Satisfaction after the Pilot Year." Education Resources Information Center, 1992, 1–28.

Lindlof, T. R., and M. J. Shatzer. "Media Ethnography in Virtual Space." *Journal of Broadcasting and Electronic Media* 42, no. 2 (1998): 170–89.

Little, Jo. *Gender and Rural Geography: Identity, Sexuality and Power in the Countryside.* Harlow, UK: Prentice Hall, 2002.

Livingstone, Sonia M. *Young People and New Media: Childhood and the Changing Media Environment.* London: Sage, 2002.

———. "Taking Risky Opportunities in Youthful Content Creation: Teenagers' Use of Social Networking Sites for Intimacy, Privacy and Self-Expression." *New Media and Society* 10, no. 3 (2008): 392–411.

Loewen, James W. *Sundown Towns: A Hidden Dimension of American Racism.* 1st ed. New York: Touchstone, 2006.

Loffreda, Beth. *Losing Matt Shepard: Life and Politics in the Aftermath of Anti-Gay Murder.* New York: Columbia University Press, 2000.

Low, Setha M., and Denise Lawrence-Zúñiga. *The Anthropology of Space and Place: Locating Culture.* Malden, MA: Blackwell, 2003.

Lyman, Peter, and Nina Wakeford. "Going in the (Virtual) Field." *American Behavioral Scientist* 43, no. 3 (1999): 359–76.

Lyson, Thomas A., and William W. Falk. *Forgotten Places: Uneven Development in Rural America.* Lawrence: University Press of Kansas, 1993.

Mahar, Cheleen. "On the Moral Economy of Country Life." *Journal of Rural Studies* 7, no. 4 (1991): 363–72.

Maimon, Alan. "Attempt to Block Gay-Rights Club at Boyd High School Is Stymied." *Courier-Journal*, December 18, 2002.

———. "Boyd Bans Club Meetings at Schools: Gay-Rights Group Sparked Controversy." *Courier-Journal*, December 21, 2002.

Maines, David R. *The Faultline of Consciousness: A View of Interactionism in Sociology.* Sociological Imagination and Structural Change. New York: Aldine de Gruyter, 2001.

Maines, David R., and Carl J. Couch. *Communication and Social Structure.* Springfield, IL: C.C. Thomas, 1988.

Maloney, Michael E., and Phillip J. Obermiller, eds. *Appalachia: Social Context Past and Present.* 5th ed. Dubuque, IA: Kendall/Hunt, 2007.

Manalansan, Martin F., IV. *Global Divas: Filipino Gay Men in the Diaspora.* Perverse Modernities. Durham, NC: Duke University Press, 2003.

———. "Colonizing Time and Space: Race and Romance in *Brokeback Mountain*." *GLQ: A Journal of Gay and Lesbian Studies* 13, no. 1 (2006): 97–100.

Mann, Chris, and Fiona Stewart. *Internet Communication and Qualitative Research: A Handbook for Researching Online.* New Technologies for Social Research. London: Sage, 2000.

Marcus, George E. "Ethnography in/of the World System: The Emergence of Multi-Sited Ethnography." *Annual Review of Anthropology* 24 (1995): 95–117.

———. *Connected: Engagements with Media.* Late Editions 3. Chicago: University of Chicago Press, 1996.

Marcus, George E., and Michael M. J. Fischer. *Anthropology as Cultural Critique: An Experimental Moment in the Human Sciences.* 2d ed. Chicago: University of Chicago Press, 1999.

Markowitz, Fran, and Michael Ashkenazi. *Sex, Sexuality, and the Anthropologist.* Urbana: University of Illinois Press, 1999.

Marvin, Carolyn. *When Old Technologies Were New: Thinking About Electric Communication in the Late Nineteenth Century.* New York: Oxford University Press, 1988.

Massey, Doreen B. *Space, Place and Gender.* Cambridge: Polity Press, 1994.

———. *Spatial Divisions of Labor: Social Structures and the Geography of Production.* 2d ed. New York: Routledge, 1995.

McAreavey, Ruth. "Getting Close to the Action: The Micro-Politics of Rural Development." *European Society for Rural Sociology* 46, no. 2 (2006): 87–103.

McBride, Dwight A. "Why I Hate That I Loved *Brokeback Mountain.*" *GLQ: A Journal of Gay and Lesbian Studies* 13, no. 1 (2006): 95–97.

McCarthy, Linda. "Poppies in a Wheat Field." *Journal of Homosexuality* 39 (2000): 75–94.

McDonough, Kevin, and Walter Feinberg. *Education and Citizenship in Liberal-Democratic Societies: Teaching for Cosmopolitan Values and Collective Identities.* Oxford: Oxford University Press, 2003.

McKenna, Katelyn, and John Bargh. "Coming Out in the Age of the Internet: Identity 'Demarginalization' through Virtual Group Participation." *Journal of Personality and Social Psychology* 75, no. 3 (1998): 681–94.

McLuhan, Marshall. *Understanding Media; the Extensions of Man.* 1st ed. New York: McGraw-Hill, 1964. Reprint. Cambridge: MIT Press, 1994.

McLuhan, Marshall, and Eric McLuhan. *Laws of Media: The New Science.* Toronto: University of Toronto Press, 1988.

Mead, George Herbert. *On Social Psychology; Selected Papers.* Rev. ed. Heritage of Sociology Series. Chicago: University of Chicago Press, 1964.

Mead, George Herbert, and Charles W. Morris. *Mind, Self & Society from the Standpoint of a Social Behaviorist.* Chicago: University of Chicago Press, 1934.

Mead, Margaret. *Coming of Age in Samoa; a Psychological Study of Primitive Youth for Western Civilization.* New York: Blue Ribbon Books, 1932.

Meeker, Martin. *Contacts Desired: Gay and Lesbian Communications and Community, 1940s–1970s*. Chicago: University of Chicago Press, 2006.

Meyerowitz, Joanne J. *How Sex Changed: A History of Transsexuality in the United States*. Cambridge: Harvard University Press, 2002.

Miceli, Melinda. *Standing Out, Standing Together: The Social and Political Impact of Gay-Straight Alliances*. New York: Routledge, 2005.

Miller, Daniel, and Don Slater. *The Internet: An Ethnographic Approach*. Oxford: Berg, 2000.

Mills, C. Wright. *The Sociological Imagination*. New York: Oxford University Press, 1959.

Mingay, G. E. *The Rural Idyll*. London: Routledge, 1989.

Mitchell, W. J. Thomas. *On Narrative*. Chicago: University of Chicago Press, 1981.

Mittell, Jason. "A Cultural Approach to Television Genre Theory." *Cinema Journal* 40, no. 3 (Spring 2001): 3–24.

Moraga, Cherríe, and Gloria Anzaldúa. *This Bridge Called My Back: Writings by Radical Women of Color*. 2d ed. New York: Kitchen Table, Women of Color Press, 1983.

Morley, David, and Kevin Robins. *Spaces of Identity: Global Media, Electronic Landscapes and Cultural Boundaries*. London: Routledge, 1995.

Morris, Debra. "Privacy, Privation, Perversity: Toward New Representations of the Personal." *Signs* 25, no. 2 (Winter 2000): 323–51.

Morrison, Toni. *Playing in the Dark: Whiteness and the Literary Imagination*. Cambridge: Harvard University Press, 1992.

Mumford, Kevin J. *Interzones: Black/White Sex Districts in Chicago and New York in the Early Twentieth Century*. Popular Cultures, Everyday Lives. New York: Columbia University Press, 1997.

Muñoz, José Esteban. *Disidentifications: Queers of Color and the Performance of Politics*. Cultural Studies of the Americas. Minneapolis: University of Minnesota Press, 1999.

Murray, Stephen O. "The Institutional Elaboration of a Quasi-Ethnic Community." *International Review of Modern Sociology* 9 (1979): 165–78.

———. *American Gay*. Worlds of Desire. Chicago: University of Chicago Press, 1996.

Murray, Susan, and Laurie Ouellette, eds. *Reality TV: Remaking Television Culture*. New York: New York University Press, 2004.

Nagel, Joane. *Race, Ethnicity, and Sexuality: Intimate Intersections, Forbidden Frontiers*. New York: Oxford University Press, 2003.

Nakamura, Lisa, Gilbert B. Rodman, and Beth E. Kolko. *Race in Cyberspace*. New York: Routledge, 2000.

Newton, Esther. *Mother Camp: Female Impersonators in America*. Englewood Cliffs, NJ: Prentice Hall, 1972.

———. *Cherry Grove, Fire Island: Sixty Years in America's First Gay and Lesbian Town*. Boston: Beacon Press, 1993.

———. *Margaret Mead Made Me Gay: Personal Essays, Public Ideas.* Series Q. Durham, NC: Duke University Press, 2000.

Nichols, Bill. *Representing Reality: Issues and Concepts in Documentary.* Bloomington: Indiana University Press, 1991.

Nye, David E. *Electrifying America: Social Meanings of a New Technology, 1880–1940.* Cambridge: MIT Press, 1990.

O'Riordan, Kate, and David J. Phillips, eds. *Queer Online: Media Technology & Sexuality.* Digital Formations. New York: Peter Lang, 2007.

Obermiller, Phillip J. "Introduction to Appalachia Counts: The Region in the 2000 Census, a Special Issue of the Journal of Appalachian Studies." *Journal of Appalachian Studies* 10, no. 3 (2004): 245–54.

Oswald, Ramona. "Who Am I in Relation to Them? Gay, Lesbian, and Queer People Leave the City to Attend Rural Family Weddings." *Journal of Family Issues* 23, no. 3 (2002): 323–48.

Otis, Melanie D. "One Community's Path to Greater Social Justice: Building on Earlier Successes." *Journal of Gay & Lesbian Social Services* 16, no. 3/4 (2004): 17–33.

Paccagnella, L. "Getting the Seats of Your Pants Dirty: Strategies for Ethnographic Research on Virtual Communities." *Journal of Computer Mediated Communication* 3, no. 1 (1997).

Padilla, Mark. *Caribbean Pleasure Industry: Tourism, Sexuality, and AIDS in the Dominican Republic.* Worlds of Desire. Chicago: University of Chicago Press, 2007.

Padilla, Yolanda C. *Gay and Lesbian Rights Organizing: Community-Based Strategies.* New York: Harrington Park Press, 2004.

Panelli, Ruth. "Young Rural Lives: Strategies Beyond Diversity." *Journal of Rural Studies* 18, no. 2 (2002): 113–22.

Papacharissi, Zizi. "The Virtual Sphere: The Internet as Public Sphere." *New Media and Society* 4, no. 1 (2002): 9–27.

Parker, Richard G. *Bodies, Pleasures, and Passions: Sexual Culture in Contemporary Brazil.* Boston: Beacon Press, 1991.

———. "Sexuality, Culture, and Power in HIV/AIDS Research." *Annual Review of Anthropology* 30 (2001): 163–79.

Parker, Richard G., Regina Maria Barbosa, and Peter Aggleton. *Framing the Sexual Subject: The Politics of Gender, Sexuality, and Power.* Berkeley: University of California Press, 2000.

Pascoe, C. J. *Dude, You're a Fag: Masculinity and Sexuality in High School.* Berkeley: University of California Press, 2007.

Patton, Cindy. "Tremble, Hetero Swine!" In *Fear of a Queer Planet*, edited by Michael Warner, 143–77. Minneapolis: University of Minnesota Press, 1993.

Pauly, Ira B. "Terminology and Classification of Gender Identity Disorders." In *Gender Dysphoria: Interdisciplinary Approaches in Clinical Management*, edited by Walter O. Bockting and Eli Coleman, 1–14. New York: Haworth Press, 1992.

Phelan, Shane. *Identity Politics: Lesbian Feminism and the Limits of Community.* Philadelphia: Temple University Press, 1989.

———. "(Be)Coming Out: Lesbian Identity and Politics." *Signs* 18, no. 4 (1993): 765–90.

———. "The Shape of Queer: Assimilation and Articulation." *Women and Politics* 18, no. 2 (1997): 55–73.

Phillips, D. J. "Defending the Boundaries: Identifying and Countering Threats in a Usenet Newsgroup." *Information Society* 12, no. 1 (1996): 39–62.

Phillips, Richard, Diane Watt, and David Shuttleton, eds. *De-Centring Sexualities: Politics and Representations Beyond the Metropolis.* London: Routledge, 2000.

Piontek, T. "Kinging in the Heartland; or, the Power of Marginality." *Journal of Homosexuality* 43, no. 3–4 (2002): 125–43.

Pitsch, Mark. "Gay-Straight Group Wants to Meet at Boyd School; Council Denied Request, Will Reconsider Tonight." *Courier-Journal,* October 28, 2002.

———. "Gay-Rights Decision Protested at E. Kentucky School: Allowing Group to Meet Sparks Student Boycott," *Courier-Journal,* November 5, 2002.

———. "'We Have to Protect Our Children' Rally Targets Gay-Rights Group: Boyd High Urged to Change Curriculum," *Courier-Journal,* November 11, 2002.

———. "ACLU Files Gay-Rights Suit against Boyd School Leaders." *Courier-Journal,* January 23, 2003.

———. "Boyd Gay-Rights Club to Meet Again; School District Ponders Appeal of Ruling against Ban." *Courier-Journal,* April 23, 2003.

Plummer, Kenneth. *Sexual Stigma: An Interactionist Account.* London: Routledge & Kegan Paul, 1975.

———. *Telling Sexual Stories: Power, Change, and Social Worlds.* London: Routledge, 1995.

Pollard, Kelvin. "Appalachia at the Millennium: An Overview of Results from Census 2000." Washington D.C.: Appalachian Regional Commission/Population Reference Bureau, 2003.

Ponse, Barbara. *Identities in the Lesbian World: The Social Construction of Self.* Contributions in Sociology, no. 28. Westport, CT: Greenwood Press, 1978.

Prieur, Annick. *Mema's House, Mexico City: On Transvestites, Queens, and Machos.* Chicago: University of Chicago Press, 1998.

Prosser, Jay. *Second Skins: The Body Narratives of Transsexuality.* Gender and Culture. New York: Columbia University Press, 1998.

Pullen, Christopher. *Documenting Gay Men: Identity and Performance in Reality Television and Documentary Film.* Jefferson, NC: McFarland, 2007.

Puri, Jyoti. *Woman, Body, Desire in Post-Colonial India: Narratives of Gender and Sexuality.* New York: Routledge, 1999.

Qvortrup, Jens. *Childhood Matters: Social Theory, Practice and Politics.* Public Policy and Social Welfare. Aldershot, UK: Avebury, 1994.

Raffo, Susan. *Queerly Classed.* Cambridge, MA: South End Press, 1997.

Raphael, Chad. "The Political Economic Origins of Reali-TV." In *Reality TV: Remaking Television Culture*, edited by Susan Murray and Laurie Ouellette, 119–36. New York: New York University Press, 2004.

Reid, E. "Informed Consent in the Study of On-Line Communities: A Reflection of the Effects of Computer-Mediated Social Research." *Information Society* 12, no. 2 (1996): 169–74.

Remafedi, Gary. *Death by Denial: Studies of Suicide in Gay and Lesbian Teenagers*. 1st ed. Boston: Alyson Publications, 1994.

Rheingold, Howard. *The Virtual Community: Homesteading on the Electronic Frontier*. New York: HarperPerennial, 1994.

Ribeiro, Gustavo Lins. "IRBs Are the Tip of the Iceberg: State Regulation, Academic Freedom, and Methodological Issues." *American Ethnologist* 33, no. 4 (2006): 529–31.

Rich, Adrienne. "Compulsory Heterosexuality and Lesbian Existence." *Signs: Journal of Women in Culture and Society* 5 (Summer 1980): 631–60.

Rodriguez, Juana Maria. *Queer Latinidad: Identity Practices, Discursive Spaces*. Sexual Cultures. New York: New York University Press, 2003.

Rosario, M., J. Hunter, S. Maguen, M. Gwadz, and R. Smith. "The Coming-Out Process and Its Adaptational and Health-Related Associations among Gay, Lesbian, and Bisexual Youths: Stipulation and Exploration of a Model." *American Journal of Community Psychology* 29, no. 1 (2001).

Rose, Arnold Marshall. *Human Behavior and Social Processes; an Interactionist Approach*. Boston: Houghton Mifflin, 1962.

Ross, Marlon B. "Beyond the Closet as Raceless Paradigm." In *Black Queer Studies: A Critical Anthology*, edited by E. Patrick Johnson and Mae G. Henderson, 161–89. Durham, NC: Duke University Press, 2005.

Rostosky, S., G. Owens, R. Zimmerman, and E. Riggle. "Associations among Sexual Attraction Status, School Belonging, and Alcohol and Marijuana Use." *Journal of Adolescence* 26, no. 6 (December 2003): 741–51.

Rust, Paula C. *Bisexuality in the United States: A Social Science Reader*. Between Men—Between Women. New York: Columbia University Press, 2000.

Sammond, Nicholas. *Babes in Tomorrowland: Walt Disney and the Making of the American Child, 1930–1960*. Durham, NC: Duke University Press, 2005.

Savin-Williams, Ritch C. *Adolescence: An Ethological Perspective*. New York: Springer-Verlag, 1987.

———. *Gay and Lesbian Youth: Expressions of Identity*. Series in Clinical and Community Psychology. New York: Hemisphere, 1990.

———. *"— and Then I Became Gay": Young Men's Stories*. New York: Routledge, 1998.

———. *Mom, Dad. I'm Gay: How Families Negotiate Coming Out*. 1st ed. Washington, D.C.: American Psychological Association, 2001.

———. "A Critique of Research on Sexual-Minority Youths." *Journal of Adolescence* 24 (2001): 5–13.

———. *The New Gay Teenager*. Adolescent Lives, no. 3. Cambridge: Harvard University Press, 2005.

Savin-Williams, Ritch C., and Lisa M. Diamond. "Sexual Identity Trajectories among Sexual-Minority Youths: Gender Comparisons." *Archives of Sexual Behavior* 29, no. 6 (2000): 419–40.

Schatzman, Leonard, and Anselm L. Strauss. *Field Research; Strategies for a Natural Sociology*. Englewood Cliffs, NJ: Prentice Hall, 1973.

Schudson, Michael. *The Good Citizen: A History of American Civic Life*. New York: Martin Kessler Books, 1998.

Scott, Joan W. "Gender: A Useful Category of Analysis." *American Historical Review* 91, no. 5 (December 1986): 1053–75.

Sears, James T. *Rebels, Rubyfruit, and Rhinestones: Queering Space in the Stonewall South*. New Brunswick, NJ: Rutgers University Press, 2001.

Sedgwick, Eve Kosofsky. *Epistemology of the Closet*. Berkeley: University of California Press, 1990.

Seidman, Steven, ed. *Queer Theory/Sociology*. Twentieth-Century Social Theory. Cambridge, MA: Wiley-Blackwell, 1996.

Seidman, Steven. *Beyond the Closet: The Transformation of Gay and Lesbian Life*. New York: Routledge, 2002.

Seiter, Ellen. *Remote Control: Television, Audiences, and Cultural Power*. London: Routledge, 1989.

———. *Sold Separately: Children and Parents in Consumer Culture*. Rutgers Series in Communications, Media, and Culture. New Brunswick, NJ: Rutgers University Press, 1993.

———. *Television and New Media Audiences*. Oxford Television Studies. Oxford: Clarendon Press, 1999.

———. *The Internet Playground: Children's Access, Entertainment, and Mis-Education*. Popular Culture & Everyday Life. New York: Peter Lang, 2005.

Sender, Katherine. "Sex Sells: Sex, Class, and Taste in Commercial Gay and Lesbian Media." *GLQ: A Journal of Gay and Lesbian Studies* 9, no. 3 (2003): 331–65.

———. *Business, Not Politics: The Making of the Gay Market*. Between Men—Between Women. New York: Columbia University Press, 2004.

Sennett, Richard. *The Fall of Public Man*. 1st ed. New York: Knopf, 1977. Reprint. New York: Penguin Books, 2002.

Seufert, Robert L., and Mark A. Carrozza. "Economic Advances and Disadvantages in Appalachia: Occupation, Labor Force Participation, and Unemployment." *Journal of Appalachian Studies* 10, no. 3 (2004): 331–40.

Shapin, Steven, Simon Schaffer, and Thomas Hobbes. *Leviathan and the Air-Pump: Hobbes, Boyle, and the Experimental Life: Including a Translation of Thomas Hobbes, Dialogus Physicus De Natura Aeris by Simon Schaffer*. Princeton, NJ: Princeton University Press, 1985.

Shapiro, Eve. "'Trans'cending Barriers: Transgender Organizing on the Internet." *Journal of Gay & Lesbian Social Services* 16, no. 3/4 (2004): 165–79.

Shapiro, Henry D. *Appalachia on Our Mind: The Southern Mountains and Mountaineers in the American Consciousness, 1870–1920.* Chapel Hill: University of North Carolina Press, 1978.

Shaw, D. F. "Gay Men and Computer-Communication: A Discourse of Sex and Identity in Cyberspace." In *Virtual Culture: Identity and Communication in Cybersociety*, edited by Steve Jones, 133–45. London: Sage, 1997.

Sherrill, Kenneth S., and Alan S. Yang. "From Outlaws to In-Laws: Anti-Gay Attitudes Thaw." *Public Perspective* 11, no. 1 (2000): 20–31.

Shibutani, Tamotsu. *Society and Personality; an Interactionist Approach to Social Psychology.* Englewood Cliffs, NJ.: Prentice Hall, 1961.

Shields, R., ed. *Cultures of Internet: Virtual Spaces, Real Histories, Living Bodies.* London: Sage, 1996.

Shilt, Kristen. "'AM/FM Activism': Taking National Media Tools to a Local Level." *Journal of Gay & Lesbian Social Services* 16, no. 3/4 (2004): 181–92.

Shome, Raka. "Space Matters: The Power and Practice of Space." *Communication Theory* 13, no. 1 (2003): 39–56.

Short, John R. *Imagined Country: Environment, Culture, and Society.* London: Routledge, Chapman, and Hall, 1991.

Shuetz, Alfred. "The Stranger: An Essay in Social Psychology." *American Journal of Sociology* 49, no. 6 (1944): 499–507.

Silver, David, and Adrienne Massanari, eds. *Critical Cyberculture Studies.* New York: New York University Press, 2006.

Silverman, Victor, and Susan Stryker. *Screaming Queens: The Riot at Compton's Cafeteria.* San Francisco: Frameline, 2005. Video recording.

Silverstone, Roger. *Television and Everyday Life.* London: Routledge,1994.

Silverstone, Roger. "Domesticating Domestication: Reflections on the Life of a Concept." In *Domestication of Media and Technology*, edited by Thomas Berker, Maren Hartmann, Yves Punie, and Katie Ward, 229–48. Maidenhead, UK: Open University Press, 2006.

Silverstone, Roger, and Eric Hirsch, eds. *Consuming Technologies: Media and Information in Domestic Spaces.* London: Routledge, 1992.

Simmel, Georg. *On Individuality and Social Forms; Selected Writings.* Heritage of Sociology Series. Chicago: University of Chicago Press, 1971.

——. *The Sociology of Georg Simmel.* Translated by Kurt H. Wolff. Glencoe, IL: Free Press, 1950.

Sinnott, Megan. *Toms and Dees: Transgender Identity and Female Same-Sex Relationships in Thailand.* Honolulu: University of Hawai'i Press, 2004.

Siu, Paul C. P. "The Sojourner." *American Journal of Sociology* 58, no. 1 (1952): 34–44.

Skelton, Tracey, and Gill Valentine. *Cool Places: Geographies of Youth Cultures.* London: Routledge, 1998.

Smith, Barbara H. "Narrative Versions, Narrative Theories." In *On Narrative*, edited by W. J. Thomas Mitchell, 209–32. Chicago: University of Chicago Press, 1981.

Smith, Daniel A., Matthew DeSantis, and Jason Kassel. "Same-Sex Marriage Ballot Measures and the 2004 Presidential Election." *State and Local Government Review* 38, no. 2 (2006): 78–91.

Smith, Darren, and Louise Holt. "Lesbian Migrants in the Gentrified Valley and Other Geographies of Rural Gentrification." *Journal of Rural Studies* 21, no. 3 (2005): 313–22.

Smith, James Donald, and Ronald J. Mancoske, eds. *Rural Gays and Lesbians: Building on the Strengths of Communities*. New York: Haworth Press, 1997.

Smith, M. A. "Invisible Crowds in Cyberspace: Mapping the Social Structure of Usenet." In *Communities in Cyberspace*, edited by P. Kollock and M. A. Smith, 134–63. London: Routledge, 1999.

Smith, R. R. "Queer Theory, Gay Movements, and Political Communication." *Journal of Homosexuality* 45, no. 2–4 (2003): 345–48.

Snitow, Ann Barr, Christine Stansell, and Sharon Thompson. *Powers of Desire: The Politics of Sexuality*. New York: Monthly Review Press, 1983.

Snively, Carol A. "Building Community-Based Alliances between GLBTQQA Youth and Adults in Rural Settings." *Journal of Gay & Lesbian Social Services* 16, no. 3/4 (2004): 99–112.

Spigel, Lynn. *Make Room for TV: Television and the Family Ideal in Postwar America*. Chicago: University of Chicago Press, 1992.

Spitulnik, Debra. "Mobile Machines and Fluid Audiences: Rethinking Reception through Zambian Radio Culture." In *Media Worlds: Anthropology on New Terrain*, edited by Faye D. Ginsburg, Lila Abu-Lughod and Brian Larkin, 337–54. Berkeley: University of California Press, 2002.

Stacey, Judith. *In the Name of the Family: Rethinking Family Values in the Postmodern Age*. Boston: Beacon Press, 1996.

Staiger, Janet. *Media Reception Studies*. New York: New York University Press, 2005.

Star, Susan Leigh. "The Structure of Ill-Structured Solutions: Heterogeneous Problem-Solving, Boundary Objects and Distributed Artificial Intelligence." Paper presented at the 8th AAAI Workshop on Distributed Artificial Intelligence, Department of Computer Science, University of Southern California, 1988.

———. "The Ethnography of Infrastructure." *American Behavioral Scientist* 43, no. 3 (1999): 377–91.

Star, Susan Leigh, and James Griesemer. "Institutional Ecology, 'Translations,' and Boundary Objects: Amateurs and Professionals in Berkeley's Museum of Vertebrate Zoology, 1907–1939." *Social Studies of Science* 19 (1989): 387–420.

Stein, Arlene. "Sisters and Queers: The Decentering of Lesbian Feminism." *Socialist Review* 22, no. 1 (1992): 33–55.

———. *The Stranger Next Door: The Story of a Small Community's Battle over Sex, Faith, and Civil Rights*. Boston: Beacon Press, 2001.

Stein, Marc. *City of Sisterly and Brotherly Loves: Lesbian and Gay Philadelphia, 1945–1972*. Chicago Series on Sexuality, History, and Society. Chicago: University of Chicago Press, 2000.

Stewart, Kathleen. *A Space on the Side of the Road: Cultural Poetics in an "Other" America*. Princeton, NJ: Princeton University Press, 1996.

Strathern, Marilyn. *Kinship at the Core: An Anthropology of Elmdon, a Village in North-West Essex in the Nineteen-Sixties*. Cambridge: Cambridge University Press, 1981.

Strauss, Anselm L. *Mirrors and Masks: The Search for Identity*. Glencoe, IL: Free Press, 1959.

———. *The American City; a Sourcebook of Urban Imagery*. Chicago: Aldine, 1968.

———. *Negotiations: Varieties, Contexts, Processes, and Social Order*. 1st ed. San Francisco: Jossey-Bass, 1978.

———. *Continual Permutations of Action*. Communication and Social Order. New York: Aldine de Gruyter, 1993.

Strauss, Anselm L., and Juliet M. Corbin. *Basics of Qualitative Research: Techniques and Procedures for Developing Grounded Theory*. 2d ed. Thousand Oaks, CA: Sage, 1998.

Stryker, Susan. "Transgender History, Homonormativity, and Disciplinarity." *Radical History Review* 100 (Winter 2008): 145–57.

Suppe, Frederick. "Classifying Sexual Disorders: The Diagnostic and Statistical Manual of the American Psychiatric Association." *Journal of Homosexuality* 9, no. 4 (1984): 9–28.

Taylor, T. L. *Play between Worlds: Exploring Online Game Culture*. Cambridge: MIT Press, 2006.

Terry, Jennifer. *An American Obsession: Science, Medicine, and Homosexuality in Modern Society*. Chicago: University of Chicago Press, 1999.

Theall, Donald F. *The Virtual Marshall McLuhan*. Montreal: McGill-Queen's University Press, 2001.

Thomas, Jim. "When Cyberresearch Goes Awry: The Ethics of the Rimm 'Cyberporn' Study." *Information Society* 12, no. 2 (1996): 189–98.

Thorne, Deborah, Ann Tickamyer, and Mark Thorne. "Poverty and Income in Appalachia." *Journal of Appalachian Studies* 10, no. 3 (2004): 341–58.

Tiemann, Kathleen. "Why Is Their Picture on the Wedding Page? A Rural Community Responds to a Union Announcement." *Journal of Homosexuality* 51, no. 4 (2006): 119–35.

Tiemann, Kathleen, Sally Kennedy, and Myrna Haga. "Rural Lesbians' Strategies for Coming Out to Healthcare Professionals." *Journal of Lesbian Studies* 2, no. 1 (1998): 61–75.

Timmermans, Stefan. "Cui Bono? Institutional Review Boards and Ethnographic Research." *Studies in Symbolic Interaction: A Research Annual* 19 (1995): 155–73.

Tolman, Deborah L. *Dilemmas of Desire: Teenage Girls Talk about Sexuality.* Cambridge: Harvard University Press, 2002.

Tucker, Faith, and Hugh Matthews. "'They Don't Like Girls Hanging around There': Conflicts over Recreational Space in Rural Northamptonshire." *Area* 33, no. 2 (2001): 161–68.

Turkle, Sherry. *The Second Self: Computers and the Human Spirit.* New York: Simon & Schuster, 1984.

———. *Life on the Screen: Identity in the Age of the Internet.* London: Weidenfeld & Nicolson, 1995.

———. "Parallel Lives: Working on Identity in Virtual Space." In *Constructing the Self in a Mediated World,* edited by D. Grodin and T. R. Lindlof, 156–75. Thousand Oaks, CA: Sage, 1996.

Turner, Fred. *From Counterculture to Cyberculture: Stewart Brand, the Whole Earth Network, and the Rise of Digital Utopianism.* Chicago: University of Chicago Press, 2006.

Vaid, Urvashi. "Foreword." *Journal of Gay & Lesbian Social Services* 16, no. 3/4 (2004): 1–1.

Valentine, David. *Imagining Transgender: An Ethnography of a Category.* Durham, NC: Duke University Press, 2007.

Valentine, Gill. *From Nowhere to Everywhere: Lesbian Geographies.* New York: Harrington Park Press, 2000.

———. *Public Space and the Culture of Childhood.* Aldershot, UK: Ashgate, 2004.

Van Meter, Eddy J. "Implementing School-Based Decision Making in Kentucky." *National Association of Secondary School Principals (NASSP) Bulletin* 78 (1994): 61–70.

Wakeford, Nina. "Cyberqueer." In *The Cybercultures Reader,* edited by David Bell and Barbara M. Kennedy, 403–15. London: Routledge, 2000.

Waldrep, Christopher. *Lynching in America: A History in Documents.* New York: New York University Press, 2006.

Walker, Lisa M. "How to Recognize a Lesbian: The Cultural Politics of Looking Like What You Are." *Signs* 18, no. 4 (1993): 866–90.

Waller, Gregory A. "Situating Motion Pictures in the Prenickelodeon Period: Lexington, Kentucky, 1897–1906." *Velvet Light Trap* 29 (Spring 1990): 12–28.

Walters, Suzanna Danuta. *All the Rage: The Story of Gay Visibility in America.* Chicago: University of Chicago Press, 2001.

———. "Threat Level Lavender: The Truthiness of Gay Marriage." *Chronicle of Higher Education,* January 19, 2007, B12.

Warner, Michael. *The Trouble with Normal: Sex, Politics, and the Ethics of Queer Life*. 1st ed. New York: Free Press, 1999. Reprint. Cambridge: Harvard University Press, 2000.

———. *Publics and Counterpublics*. New York: Zone Books, 2002.

Warner, Michael, and Social Text Collective. *Fear of a Queer Planet: Queer Politics and Social Theory*. Minneapolis: University of Minnesota Press, 1993.

Waskul, Dennis, and Mark Douglass. "Considering the Electronic Participant: Some Polemical Observations on the Ethics of On-Line Research." *Information Society* 12, no. 2 (1996): 129–39.

Weeks, Jeffrey. *Coming Out: Homosexual Politics in Britain from the Nineteenth Century to the Present*. London: Quartet Books, 1979.

Wenger, Etienne. *Communities of Practice: Learning, Meaning, and Identity*. Cambridge: Cambridge University Press, 1998. Reprint. 1999.

Werner, Tammy, and Joanna Badagliacco. "Appalachian Households and Families in the New Millennium: An Overview of Trends and Policy Implication." *Journal of Appalachian Studies* 10, no. 3 (2004): 373–88.

Weston, Kath. *Families We Choose: Lesbians, Gays, Kinship*. Between Men—Between Women. New York: Columbia University Press, 1991.

———. "Lesbian/Gay Studies in the House of Anthropology." *Annual Review of Anthropology* 22 (1993): 339–67.

———. "Get Thee to a Big City: Sexual Imaginary and the Great Gay Migration." *GLQ: Gay and Lesbian Quarterly* 2 (1995): 253–77.

———. *Long Slow Burn: Sexuality and Social Science*. New York: Routledge, 1998.

White, Mel. *Stranger at the Gate: To Be Gay and Christian in America*. New York: Simon & Schuster, 1994.

Whittier, David Knapp. "Social Conflict Among 'Gay' Men in a Small(er) Southern Town." In *Rural Gays and Lesbians: Building on the Strengths of Communities*, 53–71. New York: Haworth Press, 1997.

Whyte, William Foote. *Street Corner Society; the Social Structure of an Italian Slum*. Chicago: University of Chicago Press, 1943.

Wiederman, Michael W., and Bernard E. Whitley. *Handbook for Conducting Research on Human Sexuality*. Mahwah, NJ: Lawrence Erlbaum Associates, 2002.

Williams, Juan. *Eyes on the Prize: America's Civil Rights Years, 1954–1965*. New York: Penguin Books, 1988.

Williams, Raymond. *The Country and the City*. New York: Oxford University Press, 1973.

———. *Marxism and Literature*. Oxford: Oxford University Press, 1977.

Williamson, J. W. *Hillbillyland: What the Movies Did to the Mountains and What the Mountains Did to the Movies*. Chapel Hill: University of North Carolina Press, 1995.

Wittig, Monique. "One Is Not Born a Woman." In *The Lesbian and Gay Studies Reader*, edited by Henry Abelove, Michèle Aina Barale, and David M. Halperin, 103–109. New York: Routledge, 1993.

Woolgar, Steve. *Virtual Society? Technology, Cyberbole, Reality*. Oxford: Oxford University Press, 2002.

Woolwine, David. "Community in Gay Male Experience and Moral Discourse." *Journal of Homosexuality* 38, no. 4 (2000): 5–37.

Wysocki, Diane. "'Growing Up Gay in Rural Nebraska,' or a Feminist Relocates to the Midwest." *Sexuality and Culture* 4, no. 3 (2000): 57–64.

Index

ACLU (American Civil Liberties Union): Boyd County High School GSA, 73, 76, 77, 78, 80–81, 82; Gay-Straight Alliances (GSAs), 81; high-profile, impact litigation, 72; suit against Ten Commandments on courthouse wall, 46

activism, voicing your opinion and, 117

Adam, Barry, 174

Adkins, Gary, 80

adolescence, 18

The Advocate (magazine), 16

Advocates for Youth, 124

"affective communities," 197n3

African Americans, 64–65, 132

Agee, James, 209n62

AIDS Volunteers of Lexington, 99

AJ (a rural youth participant): blog, his personal, 103, 105–106, 118; as a boundary public, 103; documenting his transition, 105–106; experience of *What Sex Am I?*, 144–145, 157–159, 162–164, 172; family, 156, 158, 162–163; staying in rural town, 168, 182; trans identity, 156–157, 182

Alyson Books, 16

Amanda (a rural youth participant), 101–102, 127

Amendment 2 initiative (Kentucky, 2004), 177–179, 226n1, 227n2

America Undercover (*AU*) documentary series, 148, 149, 153, 154

American Psychiatric Association, 7, 18

Amnesty International, 187

Amp Space (alternative music venue), 111–112

Amy (a rural youth participant), 121, 168, 180, 181

An American Family (documentary series), 151

Anderson, Benedict, 10, 211n69

Anti-Defamation League, 70

Appalachia, 208n60. *See also* Central Appalachian Region

Ashland, Kentucky, 61, 62, 75, 79–80

Ashland Human Rights Commission, 79

Ashley (a rural youth participant): experience of *What Sex Am I?*, 144–145, 155, 156, 160–164, 172; family, 159–160, 162–163; staying in rural town, 168

assimilationist strategy, 7

Atherton High School (Louisville), 213n1

Austin, J. L., 200n15

Tri-State Alliance, 130, 186
Tyler M. (a rural youth participant),
    80

U.S. Department of Education: Office
    for Civil Rights (OCR), 68
U.S. Department of Health and Hu-
    man Services, 68
Unity Rally (Ashland, Kentucky),
    79–82, 84
University of Kentucky, 43, 44, 213n15
University of Kentucky Cooperative
    Extension Service, 43–45, 56–57
Urbach, Stuart, 52
urban areas. *See* cities/urban areas
urban gay youth: access to social ser-
    vices, 5; queer-identity work, 21;
    rural gay youth compared to, 5, 21,
    31, 114, 168
Uriah (a rural youth participant), 80
Uribe, Virginia, 69–70

Valentine, David, 9, 28, 63
Valentine, Gil, 10
Vessels, Jeff, 78, 81
violence: anti-transgender hate vio-
    lence, 225n17; hate e-mail, 112–
    113, 114; urban compared to small-
    town violence, 90, 115, 221n19
visibility. *See* gay visibility; politics of
    visibility
voting patterns, 40–41

Wal-Mart (Springhaven, Kentucky): as
    boundary public, 107, 108; custom-
    ers as "guests," 98; domestic-partner
    benefits, 98; dragging at, 88, 96–98,
    108–110, 112–113, 116, 182; drag-
    ging at, photos of, 109, 112–113;
    harassment at, 109–110, 114; shop-
    ping at, 110
Walker, Paul A., 149

Waller, Greg, 12–13
Walters, Suzanna, 30, 122, 180–181,
    211n4
Warner, Carita, 53
Warner, Michael, 26, 94–95
Watt, Diane, 10
websites: as boundary publics, 103–
    104, 113; coming-out stories (*see*
    coming-out stories on the Internet);
    frequented by rural gay youth,
    123–124; naming desires, 137–138;
    personal ads (*see* personal ads on
    the Internet); personal websites,
    105–106; queer-identity work, 113;
    as queer public spaces, 170–171;
    realness found in online narratives,
    124; sense of public presence, 118
Weimer, Judy, 53, 54
Weitz, Rose, 25
Welch, David, 80
Wellman, Joyce, 74
Westboro Baptist Church (Kansas),
    79–80
Western Kentucky Research and Edu-
    cation Center, 43
Weston, Kath: gay/lesbian scholarship,
    7–8; kinship, 58; polarization of gay
    and straight families, 51; rural to
    urban migration of gays, 10; schol-
    arly attention to homosexuality,
    199n14
What Sex Am I? (documentary),
    148–153; *America Undercover* (AU)
    documentary series, 148; context of
    reception, 162–163, 172; Discovery
    Channel, 154–155, 157–159, 160;
    Discovery Health channel rebroad-
    cast, 144–145, 155; DVD versions,
    225n16; in explaining gender transi-
    tions to family members, 158–159;
    female-to-male transsexuals, 149,
    150; HBO (Home Box Office), 148,

154, 155; Jorgensen, Christine, 149; male-to-female transsexuals, 149, 150; medical experts in, 149, 151; narrator, 148; premiere, 148; producer, 148; production values, 153–156; queer-identity work, 163, 172; queer realness, 145, 163–164; reactions to, 152–153; sameness doctrine, 151; significance, 155–156; subjects, 150; viewers' recognition of themselves as transsexual, 157–162

Will and Grace (television show), 121
Williams, Raymond, 5, 39, 197n3
Woolwine, David, 205n45
Word Is Out (documentary), 151

York, Tim, 74, 78
youth culture, cars in, 208n58
youth research, 185

Zimmerman, Rick, 228n2

About the Author

MARY L. GRAY is Assistant Professor in the Department of Communication and Culture and Adjunct Professor of American Studies, Anthropology, and Gender Studies at Indiana University, Bloomington. She is the author of *In Your Face: Stories from the Lives of Queer Youth*.